THE NYPD'S FIRST FIFTY YEARS

THE NYPD'S FIRST FIFTY YEARS

Politicians, Police Commissioners, and Patrolmen

BERNARD WHALEN AND JON WHALEN

Foreword by William J. Bratton

POTOMAC BOOKS

An imprint of the University of Nebraska Press

Library of Congress Cataloging-in-Publication Data
Whalen, Bernard.
The NYPD's first fifty years: politicians, police
commissioners, and patrolmen / Bernard Whalen and
Jon Whalen; foreword by William J. Bratton.
pages   cm
Includes bibliographical references and index.
ISBN 978-1-61234-656-4 (cloth: alk. paper)
ISBN 978-1-61234-657-1 (pdf)
1. New York (N.Y.). Police Department—History.
2. Police—New York (State)—New York—History.
I. Whalen, Jon. II. Title.
HV8148.N5W43 2014
363.209747'109041—dc23
2014031611

Set in Minion Pro by Renni Johnson.
Designed by Rachel Gould.

On July 4, 1940, NYPD personnel responded to investigate what was presumed to be a bomb hidden in a suitcase planted inside the British Pavilion at the World's Fair in Flushing Meadows, Queens. The bomb detonated as it was being examined, killing two detectives assigned to the Bomb Squad: Joseph Lynch and Ferdinand "Freddy" Socha. The explosion also severely injured several other members of the force: Detective William Federer, Detective Joseph Gallagher, Detective Martin Schuchman, and Patrolman Emil Vyskocil. This book, in which their story is included, is dedicated to them in recognition of the heroism they displayed that fateful afternoon in the finest tradition of the NYPD.

*It is better to be governed by good men
than by good laws.*

PLATO

CONTENTS

ILLUSTRATIONS

FOREWORD

I have always been interested in the NYPD, even before I became police commissioner. When I was a young boy, one of my favorite pastimes was reading a book illustrated with pictures of the NYPD called *Your Police*, by George Zaffo. Years later, when I became police commissioner, I put together an exhibit for the 150th anniversary of the establishment of the Municipal Police in New York City. My officers were issued distinctive breast bars to wear above their shields to commemorate the anniversary.

I was intrigued when Lieutenant Bernard Whalen approached me to consider writing the foreword for this book. As I began reading a draft of the manuscript, I realized that he and his father and coauthor, Jon Whalen, had taken a far different approach in telling the story of the department's early history than any other authors by looking at the relationship among the city's politicians, the police commissioner, and the patrol force.

As much as policing has changed since 1898, when the five boroughs merged and eighteen separate police departments joined to form the NYPD that we know today, the nature of the work has not changed. The problems with which patrolmen dealt yesteryear are still problems for the police officers of today.

During the fifty-year period this book covers, mayors (often times at the direction of their political benefactors) selected hacks, military men, lawyers, businessmen, career police officers, and, on occasion, outsiders to run the department. Although the police commissioners themselves are not politicians, they are political appointees who need to be politically savvy in order to succeed. Since the position of police commissioner was established in 1901, their tenures have been as short as twenty-eight days and as long as twelve years, but on average they last about three years, even though the term of office is five years. This is because the police commissioner serves at the pleasure of the mayor, and performance, whether it is good or bad, is not always the most important consideration. This was especially true in the early days of the NYPD.

I think the reader of this book will gain a new appreciation for the complexities involved in policing America's largest and greatest metropolis. At times it has been a two-steps-forward-and-one-step-backward approach to solving problems of crime, corruption, deployment of resources, use of technology, and maintenance of the public trust. By looking at how each mayor, each police commissioner, and the policemen themselves have addressed such issues—sometimes with success, sometimes without—one can get a true sense of why things are the way they are today in the NYPD.

Although we all come from different walks of life, as a police commissioner, with few exceptions, I share with my predecessors and successors many of the same feelings. We desire a corruption-free police force. We want to reward properly those officers who have distinguished themselves. We strive to provide the best police service to the public that we possibly can. We try to be innovative. We all love the job. We believe that Cops Count, Police Count. Lieutenant Bernard Whalen and Jon Whalen have captured the essence of that belief.

William J. Bratton
NYPD Police Commissioner, 1994–96, 2014–

PREFACE

I have been with the NYPD for thirty-three years. During that time I have served under five mayors and nine police commissioners (two have served twice). In the twenty-five years that I have been a lieutenant working at Police Headquarters, I have had an insider's view of the department's decision-making process. It was with this viewpoint in mind that my father and I wrote this book about the first fifty years of the NYPD.

Police Headquarters has always been within walking distance of City Hall for a reason. To paraphrase Mayor Fiorello LaGuardia, if you control the police department, you control the city. The mayor has power over the police department because the police commissioner serves at his pleasure. Police commissioners have power over the force because they have the statutory authority to assign and/or discipline police officers as they see fit. Police officers have power over the public because they are the ones who arrest lawbreakers and have the option in some situations to warn and admonish violators. The public has power over candidates seeking to become mayor because its votes ultimately decide which candidate will be elected. The process begins anew with each election cycle. With each new mayor comes a new police commissioner with a new agenda for the police to implement.

As a police officer, I have often heard that things were better in the past. I was surprised to discover while writing this book that they were not better; rather they were quite the same. A patrolman's lot is not much different today than it was back in 1898, when the five boroughs merged to create the Greater City of New York. The scandals of today are no different than the scandals of yesteryear. There have always been good cops and bad cops. Fortunately, then as now, there have been a lot more good cops in the NYPD.

This book is the story of how it all started.

Bernard Whalen

CHRONOLOGY

1629: A "Shout" fiscal (sheriff attorney) is appointed by the Dutch governor.

1664: The English take control of New York from the Dutch. British army regulars police the port colony.

1700: Abolishment of Militia Watch and installation of a Constable's Watch, consisting of a high constable and twelve sub-constables. (The twelve stars on today's NYPD Medal of Honor represent the original twelve sub-constables.)

1786: The Night Watch is established when the town fathers in the city, now with a population of twenty-five thousand, appoint a night watch consisting of a captain and twenty-eight men.

1802: Jacob Hays is appointed high constable. He will hold the position for fifty years.

1836: The number of watchmen is increased. Formation of a detective bureau. The law provides for the appointment of 192 men to perform duty as roundsmen in civilian clothes.

1838: Reorganization of the Night Watch.

1842: Powers of the mayor over the Night Watch are revoked and transferred to Common Council.

1843: Mayor reinvested with supreme police authority. Marshals formed into a Day Police. The total force numbers 1,000 men for a population of 350,000. The patrol is limited south of an irregular line extending from the East River and Twenty-Eighth Street to the Hudson River and Fortieth Street.

1844: The old Night Watch is abolished. The law is amended to provide for a chief of police to command the police force of the city, which now has a population of four hundred thousand.

1845: The Municipal Police, a day and night police force of eight hundred officers, is established to enforce the laws. The municipal policemen are issued brass or copper stars to wear on their chests, but they refuse to wear uniforms because they consider them to be "badges of servitude."

1847: Entire police force directed to patrol day and night. Telegraph Bureau is established.

1853: Police force is reorganized. Tenure established. Police Commission appointed. Reserve corps created.

1857: Police Commission repealed. Five commissioners appointed. Municipal Police Force declared unable to keep the peace in the city on its own. Republicans in the state legislature create the Metropolitan Police Force to patrol New York, Brooklyn, Westchester, and Staten Island. Five commissioners reduced to three. The two forces share patrol responsibilities, but when the state-created force tries to arrest the mayor, a brawl between the two departments breaks out on the steps of City Hall. Before the end of the year, the Municipal Police Force is abolished in favor of the Metropolitan Police Force.

1858: The *Seneca*, a side-wheel steamboat, takes its first cruise in New York Harbor for the newly created Harbor Precinct. Police Headquarters is located at the corner of Broome and Elm Streets in Manhattan. The city has a population of 820,000. The police force numbers 1,420 men.

1860: The Metropolitan Police District is extended to include the towns of Newtown, Flushing, and Jamaica in the borough of Queens.

1863: Police Headquarters for the Metropolitan Police Force is relocated to 300 Mulberry Street. The new building costs $230,860 to construct. The population of the city is 1,400,000 residents living below 152nd Street, and the police force numbers 1,856 men.

1864: A police life-insurance fund is established.

1866: New station houses are erected.

1867: The Central Office at Police Headquarters is established.

1869: Reorganization of the Metropolitan Police Force takes place.

1870: A new charter reorganizes the police department. A board of four commissioners is given the power to appoint a superintendent of police. Police officers begin to wear shields over the left breast.

1871: First Mounted Police Unit formed and deployed in the city.

1872: The police are given the responsibility for cleaning the streets.

1873: Board of Police to consist of five members. Board of Surgeons created. Police Board reduced to four members.

1881: Street Cleaning Department created. Police force relieved of cleaning responsibilities.

1882: Board of Police authorized by act of legislature to establish a new detective bureau of not more than forty members. Inspector Thomas Byrnes becomes first commanding officer and is placed in charge of thirty-one men.

1883: The police force is made subject to civil service rules concerning appointment and promotion.

1887: The force numbers 3,232 men.

1888: Provisions authorize department to appoint matrons.

1891: First four matrons appointed.

1894: Eastchester, Westchester, and Pelham become part of New York City. Voters approve referendum to merge five boroughs into one city to be called the Greater City of New York.

1895: Theodore Roosevelt appointed to the Police Board. The office of the Chief Surgeon to the Police Department is created.

1898, January 1: Five boroughs consolidate into one city. The population is reported to be 3,272,418. New York Police Department, with 6,382 men (other sources put the number at 6,396), is formed by combining other police departments in the area and is placed under the control of a four-commissioner bipartisan police board that selects the chief of police.

Source: NYPD Annual Report

THE NYPD'S FIRST FIFTY YEARS

1

THE BIRTH OF THE NYPD

In November 1897 the most important election in the United States was to select a mayor for a city that did not yet exist. Four years earlier, voters of New York City, which at the time consisted of Manhattan and the Bronx, and those of Brooklyn, Queens, and Staten Island approved a referendum to merge their five separate boroughs into a single metropolis that would be called the "City of Greater New York."

While the impetus for consolidation as first proposed by prominent New York attorney and civic planner Andrew H. Green appears to have been rooted in fiscal logic, such as an effort to lower taxes and reduce the duplication of services caused by a number of independent municipal governments sharing similar resources in the same geographic area, New York State Republican Party leader Thomas Platt had his own motivation for pushing Green's plan through the state legislature. Platt, an astute politician who hailed from upstate New York, realized that the residents of Brooklyn (Kings County) and the more rural counties of Queens and Richmond (Staten Island) were predominantly Republican, while Manhattan and the Bronx were solidly Democratic. For years what was considered New York City had been controlled by Democrats affiliated with a powerful but corrupt political organization known as Tammany Hall. By tying the counties together, Platt hoped to wrest control of Manhattan from the Democrats and deposit it directly into the pockets of the Republicans. History has shown, however, that at least as far as his gerrymandering scheme was concerned, Platt seriously underestimated the tenacity of Tammany Hall. Like a great octopus, the political organization reached its long tentacles into the homes and minds of the less sophisticated folk in the outer boroughs, seized their votes, and added them to its own. As a result, Republicans often were left with virtually no voice in the political affairs of the largest city in America, one that they had helped create.

For the new metropolis's first mayoral election, Platt nominated Benjamin Tracy as the Republican candidate, but a faction of disgruntled Republicans, disaffected Democrats, and Independents formed a fusion party called the Citizens' Union, with the express intent of placing a bipartisan candidate on the ballot. A major part of their platform called for the fair enforcement of local statutes and ordinances by the police. The fusionists selected Seth Low, the former mayor of the City of Brooklyn, because his reform ethic compared favorably to that of William Strong, the well-respected mayor of "old" New York City who said that he was retiring from politics because battling corruption had left him exhausted.

While the Republicans split their support between two candidates, the Democrats united solidly behind Robert Van Wyck, a malleable city court judge plucked from the bench by the sachem of Tammany Hall, Richard Croker. In return Van Wyck agreed that if he won, he would allow "Boss" Croker total control of the forty thousand patronage appointments in the new municipality.

Van Wyck was born in New York City in 1849. Although the New York newspapers portrayed the forty-eight-year-old candidate for mayor as little more than a Tammany stooge, the Democrats touted his educational background (Van Wyck had graduated first in his class at the prestigious Columbia Law School) and his family's strong Dutch and German ties, which Croker believed would appeal to New York's large immigrant population.

Although Van Wyck did not make a single public appearance during the campaign, he routed runner-up Seth Low and Platt's handpicked candidate, thanks to Tammany Hall's support and a memorable campaign slogan: "To Hell with Reform." Commenting on Low's crushing defeat, an East Side gang member opined, "These reform movements are like hornets. They sting once and then they die."

During December 1897 mayor-elect Van Wyck and Croker sojourned to the Lakewood Hotel, a New Jersey resort, to determine who would be rewarded. Among the many important political appointments to be made by the incoming administration were the four commissioners of the Police Board. The drafters of the City Charter, the constitutional document for the new city, were very concerned of the detrimental effect one-party control could have on the new municipal police department and took precautions to prevent any one party from seizing control of the force for its own political purposes. Although the mayor appointed the four commissioners—each at a salary of $5,000 per year—no more than two appointees from any one political party could serve at the same time. The terms of office were intended to be four years, but an important caveat in the City Charter permitted the mayor to remove any or all of the commissioners at his discretion. This provision would prove to be very useful in the months to come.

At Croker's behest Van Wyck appointed two Democrats: Bernard York, a lawyer, former Kings County clerk for Court Special Sessions, and chairman of the Kings County Democratic Executive Committee, to serve as the president of the Police Board, and John Sexton, the former under-sheriff of New York County. Their Republican counterparts were Thomas Hamilton, a New York contractor, and William Phillips, a produce wholesaler from Brooklyn.

The City Charter also provided the framework to consolidate the region's eighteen police departments into a single large department of 6,396 patrolmen that would become the world renowned NYPD. The former departments included the old New York Police (from which the bulk of the force would come), the City of Brooklyn Police, the Long Island City Police, the Brooklyn Bridge Police, the Park Police, the County of Richmond Police, a handful of small village police departments and constabularies from Queens, and the Telegraph Force, a unit responsible for maintaining the citywide communications link.

At the stroke of midnight, January 1, 1898, with snow falling and celebratory fireworks bursting in air above the dome of the *New York World*, a newspaper owned by Joseph Pulitzer, New York City grew from 60 square miles to 320 square miles, with a population estimated to be 3,400,000. The combined municipal budget for the five boroughs swelled to $90 million, of which $10 million was allotted to the new police force.

During Van Wyck's swearing-in ceremony, outgoing mayor Strong offered his congratulations, from which Van Wyck turned away and said, "The people have chosen me to be mayor. I shall say whatever I have to say to them." Later that day, Police Board president York addressed the ranking officers for the first time. "There will be no politics permitted in the administration of this department, so far as the commissioners are concerned.

Political considerations will not be permitted to weigh anything. We will stand by you and we expect you to stand by us." But it soon became apparent that nothing he said could have been farther from the truth.

The Police Board was vested with the power to appoint a chief of police to head the consolidated force, at an annual salary of $6,000, but the City Charter required the initial selection be one of four men: the chief of police or deputy chief of police from the old New York City Police Department or the superintendent of police or deputy superintendent of police from the old Brooklyn Police Department. The board selected John McCullagh, a fifty-two-year-old Irishman who had previously served as chief of police for New York City. McCullagh had joined the force in 1870. Six years later he placed first in a field of fifty candidates for promotion to sergeant. By 1883 he was a captain. Over the next fifteen years he commanded some of Manhattan's toughest precincts. He was an avowed Republican and a favorite of Theodore Roosevelt during the latter's days as president of the Police Board. Over his career McCullagh had distinguished himself as honest, brave, and capable. As he took the reins of the new department, McCullagh said wistfully, "Let us start fairly and do best for this city."

The consolidated force operated out of the original Police Headquarters of the former Metropolitan Police at 300 Mulberry Street. The four-story building had been erected during the Civil War, when the entire police force consisted of 1,900 men. As soon as he was sworn in, McCullagh declared the dilapidated structure woefully inadequate and recommended that it be replaced as soon as possible. The detention cells in the basement were in such poor condition that the officers referred to them as dungeons and called the building itself the "Castle of Joy and Sorrow"—"Joy" for the fortunate few who reported there to receive their promotion orders and "Sorrow" for the many who reported there to attend disciplinary hearings, where the outcomes were seldom in their favor.

In regard to the newly acquired stationhouses in the outer boroughs, the situation was even worse. After visiting several of them for the first time, McCullagh determined that several were entirely unfit for use and dangerous to the health of the officers assigned to work in them. Despite their poor condition, many of the former police department heads were reluctant to surrender their facilities to their new tenants. It took more than a month for McCullagh to resolve issues of ownership. Once he did, he began to renumber all of city's stationhouses because many shared the same numerical designations. The boroughs of Manhattan, Brooklyn, Long Island City, and Staten Island, for example, each had their own First Precinct. Under McCullagh's system there was only one First Precinct, and it was located in Lower Manhattan. From there the numbered precincts rose sequentially up Manhattan and into the Bronx, followed by Brooklyn, Queens, and Staten Island in that order. Although the number of precinct stationhouses has changed over the years, the numbering order has remained virtually the same ever since.

The chain of command in 1898 was such that police precincts were commanded by captains assisted by plainclothes wardsmen whom they appointed. Captains reported to inspectors stationed at Headquarters who oversaw districts or groups of precincts. The rank of lieutenant did not yet exist, so sergeants were in charge of the stationhouses in the captain's absence, while roundsmen "made the rounds" and inspected patrolmen in the field. The roundsmen's work schedule conformed to that of the patrolmen, but since the authorized department staffing-level called for just four roundsmen per precinct, meaningful supervision was virtually impossible. To alleviate the situation somewhat, McCullagh transferred a special squad of seventeen plainclothes roundsmen assigned to the Headquarters Central Squad back to patrol precincts. In police vernacular they were known as "shooflies." They roamed the city streets in civilian clothes to spy on delinquent patrolmen. McCullagh explained, "This is not Russia; this is America, and our police force is composed of good, red-blooded Americans." He hoped the move would improve morale, but in reality the "shoofly" system would come and go on a regular basis, depending on who was in charge of the force.

McCullagh issued each patrolman a pocket pamphlet explaining the regulations of the unified department and required that they carry it at all times while in uniform. Failure to do so was a violation in itself.

The Detective Bureau consisted of 271 detective sergeants (a number fixed by the charter), who operated out of the Central Office at Headquarters.

Detective sergeants were patrolmen and roundsmen detailed by the chief of police to perform investigative duties. Although they received the same pay as regular sergeants and could act as supervisors when necessary, they did not have the same civil service protection and therefore could be demoted for any reason. McCullagh recommended that only one hundred of these investigators remain assigned to Headquarters and the rest be transferred in groups of three to local precincts to investigate crimes as sub-units of his proposed reconfiguration of the Detective Bureau. Detective sergeants, however, in addition to their investigative role, traditionally functioned as important links in the chain of graft between Police Headquarters and illegal businesses, so the Police Board did not act upon McCullagh's proposal.

Among the legitimate perks that patrolmen were permitted was free public transportation on streetcars and trolleys, provided that only one officer was on board at a time and that he stood outside on the rear platform. Otherwise conductors were expected to collect a fare or eject the officer. In reality most infractions were ignored because there was nobody a conductor could turn to if the patrolman refused to pay or get off.

In the old police departments of New York and Brooklyn patrolmen received a half-pay retirement pension after completing twenty years of service. But that was a cause for public outcry, as evidenced in a letter to *Outlook* magazine by a disgruntled former police surgeon, Dr. George Hopkins. "We are paying many able-bodied men half their full pay, when they were in perfect health from forty-one years and upward," he wrote. "Why such a law has not been exposed, and the Legislature compelled by the force of public sentiment to repeal it, is an enigma to me."

After consolidation the number of years required for a patrolman to work in order to qualify for a police pension was raised to twenty-five, and the officer had to be at least fifty-five years old to be eligible to collect a pension. Since the average life span in America for a male at the time was only forty-seven years, many patrolmen never saw a single penny of their pensions. Patrolling tenements around the clock, where tuberculosis and small pox were rampant, meant that a great number of them succumbed to disease. In 1898 alone, 114 active New York City police officers died in service.

This high mortality rate was the impetus for the formation of the Patrolmen's Benevolent Association in 1894. Patrolmen paid twenty-five cents each month to the association for the purpose of providing the widows and orphans of deceased patrolmen a $175 death benefit.

Although no new patrolmen were appointed during the consolidated department's first year because the size of the force was stipulated in the City Charter, the civil service set about establishing standards for future hires. Candidates had to be U.S. citizens and city residents. They had to be between twenty-one and thirty years of age, at least five feet seven and one-half inches tall, and weigh no less than 138 pounds. They had to be able to read, write, and speak English and score a minimum of 70 percent on a written test. They had to pass a physical exam and provide references. Any candidate convicted of a felony or who had a heart murmur, bad eyesight, syphilis, fits, or a physical ailment such as piles or a crooked spine was automatically disqualified. If a candidate met all of the qualifications, he was hired as probationary patrolman. His first month on the job was spent in the classroom. It was only after he graduated from training that he achieved permanent status as a patrolman.

In preparation for new hires McCullagh founded the School of Instruction and put it under the command of Captain Anthony Allaine, who was designated "Drill Master." Until new patrolmen were hired, the School of Instruction trained members who came over from the smaller departments in the rules and procedures of the consolidated force.

A year later, when the first class of probationary patrolmen was appointed, recruits were instructed in the duties of a patrolman and educated in the laws of the city and the state. The course of study ran Monday through Saturday for a period of thirty days. A morning session consisted of classroom instruction, an afternoon session of physical training. After graduation senior officers, called "trainers," were charged with keeping a watchful eye on the rookies. Once a month the trainers filed a report to the School of Instruction on the proficiency, character, and capacity for police duties of each of their charges.

Despite his obvious commitment to the force, by early May 1898 rumors that McCullagh was about to be removed proved true. The method in which it was done had negative repercussions in the department for years to come.

Just before sailing off to England, the head of Tammany Hall, Richard Croker, gave instructions to Commissioner Sexton to introduce a motion to the board calling for the retirement of Chief McCullagh. Republican commissioners Hamilton and Phillips balked. President York refused to vote until he had a chance to discuss the matter with Croker in person. When it became apparent that the two Republican board members intended to stand firm, Mayor Van Wyck exercised his executive privilege and ousted both of them. In their stead he appointed a more pliable Republican, Jacob Hess, a fifty-two-year-old former member of the Subway Commission. To ensure that the reconfigured Police Board did not find itself deadlocked again, Van Wyck left the fourth commissionership vacant. The three commissioners acted swiftly. They retired McCullagh on a $3,000-a-year pension and replaced him with Croker's original choice, Deputy Chief William Devery.

Devery was born in New York City in 1854. At age twenty-four he gave up a career as a bartender to join the Police Department in 1878. At the time there were no civil service exams. To secure a municipal job it was necessary only to bribe a connected politician.

It was not until 1894, at Theodore Roosevelt's urging, that civil service rules were enacted to more fairly control appointments and promotions in the police department. But crooked politicians simply changed their tactics. To secure a seat to take the exam cost $300, and to advance in rank required payments ranging from $1,000 (to make sergeant) to $12,000 (to be become a captain), even when a candidate had passed the written test with high marks. Then it cost a captain another $15,000 to reach the rank of inspector. During its investigation into municipal corruption in 1894, the Lexow Commission estimated that the police promotion racket alone put $7 million per year in the pockets of unscrupulous politicians.

Patrolman John Hickey, a board officer in the early years of the Patrolmen's Benevolent Association, recalled in his book, *Our Police Guardians*, that his name was way down at the bottom of the promotion list, where it would never be reached. A politician's representative approached him on patrol and said, "John, if you can raise two hundred bucks by Tuesday night [the promotion list was scheduled to be released the next morning], I promise you that your name will be among the first one hundred and fifty called." Hickey shook his head and said, "There isn't a chance." He was already deeply in hock because of his wife's medical bills. The representative suggested the name of a shylock, but Hickey already owed him a considerable sum. Although Hickey never got promoted, Devery was more than willing to trade dollars for rank because he knew that once he became a precinct commander, he could easily recover his "fees."

It was said that when Devery took command of the Eldridge Street stationhouse on the Lower East Side in Manhattan, he told his subordinates, "They tell me there's a lot of grafting going on in this precinct. They tell me you fellows are the fiercest ever on graft. Now that's going to stop! If there's any grafting to be done, I'll do it. Leave it to me." Lincoln Steffens, a popular journalist of the day, wrote of Devery, "As Chief of Police he is a disgrace, but as a character he is a work of art."

Devery's very first order as the new chief of police set the low moral standard that would be the hallmark of his stewardship. McCullagh had been under pressure from Tammany Hall to reprimand a police captain who had made a name for himself raiding so-called "protected" establishments, illicit businesses involved in gambling and prostitution that paid off the police. McCullagh had used his position to shield the captain from the political fallout. As soon as Devery took office, he gave that captain just two and a half hours to remove his personal effects from his Lower Manhattan precinct and report for duty to the Kingsbridge precinct in the Bronx. Given the state of transportation in the city at the time, the order was impossible to follow. When the captain failed to arrive at the Kingsbridge precinct on time, Devery charged him with being AWOL. The not-too-subtle message was directed at any McCullagh supporters who harbored thoughts of defying him.

The concept of a forty-hour work week with regularly scheduled time off was foreign to people in 1898. The sheer number of hours per year that police officers were required to work, coupled with a convoluted rotating duty schedule (which included an odd two-hour shift that started at 6 a.m. called the "Dog Watch"), was physically debilitating. Patrolman Hickey pointed out that during their careers policemen spent more time protecting strangers than they did in the company of their own families.

During the ninety-six hours it took patrolmen to rotate completely through the four-day work schedule of days and nights, they spent sixty-four hours either on patrol or reserve and thirty-two hours off duty, which was called "home time." After ninety-six hours patrolmen were given sixteen hours off before the rotation began anew. Once every twenty days—or the equivalent of five ninety-six-hour cycles—an officer was supposed to get a full day off. But even that was subject to the discretion of the precinct captain since the need for manpower was often unpredictable.

Patrolmen received five vacation days per year and began their careers with a salary of $800, from which $150 was spent during the first year to buy uniforms and equipment and pay separate deductions for a society tax to the Patrolmen's Benevolent Association and a stationhouse tax to clean the bed linen in the precinct dormitory.

After five years on the force a patrolmen's salary topped out at $1,400 only because several years before the Patrolmen's Benevolent Association had collected $15 from each of its members to hire a law firm with Tammany Hall connections to represent their financial interests in Albany. The firm's lobbying efforts resulted in the State Legislature's passing a bill to raise police salaries. It was rumored that most of the $87,500 collected by the association went directly into the pockets of the "concerned" politicians who voted in favor of the bill.

For patrolmen seeking to supplement their incomes illegally, the opportunities were boundless, even in the sparsely populated outer boroughs. But the proverbial pot of gold was in the old Nineteenth Precinct, which covered a section of Midtown known as the "Tenderloin," between Broadway and Ninth Avenue, from Twenty-Third Street to Forty-Second Street. A former commanding officer of the precinct, Captain Alexander "Clubber" Williams, was responsible for giving the area its notorious nickname when, after paying $15,000 for the assignment, he bragged, "I've had nothing but chuck steak for a long time and now I'm going to get a little bit of tenderloin."

The neighborhood was home to countless brothels, saloons, poolrooms, and gambling halls. The area's unsavory reputation made it a frequent target of reformers. To mollify them Chief Devery would occasionally direct that the precinct conduct a highly publicized sweep of prostitutes and report the arrest statistics to the newspapers.

The City Charter gave the chief of police complete authority to assign personnel. But Devery abused his power. He transferred eighty-five uniformed patrolmen into the Detective Bureau to work as detective sergeants without paying them the higher salary, even though their function was identical to that of the detective sergeants. Sixty-three of the men came from Manhattan and twenty-two from Brooklyn. When the grievants petitioned the Police Board to raise their salaries to the same $2,000 per year that their colleagues received, the commissioners denied their petition and ruled that it was within the department's prerogative to detail them to detective duties without providing them additional compensation.

As a result of their complaint, the power to assign patrolmen to detective duties was taken away from the chief of police and given to the Police Board. The eighty-five grievants were transferred back to their precincts. However, since these men had become vital to Devery's efforts to collect graft for Tammany Hall, the transfers of the sixty-three men from Manhattan were rescinded the next day. They were given the new title of "reserve detectives" and placed under Devery's direct control.

Devery claimed that the new reserve detectives would receive training and experience that would help them if and when they became full-fledged detective sergeants. His plan also allowed him to circumvent attempts by the Civil Service Board to make the detective sergeant rank one that required passing a written test instead of its being granted by appointment. When it came to solving crime, Devery said, "There is no learning the business out of books."

"Deveryism," as his antics came to be known, manifested itself in many ways, particularly in the department's selective enforcement of the law. Despite the hue and cry of prominent reformers, many ordinary citizens were glad that the police did not aggressively enforce laws banning the sale and consumption of alcohol on Sundays. This was particularly true of the German and Irish communities that were the main sources of Tammany Hall's strength.

Still, those with the least political influence often paid a high price for police indifference. In August 1900, for example, a large-scale riot broke out between Irish and blacks on the west side of Manhattan. The two ethnic groups had been vying for the same low-paying jobs since slavery had been abolished in New York State. During the melee eyewitnesses alleged that the police did nothing to restrain the Irish gangs from attacking the "coloreds."

Black leaders pressured the Police Board to investigate the matter. The board finally bowed to the political pressure and agreed to hear testimony, although it was completely one-sided because the commissioners refused to allow counsel for the black plaintiffs to cross-examine the witnesses supporting the police. After listening to the evidence, President York declared the accused members of the department "guiltless of clubbing Negroes."

Reformers believed there was no way to stem the tide of systematic corruption within the police department as long as it had control over the Election Bureau. Police brass, acting on Croker's orders, selected the polling places, divided the city into election districts, appointed inspectors and poll clerks, had ballots and registration lists printed, and tallied the votes. The police also had the authority to verify "floaters," residents of hotels and lodging houses who for a small fee voted for Tammany candidates. It did not matter whether the floaters were actually registered. Tammany Hall would provide them with names of registered voters even if these persons were long dead.

Ironically what appeared to be Tammany's strength would prove to be its Achilles' heel. In preparation for the November 1900 election, Devery issued orders that were intended to prevent the Republican-appointed state superintendent of elections from investigating voter fraud in New York City. The state superintendent happened to be the same John McCullagh, whose dismissal as chief of police had been orchestrated by Croker in order to make room for Devery.

With the threat of a grand jury indictment, Devery amended his orders and declared that the upcoming election would be the "fairest ever held in New York City." His promise, however, did not deter the crusaders who wanted to get rid of him. Under pressure from prominent reform-minded citizens, the State Legislature created the Mazet Committee, headed by Assemblyman Robert Mazet, to investigate municipal malfeasance, including allegations of police misconduct, dereliction of duty, and graft. The committee's findings echoed those of the Lexow Commission. Much of the police department's complicity in vice, gambling, and prostitution could be traced to its long-standing affiliation with Tammany Hall.

Fortunately the State Legislature had already taken steps to rein in Tammany Hall by establishing a Charter Revision Committee, led by former mayoral candidate Seth Low. In December 1900 Governor Theodore Roosevelt, in one of his final acts before leaving to become vice president, signed the committee's recommendations into law.

The original City Charter had limited the mayor to a single four-year term. An amendment in the charter called for mayoral elections every two years and permitted the incumbent to run for reelection. The revised charter also removed the Board of Elections from police department control and dissolved both the Police Board and the position of chief of police. Their powers were consolidated into a new entity called the police commissioner.

As a result of these changes, Bernard York and John Sexton sought to be appointed police commissioner. While both men had proved to be loyal Tammany soldiers, each on occasion had exhibited an independent streak that, in Croker's opinion, made them less than ideal candidates to head the police department. As for Devery, since there was no longer a chief of police, he was temporarily out of work.

On February 23, 1901, Mayor Van Wyck, as per the new charter, named the president of the Board of Health, Colonel Michael C. Murphy, as New York City's first police commissioner. Ex-commissioner Sexton accepted appointment to Colonel Murphy's former position at the Board of Health, while York reluctantly agreed to become the second deputy police commissioner, overseeing the affairs of the patrolmen assigned to Brooklyn, which, despite consolidation, was still treated in many respects as a separate department.

Michael Murphy was born in Ireland in 1841 and immigrated to the United States as an orphan in 1848. He served in the Civil War and rose to the rank of colonel. During the war his courage was called into question when he offered to surrender to an overwhelming rebel force rather than face certain defeat. Only the personal intercession of General Ulysses S. Grant saved his reputation. After the war his interest in politics and his devoted friendship to Richard Croker led to a seat in the New York State Senate.

In 1889 Murphy became afflicted with a rare gastronomical disorder that caused him to waste away. In a desperate attempt to save his life, surgeons inserted a silver metal tube directly into his stomach through which small amounts of food could be passed. The remedy worked, although Murphy was never able to eat solid food again.

It was never Croker's intent to have Murphy forsake his precarious health to devote himself entirely to the department. Croker was shrewd enough to realize that there was too much money at stake to allow a novice to take complete charge of the force, so just like the Police Board, the new police commissioner received his marching orders straight from the Tammany Hall sachem.

As soon as Murphy settled into the large second floor office at 300 Mulberry Street, one that had been previously occupied by the four members of the Police Board, he named William Devery as first deputy commissioner. Murphy explained that it was his desire to have men with "as much experience as may be possible" in the police business with him. For the record Devery accepted the post under protest because he felt that actions by the Charter Revision Committee to abolish the Police Board and the chief of police were illegal. There was also a monetary consideration. As first deputy commissioner, he was paid $2,000 less per year than he was as chief of police.

Reformers who had hoped to get rid of Devery by eliminating his position found little solace in the fact that he had accepted a pay cut to become second in command of the police force. This overt act of sedition by Murphy to circumvent the principal intent of the Charter Revision Committee outraged state Republicans, as well as a number of Tammany Hall Democrats who had sought to clean up the department. But nothing came of their protests.

Meanwhile, Colonel Murphy settled into his job by deferring most of the important decisions to his second in command. In his new post Devery also acted as trial commissioner, a responsibility that previously had fallen under the purview of the Police Board. Every Thursday morning patrolmen who had received charges during the preceding week traveled to Headquarters to face the "Big Chief," as he was still referred to by the rank and file.

Devery sat behind a large horseshoe-shaped desk. Patrolmen sat stoically before him on wooden pews, dressed in starched blue uniforms with polished brass buttons, waiting for their cases to be called. Oddly enough, officers who attempted to perform their sworn duty fared no better than those who shirked their responsibility. When a patrolman appeared before Devery sporting a deep cut over his temple, the result of a fierce struggle with a suspect who had managed to escape despite being fired at by the officer, Devery ordered a fine of "twenty days' pay for not hittin' him."

The harsh sentences meted out by Devery and the iron fist with which he ruled the department continued to undermine police morale to the point that his actions got Croker's attention. If Tammany Hall was going to secure the patrolmen's vote in the 1901 mayoral race, something had to be done other than threatening them with constant transfers.

Republicans sought to garner votes from the unhappy officers by proposing legislation for a three-platoon duty system with daily eight-hour shifts and fewer hours on reserve, long desired by the Patrolmen's Benevolent Association. The Van Wyck administration resisted at first because it estimated that $2.5 million would have to be added to the department's budget in order for the three-platoon duty system to provide the same patrol coverage as the two-platoon duty system. But money was no object for Tammany Hall when votes were at stake. In August 1901, just three months before the mayoral election took place, city Democrats surrendered their opposition and agreed to implement the three-platoon duty system before the Republicans had a chance to get the legislation passed by the state.

The new schedule went into effect on Tuesday, August 13, 1901, and forced the department to eliminate coverage on six hundred foot posts because fewer patrolmen were on duty. The new schedule also reduced the total number of hours that a patrolman was scheduled to work per year either on patrol or reserve from 5,824 to 4,046, excluding vacation and intermittent days off granted by the commanding officer

Shortly before the election, a noted reformer, the Reverend Charles H. Parkhurst, president of the Society for the Prevention of Crime, claimed to have uncovered a brazen trail of corruption that led directly to Police Headquarters. An undercover agent working for his organization discovered that the department's very own telephone line, SPR-3100, was being used to send calls from Headquarters to gambling establishments, advising them of impending police raids.

A spokesman for the Citizens' Union party declared, "The Police Department, which is paid and maintained by the people to suppress vice, is instead licensing vice and crime while collecting large fees for the benefit of Tammany Hall. The Police Department is using its great powers, under the direction and supervision of Tammany Hall leaders, to secure regular payments from gamblers and dive-keepers in return for freedom from police interference."

Although Devery was implicated in the payoff scheme, only a wardsman was convicted of any wrongdoing. But to the general public there was little doubt that Devery's leadership had deeply tarnished the badges of the city's police force.

Colonel Murphy became involved in a scandal of his own when he issued orders for patrolmen to purchase new brass buttons for their uniforms. He claimed that these distinctive removable buttons would allow the public to more easily tell the difference between a policeman and a trolley conductor because the words "New York City Police" were embossed on them. The buttons cost only five cents apiece, but patrolmen needed several for each of their uniform coats and had to pay for them out of pocket. The buttons were referred to derogatorily as "Murphy Buttons" when it was disclosed that Murphy shared the patent of the button with a friend and made money on each button purchased.

With Van Wyck ineligible for reelection in 1901, Croker threw his support behind Brooklyn lawyer Edward Shepard, whose political appeal lay in his reputation as an independent Democrat who insisted that he would be able to reform the police department from within. But this time around the blatant acts of corruption alleged to have been committed at Tammany Hall's behest caused many Democrats to throw their support to Seth Low, who was running again as a Fusion Party candidate and who pledged that if elected, he would dismiss both Police Commissioner Murphy and First Deputy Commissioner Devery on his first day in office.

The Shepard campaign was doomed when Shepard failed to make the same promise from the start. Whatever reputation Shepard had as a reformer was immediately forfeited under the presumption that he was merely another Tammany Hall puppet. When it became apparent on Election Day that Shepard would be defeated, Croker mused, "A change is good sometimes. But Tammany Hall will be here when we are all gone."

For his loyal service, Croker had seen to it that Van Wyck was placed on the ballot for City Supreme Court justice. From a field of six candidates, voters were asked to select three. Van Wyck came in dead last, twenty thousand ballots behind the fifth-place candidate. On his final day in office the *New York Times* wrote that it was an occasion for thankfulness because Van Wyck "delivered over the whole power of City Government into the hands of about the most conscienceless gang of knaves that ever disgraced the human family. There is nothing to do but loathe such a man." Of Devery the paper asserted, "The proved connivance with crime that has blackened the whole police department has not caused him to raise an eyelid or lift a finger."

Van Wyck never again achieved political prominence. A few years after leaving office, he married and moved to Paris, where he remained until his death in 1918. His estate at the time was estimated to be worth in excess of $5 million.

After the election loss Richard Croker retired to Ireland to pursue the gentlemen's sport of horse racing. In 1907 his horse won England's famous Epsom Derby. He passed away in Ireland in 1922, barely remembered for the prominent role he had played in the early days of the Greater City of New York and the formation of the NYPD.

With Croker out of the picture, the new leadership of Tammany Hall had little use for the "Big Chief." Nevertheless, Devery managed to get himself elected as a Democratic Party district leader and even ran for mayor in 1903 on the Independent People's Party line. He considered himself a viable candidate, but after the votes were tallied he received only 2,900 out of some 600,000 votes cast. Despite being trounced in the mayoral race, he remained a fixture in the New York political scene for years, often battling the same organization that he had once served so enthusiastically. Before he passed away from apoplexy in 1919, Devery became a part-owner of the New York Highlanders before they became the Yankees and operated a very successful real estate business in the Rockaways. Today his photograph is prominently displayed on the walls of both the first deputy commissioner's office and the chief of department's conference room at One Police Plaza.

In addition to serving as superintendent of elections, New York's first chief of police, John McCullagh, traveled to Havana at President William McKinley's behest to help reorganize the Cuban police force after the Spanish-American War. His commanding officer was Major General Francis Vinton Greene, who would become police commissioner in 1903. McCullagh died in 1917, the result of a stomach ailment. He was seventy-one years old. Several years later his admirers erected a memorial in his honor at Woodlawn Cemetery in the Bronx.

After leaving the department, Second Deputy Commissioner Bernard York returned to the practice of law and remained active in Brooklyn politics until his death in 1925 at the age of eighty. Occasionally he was mentioned as a possible candidate for police commissioner, but he was never actually offered the job.

Colonel Murphy never returned to public office. Unlike his associates, he did not enjoy the fruits of his labors. He died in 1903 of a heart attack attributed to his eating disorder. He had no children, and although a woman came forward claiming to be his widow, he left his meager estate of $2,000 to the man who had prepared his food for the last fourteen years of his life.

What can best be said about the first four years of the NYPD is that it survived. The force had been unified, and the adoption of a single police commissioner established a modicum of accountability. But the system also proved that unless the persons placed in charge were willing to provide leadership, the men on patrol were more than willing to compromise not only their oath to uphold the law but their ethics as well.

2

THE GHOST OF
WILLIAM DEVERY

One of the drawbacks of a free election system is that sometimes the better candidate loses. When Seth Low ran for mayor against Robert Van Wyck the first time in 1897, his superior credentials should have made him the obvious choice. He already had experience running a large municipal government as mayor of Brooklyn; he helped draft the City Charter, the document that would be used to govern the new Greater City of New York; and he served as president of Columbia University. Although Low could not overcome the forces of Tammany Hall, there was a silver lining in his loss. His votes combined with those of Republican candidate Benjamin Tracy were greater than Van Wyck's.

After the election Low resumed his duties at Columbia University but stayed active in politics. In particular, he served on the 1900 City Charter Revision Committee that abolished the unwieldy four-man Police Board and replaced it with a single police commissioner. The Citizens' Union renominated him as candidate for mayor in 1901. Low pledged that if he won, both Police Commissioner Murphy and First Deputy Devery would be removed as soon as he took office. This time New Yorkers rewarded him with a victory.

The new mayor-elect was born in Brooklyn in 1850. His family was well off, having made its fortune in the tea and silk trade with China. Low graduated from Columbia in 1870 and joined his father's import firm until the company was sold. In 1890 he became president of Columbia and donated a large portion of his personal fortune to relocate the university from Forty-Ninth Street and Madison Avenue to Morningside Heights in Upper Manhattan.

Low resigned his position at the university but did not wait until he was sworn in as mayor to start putting his administration together. Shortly after the election he announced that Colonel John Nelson Partridge, U.S. Army (retired), would succeed Police Commissioner Murphy.

John Partridge was born in Leicester, Massachusetts, in 1838. He served with distinction in the Union army during the Civil War and later was head of the Brooklyn police force from 1884 to 1885, during Low's tenure as mayor of Brooklyn. In addition to his police experience, Partridge's public service career included stints as fire commissioner for Brooklyn and superintendent of public works for the State of New York.

After his swearing-in ceremony at City Hall on New Year's Day 1902, Partridge traveled to Police Headquarters, where Murphy had been waiting to turn over the department. After the pair exchanged cordial greetings, Murphy introduced Partridge to First Deputy Devery, who had brought a lawyer with him to the meeting. Murphy made a pretense of offering assistance to Partridge should the need arise and then quickly excused himself. Devery then handed Partridge a letter addressed to the "So-called Commissioner of Police" and announced, "I formally present myself as a member of the uniformed force to do duty as Chief of Police."

Partridge took a moment to review the document in which Devery maintained that he was still a uniformed member of the force and could not be removed from his position as chief of police. "I cannot comply with what you ask," Partridge replied. "It's a matter for the courts. If they decide in your favor, their decision will be respected." With those words Devery's twenty-three-year association with the New York Police Department was ended, although the final outcome of his court case would not be decided for another year. In the interim Devery made himself available to the press for comment and opinion on any and all police matters.

Ridding the department of the physical presence of Devery would be Partridge's greatest achievement. Ridding it of his ghost was another matter, and it would soon become evident that he was not up to the challenge.

At his first command staff meeting Partridge confessed, "I do not believe that the most sanguine reformer expects to see a perfectly orderly condition restored to this city all in one day." He said that no drastic measures would be instituted so long as the police force towed the mark and that he intended to rely on a strict adherence to a military-style chain of command to accomplish his goals. Ultimately this meant that the lowest-ranking members of the department, the patrolmen, were destined for trouble because Partridge failed to take into account that most of the department's high-ranking officers had achieved their exalted positions as a direct result of their ties to Tammany Hall. So while Partridge preached discipline and accountability as hallmarks of his reform strategy, in truth whenever a patrolman leveled a legitimate complaint against a ranking officer, Partridge, because of his military background, was predisposed to side with the superior officer.

Just five weeks into the job Partridge unilaterally reimposed the dreaded two-platoon duty schedule. In defending his decision, he said that eight straight hours was too long for any man to be constantly patrolling and to do it faithfully. The superior officers praised his action as a victory over the Patrolmen's Benevolent Association, which had played both political parties to its advantage to get the three-platoon system implemented during the waning months of the Van Wyck administration.

After a group of patrolmen visited the mayor seeking his intervention, Low asked Partridge to determine if a better schedule could be devised. But Partridge sat on the request and did nothing. His inaction was interpreted by many precinct commanders to mean that they could resume with business as usual. Just as had been done during Devery's reign, instructions were soon being sent from Headquarters into the field to ignore the Raines Liquor Tax Law, which was part of the excise laws that controlled the sale of alcohol throughout New York State.

The statute—named after its sponsor, state senator John Raines— permitted hotels (defined as establishments serving food and having ten or more furnished rooms) to serve alcohol with meals on Sundays. Since saloons were not included, enterprising tavern owners suddenly began setting up makeshift kitchens and dividing storage space into enough bedrooms to qualify as hotels under the law. The combination of free-flowing liquor and backroom bedrooms proved to be a boon not only to the bar business, but to the prostitution trade as well. Taverns too small to be converted into "hotels" were banned from selling alcohol on the Sabbath, but for a price the police would overlook their violations as well.

When the expected police crackdown on the illegal Sunday liquor sales failed to materialize two months into Low's term, the same reformers who had so vehemently supported his candidacy for mayor suddenly denounced him. A spokesman for the Citizens' Union, the bipartisan political organization that had played such an important role in his election, noted sarcastically, "There's nothing like morality to kill reform."

As mayor of Brooklyn, Low had learned that people in the German, Irish, and Italian communities wanted taprooms open on Sunday afternoon because it was the only time they got to relax. As mayor of New York, he was willing to continue that practice so long as the "blue laws" were not flouted. In that regard he expected neighborhood taverns to keep their doors shut and windows shades drawn so as to at least appear to be closed when policemen walked by. But when the Reverend Charles H. Parkhurst convinced the politically ambitious district attorney for New York, William Travers Jerome, to use the power of his office to strictly enforce the Raines Law, it resulted in the first truly "Dry Sunday" of Low's tenure because the saloon owners were more afraid of Jerome than the police.

But just a week later, after receiving assurances from precinct commanders that they had "nothing to fear" from the district attorney, the taverns that made regular payoffs were back to serving liquor on Sundays.

Panhandling was rampant on the streets of New York. On June 14, 1902, Partridge became the first police commissioner to use the department as a force for social change by combining its resources with those of the Charity Organization Society to form the Mendicancy Police. Four specially trained patrolmen working out of Headquarters were detailed for the specific purpose of suppressing street beggars. But their duties went beyond simply arresting the indigent. The Mendicancy Police also provided temporary shelter, secondhand clothing, hot meals, and employment opportunities to the destitute. Nevertheless, such innovation did little to dispel the perception that Partridge had failed to take complete charge of the department. By midsummer the city's Jewish population joined the chorus of reformers demanding his resignation.

On July 30, 1901, Rabbi Joseph Jacob, a popular religious leader from Manhattan's Lower East Side Hebrew community, passed away. The following day the department detailed fifty patrolmen to provide security for his funeral procession. The bearded mourners in black hats and overcoats solemnly wended their way through the narrow streets of the Lower East Side without incident until they reached R. Hoe and Co., a printing press factory on Grand Street. Suddenly and without provocation, the factory workers began bombarding them with bricks.

At first the Jews begged their police escorts for help, but when the officers refused to take action against their assailants, the mourners stormed the factory. The situation quickly spiraled out of control. Police on the scene sent out a desperate call for reinforcements. Two hundred police reserves under the command of Inspector Adam Cross rushed to the location to quell the riot. Witnesses reported that the inspector took the side of the print shop workers and shouted orders for his men to club the life out of the Jewish troublemakers.

The newspapers called the disturbance a Jewish riot. Community leaders refuted the official police account. Some even claimed that the much maligned William Devery would have done better. With all his faults, Devery got some results for law and order and for the protection and security of the people, they said.

When reporters asked Partridge if he thought his patrolmen did the right thing striking the Jewish people, he shrugged and said, "What do they carry clubs for?" Then he attempted to clarify his remarks. "There are places where a policeman in quieting a disorder has to use his club. If I discipline a policeman who has used his club in a legitimate manner, I could soon get the police so that they would be afraid to use their clubs for the purpose for which they were intended."

What Partridge failed to disclose to the newspapers was that since taking over as police commissioner, he had developed a close relationship with Inspector Cross and had come to rely on him for advice. So it was with great reluctance and only after receiving explicit instructions from the mayor himself that Partridge banished his most trusted confidant to the Bronx. In keeping with his personal admiration for Inspector Cross, Partridge denied that the new assignment had anything to do with what had happened during the Jewish melee and refused to denounce the anti-Semitic acts attributed to him.

The negative publicity, however, served to further erode public confidence in Partridge's ability to lead the city's police force. It became apparent to Mayor Low that if he was to achieve a second term in office, the issue of police reform would have to take priority over all other matters. The first thing Low did was to appoint an independent civilian review board to investigate the alleged assaults by police during the rabbi's funeral. The panel concluded that the escorting officers had been negligent in their duty and were responsible for the ensuing riot. After reviewing the report, Low ordered Partridge to bring charges against Inspector Cross for his actions during the donnybrook. Partridge reluctantly scheduled a departmental hearing for later that year.

Meanwhile, the sixteen-hour workday under the two-platoon system continued to be a major bone of contention between Partridge and the patrol force. But it took a direct order from the mayor for him to finally meet with representatives of the Patrolmen's Benevolent Association to discuss the issue. After Patrolman William Drennan of the Seventeenth Precinct explained the merits of the three-platoon system versus the two-platoon system, Partridge replied that the only reason patrolmen wanted the three-platoon duty schedule was so that they could hide more easily from the roundsmen. Drennan countered that a cop could not hide from a roundsman who *really wanted* to find him. An anonymous voice from the back of the crowded room shouted, "Good boy."

When Partridge asked Patrolman John Ritter for his honest opinion, Ritter admitted, "Where a man has a long post with a bad section in one end and a quiet one at the other, he will probably seek the latter." His candor had no effect because Partridge had already made up his mind that the two-platoon system would remain in effect no matter how badly his officers wanted the three-platoon duty schedule.

It also turned out that patrolmen fared no better under Partridge than they had under Devery at the department trial room. Just about anything could subject them to charges, including allegations of spitting in public. At one hearing Partridge decreed that eight patrolmen had shown a "lack of respect for the dead" by failing to investigate the demise of a cat on a post they shared over the course of several days. He fined each officer a week's pay for ignoring the dead cat.

Precinct doormen were responsible for maintaining the department's stationhouses, many of which were in decrepit condition. They were paid $1,000 per year for sweeping floors, shoveling snow, loading coal, stoking furnaces, washing windows, painting walls, and tending to prisoners. During breaks in their daily chores, they acted as precinct receptionists and assisted complainants with everything from finding missing children to locating lost property.

As more and more duties were piled upon them, doormen had to hire their own assistants and paid them ten dollars a month out of their own salaries. They decided to form the Police Doormen's Mutual Aid and Relief Association and petitioned Partridge and then the courts for a raise, claiming that were they not only "cleaners and general custodians" but also "turnkeys and peace officers."

Partridge was adamant that they were neither peace officers nor turnkeys, just common laborers who cleaned windows only three times a year and painted walls just once. Although the courts sided with Partridge, the civil service position of doorman was subsequently decertified, and doormen were elevated to patrolmen. But since the stationhouses still had to be maintained, the former doormen ended up performing the same duties as before at the higher patrolmen's salary, which was more than they had asked Partridge for. They became known in police parlance as "brooms" and remained fixtures in precinct stationhouses for decades into the future.

In November 1902 Macy's opened its much ballyhooed new department store in Herald Square. That same month Inspector Cross was brought to department trial for his conduct during the Jewish riot. He testified under oath that on the morning in question he did not know Rabbi Jacob was dead "or that he had ever lived," for that matter. He said that by the time he arrived on the scene, many people were covered with blood, but order had been restored. Throughout the cross-examination he maintained that he had done nothing improper.

As Partridge considered the evidence against Cross, Mayor Low met in private with Governor Benjamin Odell and state Republican Party leader Thomas Platt. They convinced Low that the police commissioner had to go. Partridge saw the handwriting on the wall. Rather than suffer the embarrassment of being fired, he informed the mayor on Christmas Eve that he planned to resign from the department at the end of the year for health reasons.

The timing of Partridge's announcement left him one week to clear up old business. During his final days in office he promoted thirty-eight roundsmen, sixty sergeants, and two captains, the largest single group of promotions since the consolidation. While the long promotion lists made headlines, a small paragraph buried deep inside the Christmas Day edition of the *New York Times* reported that Police Commissioner Partridge had exonerated Inspector Cross for his actions during the funeral of Rabbi Jacobs. Unfortunately for the maligned inspector, additional allegations of misconduct would be forthcoming. Without Partridge's backing, the charges would lead to his dismissal from the department.

Low announced that he would appoint a retired army general, Francis Vinton Greene, as police commissioner, effective January 1, 1903. That morning Partridge handed over the gold commissioner's shield to General Greene and declared, "I feel sure that something has been accomplished in this department." He departed without explaining exactly what he meant by that statement.

The fifty-two-year-old Greene was born in Rhode Island. He was educated at West Point and served as an army artillery officer and later as a U.S. military attaché assigned to observe the Russian Army during the Russo-Turkish War in 1877. He volunteered for service during the Spanish-American War. As noted, after the hostilities he and former New York chief of police John McCullagh helped reorganize the Cuban police force. In between his military postings Greene served as president of the Hudson River Power Transmission Company, director of the Niagara Gorge Railroad, and director of the Seaboard National Bank. At the time of his appointment he was president of the Asphalt Company of America. It was said that he had close ties to President Theodore Roosevelt, Governor Odell, and legislator Platt.

Greene's motto was "Strike and spare not." He called all of the ranking officers to Police Headquarters on New Year's Day and told them, "I shall hold you personally to the most rigid responsibility for what takes place in your districts." It was a speech the brass had heard before, but this time a police commissioner actually meant it. In an unprecedented move Greene ordered all of the district inspectors to relocate their offices from Headquarters to suitable precincts in their districts, "so that you may be in the closest touch with the officers and members of the force under your command."

At the conclusion of his speech Greene wished them a happy new year and then promptly suspended five captains and an inspector, all of whom had unresolved charges pending from the Partridge administration. The *New York Times* reported that the suspension order struck the police brass "like a lightning bolt."

Later that morning Greene issued orders dividing the city for administrative purposes into two "Grand Divisions." The First Grand Division was Manhattan, the Bronx, and Staten Island, and the Second Grand Division was Brooklyn and Queens. Then he appointed Senior Inspector Moses Cortright to a new position he created and called the "chief inspector," which was to be the highest position in the uniformed ranks. Although Cortright's new title did not pay him any more money, as chief inspector, he was given broad authority to oversee police operations throughout the city. In addition, Cortright provided Greene with a single commander to lead the uniformed force, something that had been lacking during Partridge's tenure.

When asked for his opinion of Greene after one day in office, Devery described him as a "flash in the pan" who would not last.

The next day Greene removed all 302 wardsmen from their plainclothes details and transferred them to uniformed patrol. Although cynics predicted precinct commanders would select equally corrupt candidates to fill the vacancies, it was nonetheless a bold move by Greene because by disrupting the collection mechanism for organized payoffs, he now had the ability to enforce the Raines Law, and he did so with great enthusiasm.

Greene was the first police commissioner to require patrolmen to keep memo books to account for their daily patrol activities, a practice that continues to this day. But he was surprised to discover that when policemen got into trouble and were brought to trial, they often concocted a story that completely contradicted what they had written in their memo books. Of this he lamented, "No matter how absurd or ridiculous it may be, they will testify to it."

But unlike his predecessor, Greene understood the plight of patrolmen and sought to make their lot easier by modifying the two-platoon duty system to make it more palatable. His new six-section schedule still maintained the day and night patrols but used three squads for each platoon instead of two. It required only two of the three squads to be on patrol at any time and for no more than eight hours, with the third squad held in reserve for just four hours a day instead of seven hours, as had been the past practice. This way each patrolman was given sixteen hours off every other day and thirty-two hours off every third week. While a significant improvement over the former configuration, in which police officers were required to log in over 5,800 hours per year, the new schedule still called for patrolmen to work over 4,700 hours per year.

When the Dutch first settled New Amsterdam, little consideration was given to civic planning. As a result, narrow streets in Lower Manhattan crisscrossed in a haphazard manner, snarling traffic for blocks in all directions. The introduction of horseless carriages at the start of the twentieth century made the predicament even worse. Second Deputy Commissioner Ross Piper and Patrolman Daniel Costigan (who would one day earn the nickname "Honest Dan" for being incorruptible and later figure prominently in the career of future police commissioner Lewis Valentine) were dispatched to London to study the British method for regulating traffic.

When the pair returned to New York, they put their lessons to use for the first time on St. Patrick's Day 1903. Costigan took charge of the NYPD's first traffic control detail at the intersection of Broadway and Canal Street. At precisely 9 a.m. Costigan signaled two patrolmen to block traffic on Canal Street. Two other officers then waved through traffic traveling on Broadway. After thirty seconds Costigan signaled for them to switch duties. At first there was a great deal of confusion because drivers did not understand the new system. One disgruntled driver was even heard complaining, "Wait until Tammany gits back, and we won't have no more of this English nonsense." Nevertheless, the traffic control experiment was deemed a success and soon expanded to other busy intersections in Manhattan.

Greene's military background made him a firm believer in the adage that proper training improved performance. As a whole he observed that patrolmen were not very proficient with their firearms. To remedy the situation he established a separate curriculum in the School of Instruction just for pistol practice. For the first time patrolmen were required to fire their revolvers under the eye of a police sharpshooter. While the end-of-the-year statistics were far from spectacular, an important first step had been taken to improve accuracy of firearm discharges by patrolmen.

Proper training did not necessarily make patrolmen better citizens, however. The annual police parade took place on May 2, 1903. It was a happy occasion in which medals for heroism were presented by the mayor and the police commissioner. After a long day of celebration Sergeant Thomas Gil-hooley and two colleagues stopped off at the Lenox Hotel on Sixth Avenue and West Third Street for a nightcap. The *New York Times* described the neighborhood as "infested with about the worst colored criminals in the city."

Whether for their own amusement or as a result of too much libation, the officers began to berate their server, a black waiter named Jefferson Saunders. Around 10 p.m. the haranguing escalated into a wild brawl that spilled out onto the street. Saunders put up a fierce struggle. When the officers finally subdued him, they were so angry that they threatened to shoot him. Unbeknownst to them, Saunders had a long criminal record and was armed with a gun of his own. He fired at close range and killed Sergeant Gilhooley.

The department denied the three officers had been drinking before the fight, but after an extensive two-month investigation into the deadly encounter by District Attorney Jerome, a grand jury refused to indict Saunders for murder. After he was set free, the newspapers continued to refer to him as the "police slayer."

Sergeant Gilhooley's widow was denied a survivor's pension since her husband's death was classified as non-line-of-duty. To make matters even worse, she received nothing from her husband's $2,500 life insurance policy because Gilhooley had designated the wife of a police inspector as his beneficiary in exchange for the inspector's arranging for his promotion to sergeant. Apparently Gilhooley did not have enough cash to pay for the promotion outright. The disclosure incensed Greene so much that he vowed to get Gilhooley's widow something for her husband's fourteen years of honorable service.

In August 1903 Greene reported the Bell Telephone Company had been awarded a contract to install the first of 661 police call boxes on poles throughout Manhattan. In return the telephone company would receive $20,335 per year in maintenance and rental fees. Similar systems that allowed patrolmen to contact their stationhouses from distant patrol posts via the telephone had already proved successful in other large American cities.

That same month Low announced that a new five-story police headquarters would be built at Centre Street and Grand Street to replace 300 Mulberry Street and that $500,000 had been budgeted for its construction.

As the 1903 mayoral election approached, Greene had transformed the department into a relatively honest and efficient police force as compared to its past incarnations. Plans were under way to beef up the department by one thousand men and to divide the notorious Tenderloin district into two precincts to make it more manageable.

Ironically while it was generally conceded that a bad police department could destroy a mayor, the opposite was not necessarily true. As a result, Mayor Low's Fusion administration was in serious trouble. In an effort to build a true coalition of voter support, Low had placed reform-minded Democrats and political independents into 40 percent of his patronage appointments. He had also included a record number of Italians and Jews and had even gone so far as to appoint a black to a city clerk position. But in appeasing reformers, he had failed to strengthen his ties with the Republicans who had played such a major role in his mayoral victory. Although there was no doubt that the city was being run more efficiently, Low had inadvertently alienated a large percentage of voters who had supported him in 1901.

If his term had been four years instead of two, he may have been able to remedy the situation. Low realized too late that there was not enough time for him to accomplish all of the things he need to do to guarantee his reelection. "A bad administration grows weaker the longer it is in power," he later explained. "A good one grows stronger the longer it is in power."

Although Low had lobbied the state legislature to allow the city to determine for itself how to enforce the Sunday blue laws, he had succumbed to reformers who demanded the law be enforced as written. As a result working-class voters felt deprived of their social right to drink on their only day of leisure. It did not take much for Tammany Hall to fan these flames of discontent.

The Fusion ideal, with its high moral standards, had taken away the ability of both the good and the bad people of New York to use their connections and money as a means to get what they wanted. By being receptive to the most common complaints about the Low administration, Tammany Hall was once again able to achieve broad-based political support.

After Richard Croker's departure, the organization leadership had floundered for a short while until 1903, when it came solidly under the control of Croker disciple Charles Murphy, who had been the docks commissioner under Mayor Van Wyck. Murphy selected five-term congressman George B. McClellan Jr., the son of the famous Civil War Union general George Brinton McClellan (Lincoln's befuddled commander of the Union army), as the Democratic candidate for mayor. The younger McClellan had name recognition and the foresight to distance himself from Croker's puppet, Van Wyck.

McClellan campaigned on the principle that New York was an overwhelmingly Democratic city and therefore should be governed by the party most receptive to the needs of its people. He accused Greene of enforcing the Raines Law to the point of infringing on the personal liberty of the citizens of New York.

Low's supporters viewed the contest as a battle for the soul of New York. It pitted the mayor's honest but bland style of politics against the corrupt but flamboyant style practiced by most Tammany Hall cronies.

A third candidate, representing the Independent People's Party, made good on his promise to run for mayor. Ex-police chief William Devery campaigned around the city in a grandiose automobile. Unfortunately the touring car was temperamental and frequently broke down, causing him to miss as many campaign stops as he made. Although he was not given much of a chance, his goal was to siphon enough votes from the Democrats to help the Fusionists win. In that way he would make Tammany Hall pay for abandoning him.

The final count showed incumbent Seth Low had 252,086 votes and Democrat George McClellan had 314,782. For all his bluster Devery was never a factor. He received fewer than 3,000 votes and fared particularly poorly in Staten Island, where only eight people voted for him.

For Greene, who had taken extra measures to ensure that the election was fair, the return of Tammany Hall to City Hall was a terrible blow. "The voters have deliberately decided to reinstate the Tammany rule of crime and corruption," he sighed. "I consider this one of the most profound and significant events that have happened in this country since the Civil War."

Speaking about Mayor Low after the election, legislator Platt remarked of his old friend, "He came and went. New York is the same old town." But that was not true for either the police department or New York politics.

Mayor Low retired to become a gentleman farmer in Westchester County. Although he never again held elective office, Low continued to be a prominent voice for the reform movement. His well-deserved reputation for honesty helped him forge a career later in life as a distinguished labor arbitrator, during which he helped mediate nationwide strikes that involved coal miners and railroad workers. He was also an early proponent of developing a system of workers' compensation for employees injured on the job. Low died of cancer on his dairy farm in September 1916 at the age of sixty-six, leaving a wife but no children.

Former police commissioner John Partridge cited health concerns as the reason for his hasty retirement from the department at age sixty-two. Three years later he moved to Westport, Connecticut, and lived there until 1920, when he died at the ripe old age of eighty-two.

Although thoroughly disappointed with the election results, Greene continued to pursue his policies until the end of the term. Those ranking members of the department who appreciated his honest service presented him with a portrait of himself as a parting gift. He thanked them and said, "You know as well as I know that there are some bad men on the police force; but we all know, and it has always been a pleasure to me to say it, that the majority of the police force are upright, self-respecting men, who do their duty courageously and efficiently; and in leaving the department it will be a pleasure for me to carry away the recollection of the good deeds and the honest work performed by the great majority of the force and to forget the bad deeds of the minority."

After leaving the force, Greene lectured about his time as police commissioner, paving the way for those who followed him to start new careers in retirement on the public speaking circuit. In a speech to Columbia University students he spoke frankly about the problems of graft. "A policeman is never deterred by a sense of personal danger. No policeman would tolerate another who shrank from an assailant or from dispersing a mob. Such a man would be driven from the force in disgrace through the contempt of the rest. If such an *esprit de corps* existed in the matter of graft and truth telling, it would be a splendid influence, but it does not exist at all. The honest men are very reluctant to expose the dishonest men. They do not want to testify against them."

In 1904 Greene accepted a position as president of the Niagara, Lockport and Ontario Railroad and moved to Buffalo. He remained there until poor health forced his return to New York City in 1915. Greene spent his last six years writing articles on military and political topics for the *New York Times*. He died on May 16, 1921, at the age of seventy-one.

Perhaps Greene's greatest compliment came from hard-nosed District Attorney Jerome, who said, "There was no tiring General Greene out. If he was baffled once, he began all over again. He simply would not accept defeat. Had he been commissioner for even another term, or better, six years, it is the system that would have been worn out."

3

A ONE-LEGGED
POLICE COMMISSIONER
TAKES CHARGE

In the autumn of 1903 Congressman George B. McClellan Jr. accepted the Democratic nomination for mayor of New York. Truth be told, the thirty-eight-year-old McClellan would have preferred to remain in the House of Representatives, but Charles Murphy, who had gained control of Tammany Hall after Richard Croker's departure, convinced him that he was the only Democrat who could unseat Mayor Low. Most of the other potential candidates were tainted by their association with the political organization, but McClellan had the benefit of having been in Washington for the previous ten years. Since Tammany Hall was interested only in the affairs of New Yorkers and not the rest of America, it had little need to call on him while he was in Congress. As far as Murphy was concerned, this made McClellan an ideal candidate.

While McClellan knew that Tammany Hall was corrupt, he rationalized that so too were the Republican clubs in cities where they controlled the vote. In addition, he firmly believed that whereas a smaller, less exalted man might suffer from "evil company," a gentleman such as he remained a gentleman regardless of his associates. Still he found it necessary to distance himself from Tammany Hall. During the campaign he called fellow Democrat Robert Van Wyck the "most pitiable object who ever held great public office" for ceding control of the municipal government to Tammany Hall's "Boss" Croker. McClellan's public pronouncement, aided by some shrewd political maneuvering on the part of "Boss" Murphy (who literally stole the Fusionists slate out from under Mayor Low), incensed the reformers. The anti-Tammany factions warned the public, "The lid will come off," implying that all of the reforms the Low administration had put into place would come undone if McClellan was elected.

The reformers became especially concerned when McClellan vowed to discharge Police Commissioner Greene if he won the election. While McClellan regarded Greene a talented leader, he had no desire to have his administration hampered by an ally of Mayor Low's. The issue became moot after McClellan disclosed that Greene had been involved in what he called a "shady business deal" during his banking days and therefore had no place in his honest administration. Although the incident from Greene's past was ancient history, it silenced McClellan's opposition. McClellan won with approximately 53 percent of the total ballot.

During the campaign McClellan promised patrolmen that he would restore the three-platoon duty system that Police Commissioner Partridge had taken away. The police overwhelmingly supported his bid for office, but McClellan really owed his victory to the Tammany machine, and since he had been away from city politics for so long, McClellan left it up to Murphy to decide who should receive a patronage appointment, with the exception of two positions: his private secretary and Greene's replacement.

McClellan named former newspaper reporter John O'Brien as his private secretary. Deciding on who would be the new police commissioner proved to be more daunting. McClellan determined that the head of the police force would not come from the ranks because the last thing he wanted was an unsavory character like Bill Devery taking charge again. The possibilities were further limited by the fact that he did not want to give the job to a career politician.

By mid-December 1903 McClellan still had not made a decision. His first choice, retired major general Samuel Sumner, whose father had fought under General McClellan at Antietam, turned him down. When Murphy half jokingly suggested, "If you don't find a commissioner soon, I shall have to take the job myself," McClellan decided he could wait no longer. He beseeched a longtime Washington acquaintance, William McAdoo, to take the post. McAdoo accepted the job only after McClellan assured him that no one in or out of any political organization (namely, Tammany Hall) would come between them and that all of their dealings would be open and candid as between gentlemen. It was a decision McAdoo would come to regret.

The fifty-year-old McAdoo was born in Ireland in 1853. He had served as assistant secretary of the navy under President Grover Cleveland and, like McClellan, had been a journalist and a congressman. But whereas McClellan shared the dreams of his father to one day become president, McAdoo had given up politics to practice law.

At noon on January 1, 1904, before a crowded City Hall, Low turned the office over to his successor with these parting words: "I am glad as one of the great body of citizens to salute you and wish you well."

In his inaugural address McClellan promised an honest effort to improve the delivery of city services but conceded, "Conditions must be faced as they are and not as we should like to have them." After the brief inauguration ceremony McAdoo journeyed to 300 Mulberry Street. His first impression of Police Headquarters was that it was dirty and dingy. Years later he would describe the building as a quagmire of corruption and a chamber of horrors.

McAdoo and Greene exchanged pleasantries. If the earlier accusations McClellan had leveled bothered him, Greene did not show it. By all accounts the general was in good spirits when he presented McAdoo with the gold commissioner's badge and told him, "Your high character and conduct in life prove that you are worthy to wear it. I wish you every success." When the reporters asked for a statement, McAdoo said that he would do everything in his power to prevent blackmail, extortion, graft, or bribe taking by the police. Then after a quick tour of Headquarters, he assembled his inspectors and captains and told them, "I want to be loyal to the police, and I expect the police to be loyal to me."

McAdoo believed that with an honest man at the helm of the ship, the police would steer themselves in the right direction. He would later admit to being naive about department operations and ignorant of actual conditions. What McAdoo discovered was that an honest cop would never expose a dirty cop and that this attitude was prevalent throughout the department, a trait he attributed to the cops' shared Irish heritage.

McClellan was very cognizant of the "lid will come off" rhetoric that had been levied against him during the mayoral campaign. In his early conversations with McAdoo he made it clear that as far as he was concerned, the three most serious problems for the police to address were gambling, prostitution, and alcohol. He left it up to McAdoo to decide how to best handle them.

In the past widespread graft had made it difficult to secure evidence against gambling establishments using traditional methods of detection. McAdoo determined that a new strategy was necessary to "screw down the lid," as he put it. Little more than a week into his tenure he stationed forty detective sergeants and plainclothesmen on fixed posts directly in front of some of the Tenderloin's most notorious poolrooms (establishments suspected of taking bets on horse races). The job of the officers was to deter business simply by advising customers that they risked arrest if they entered the premises.

The blockade was so effective that the poolroom operators begged "Boss" Murphy to intercede. They had good reason to expect help since many of the Tammany Hall politicians were on their payroll. When McClellan refused Murphy's request to have McAdoo rein in the police, their relationship soured. The poolroom operators put pressure on Murphy by threatening to give the names of Democrats on the pad to the newspapers. Murphy responded by cutting off the wire services on which the bookmakers relied for their horse race results. This created a stalemate in which neither side benefited. Even Western Union complained because profits from its telegraph service in New York plummeted during the dispute.

The status quo returned after the owners of legitimate establishments operating on the same blocks as the poolrooms got Brooklyn justice William J. Gaynor to issue a restraining order against the department because the constant presence of police was having a negative impact on their businesses as well. The city appealed Gaynor's decision so that McAdoo could continue his policy of harassment, but in the interim the poolroom operators and politicians quietly resumed their previous business arrangement.

While most poolrooms were frequented by men, a handful of betting parlors in the city catered only to women. When the commander of the West Sixty-Eighth Street stationhouse learned of one operating within the confines of his precinct, he enlisted the help of a police matron for the first time to infiltrate the establishment.

Matron Mary Quinn admitted that she was "not over pleased to be dragged out of the precinct" to take part in the raid, but she played her role well nevertheless. As soon as the bell rang indicating that the horses were off, she stood up and announced, "You're all under arrest." Before the female customers could flee, her backup team came crashing through the rear window to effect the arrests.

The crackdown on poolrooms was put on hold for several weeks during the summer of 1904. On Wednesday, June 15, the popular excursion boat *General Slocum* departed from a pier on the Lower East Side of Manhattan. Nearly all of the passengers were women and children of German descent who belonged to St. Mark's Evangelical Church. The Lutheran congregation had paid $350 to charter the vessel to sail round trip to Huntington, Long Island, for its annual summer picnic.

A fire broke out below deck just as the paddle-wheeler reached the turbulent waters of Hell Gate, where the East River met Long Island Sound. As smoke began to billow up the stairwell and out onto the bow, panicky passengers at the front of the boat scrambled toward the stern seeking safety.

The captain ordered full-speed ahead, hoping to make shore before the ship became completely engulfed, but the wind only served to fan the flames. The crew attempted to douse the blaze, but they had not been properly trained, nor had the dilapidated firefighting equipment been maintained. To make matters worse, the crew could not lower the lifeboats into the water because the davits were crusted with layer upon layer of paint. Faced with certain death if they stayed on board, hundreds of women and children donned cork life vests and leapt into the swirling waters. But the cork filling in the life jackets was so old and rotten that it had no buoyancy ability to keep them afloat, especially in their period clothing.

Although members of the police Harbor Unit rushed to the scene, there were already hundreds of corpses bobbing in the water by the time they arrived at the disaster. The intense heat made it impossible for them to draw close enough to the *General Slocum* to rescue the desperate few still clinging to its outer railing, begging for help.

The captain and his crew managed to survive by jumping overboard just before the vessel crashed into North Brother's Island. The remaining passengers were not as fortunate. The violent impact caused the ship's burning superstructure to collapse on top of them, trapping them in a raging inferno. A short time later the captain and his crew were arrested trying to flee the island, along with thieves whom police caught looting the corpses that washed to shore.

McClellan placed McAdoo in charge of the investigation. During the recovery operation the police set up a temporary morgue on the island where corpses were stored on ice. When they ran out of space, the remaining corpses were removed to the Alexander Avenue stationhouse in the South Bronx and photographed in order to help with identification. Unfortunately some of the corpses were burned beyond recognition. McAdoo dispatched Inspector Max Schmittberger and several German-speaking police officers to the Lower East Side to gather information to help identify victims and console their families. Sixty-one victims ended up being buried in a mass grave of unknowns at the Lutheran Cemetery in Middle Village, Queens.

Police officials determined that 1,021 of the 1,358 passengers who had boarded the *General Slocum* that fateful morning lost their lives. The captain was ultimately found guilty of criminal negligence for failure to hold practice fire drills as required by law. He was sentenced to ten years in prison, but his sentenced was commuted after he had served half that time in jail. The community never recovered from the disaster. While speaking at a memorial service to commemorate the victims, McAdoo said, "There are no better people in New York."

While he had high regard for members of the German population, Mc-Adoo could not say the same about Italian immigrants living in Manhattan. Nearly one-quarter of New York's population was of Italian descent. Little Italy in itself had become the second largest "Italian" city in the world, smaller only than Naples. Most of its inhabitants were crammed into poverty-stricken tenements centering on Mott and Mulberry Streets. This ghetto provided a myriad of opportunities for criminal gangs from the "old country" to take advantage of the destitute residents.

In an official report to the mayor McAdoo called the situation of the Lower East Side an insoluble problem for the police. "It is simply impossible to pack human beings into these honey-combs towering over the narrow canyons of streets and then propose to turn them into citizens who respect and obey the laws."

Detective Sergeant Giuseppe "Joe" Petrosino thought otherwise. The squat Italian immigrant had joined the department in 1883 at age twenty-three, after starting out as a city street sweeper before becoming a patrolman. Though only one of a handful of policemen who could speak Italian, he was determined to make a difference in his community. Police Board president Theodore Roosevelt was so impressed with Petrosino's efforts that he promoted him to detective sergeant in 1895. But one man alone was no match for the Black Hand, the Italian mob whose methods of terror included kidnapping, extortion, and crude explosive devices.

Petrosino appealed to McAdoo. "At least give me a team of Italians. With Irishmen and Jews you'll never get a spider out of its web." It took almost a year, but Petrosino's persistence paid off. In January 1905 McAdoo informed him that the Board of Aldermen had at long last granted his request to create a special squad of Italian cops to battle the Black Hand.

Even with the new Italian squad, as it was called, finally up and running, Petrosino admitted that policing five hundred thousand people with just five police officers was a daunting task. Nevertheless, the squad's strategic use of informants resulted in the creation for the first time of a reliable list of suspected Italian criminals operating in New York.

The undercover work was extremely dangerous. On one occasion Petrosino was mistaken for a criminal after a roundsman spotted him lurking about Little Italy and made a report to Headquarters. He did not know that Petrosino's unit was operating out of a small storefront on Waverly Place to keep a closer eye on the neighborhood thugs. During the subsequent police raid of the premises, the captain in charge aimed his gun at Petrosino's head. A desperate scuffle ensued until Petrosino was finally able to convince the captain that he was a cop himself. Several days later McAdoo banished the captain to Brooklyn for his mistake and Petrosino was given an office at Headquarters, where the brass could get to know him in order to avoid future instances of mistaken identity.

As noted, McClellan had promised patrolmen that if he won the election, he would restore the three-platoon duty system that had been rescinded by the Low administration. But critics of that system were quick to point out that fewer patrolmen were on duty at any one time. McAdoo countered that it did not matter if there were two platoons or eight platoons; the present size of the force was inadequate to meet the city's needs. Before he could carry through with his promise, McClellan first had to seek permission from the state legislature and then the Board of Estimate to increase the size of the patrol force over the authorized quota. Approval for an additional 150 patrolmen came in late February 1904. McAdoo reinstated the three-platoon duty schedule on March 1. A second increase of 400 patrolmen was approved in September. Unfortunately the department's antiquated training facility could accommodate only 50 recruits per class. In order to supplement the patrol force until more officers were hired and trained, McAdoo rousted the old timers out of their cushy jobs at Headquarters. Men who had previously spent their days winding clocks, polishing brass, and emptying spittoons suddenly found themselves back on patrol.

An unintended consequence of Greene's earlier crackdown on vice was that prostitution, which had been concentrated in the Tenderloin, was now scattered into other areas of the city. McClellan preferred to have it pushed back into the Tenderloin, if for no other reason than to appease Reverend Parkhurst and his ilk. He directed McAdoo to do whatever he could to clear the area outside the Tenderloin of brothels and streetwalkers.

The main obstacle facing McAdoo was that the disorderly houses, much like the poolrooms, paid large sums of money to the police and politicians to simply ignore their existence. To get around the problem McAdoo took responsibility away from the precincts and created a special plainclothes vice squad detailed out of the Central Office at Headquarters to shut down the houses of prostitution. Since these plainclothesmen had no ties to the precincts that were home to the brothels, McAdoo thought that they would be less likely to accept unlawful gratuities for looking the other way. But once the unit was in operation and the brothel operators realized that the precinct commanders they had bribed could no longer "deliver the goods," they began to offer money directly to the members of the vice squad, forcing McAdoo to transfer officers in and out of the unit on an almost daily basis.

To clear Fifth Avenue of streetwalkers, McAdoo installed a new captain in the Tenderloin precinct. The captain took the law into his own hands by imposing a 10 p.m. curfew in the precinct. Any woman caught on the streets after 10 p.m. without a proper escort was presumed to be a prostitute. He ordered his patrolmen to arrest such women for vagrancy, a task that had previously been the responsibility of the precinct plainclothesmen. The captain reasoned that since the uniformed officers walked the same beat every night, they were in the best position to know which women were "disorderly."

Despite the fact that the patrolmen complied with the order, nearly every case was dismissed because when the patrolmen were asked by the judge why they had arrested the women, they blamed it on the captain's order rather than providing evidence of guilt in each case.

When McAdoo got wind of their shenanigans, he became the first police commissioner to visit a stationhouse specifically for the purpose of doing a bit of arm twisting. McAdoo told the officers that the stance the captain had taken was fundamentally sound and that they had to enforce the law. "You must arrest a woman whom you know and can prove has no lawful employment whereby to maintain herself," he said. He further explained that they had to produce such proof in court or he would consider their testimony an intentional effort to discredit him, the police department, and the precinct commander. "If I should become convinced that this precinct is in mutiny," he warned, "I will act suddenly so swiftly and surely that those concerned will not forget it for many a day to come."

The patrolmen got the message. Within a very short time Fifth Avenue was cleared of prostitutes and was declared as safe as a country street by the mayor.

How to best enforce the laws against the illegal sale of alcohol vexed McClellan, just as it had Mayor Low. But rather than leave the matter up to McAdoo, he decided to handle it himself. McClellan discussed the problem with Fritz Lindinger, president of the Wine, Liquor, and Beer Dealers' Association. Lindinger freely admitted that tavern owners paid off the police to stay open at times prohibited by law. McClellan was more upset with the policemen taking bribes than with the bars serving liquor on Sundays. He told Lindinger that if he got his members to stop paying bribes to the police, he would personally see to it that no harm came to their businesses.

When the two men met a few months later, McClellan asked how things were going. Lindinger advised him that his members were no longer paying protection money to the police. The mayor was delighted until Lindinger explained that a new arrangement had been made with the precinct commanders by which they would receive a nice big Christmas present.

McClellan was furious and blamed McAdoo for what had happened, even though he had never discussed the matter with him. McAdoo was so upset that the next morning he appeared at City Hall with the department's entire compliment of inspectors in tow. He lined them up in front of the mayor and asked each one on his word of honor if he knew of any case of direct or indirect payment of protection money to the police.

To a man they swore, "On my word of honor, I know of no such case." McAdoo turned to the mayor and asked, "Are you satisfied?"

"Yes," McClellan replied sarcastically, "I am satisfied that if the inspectors have told the truth, they know very little of what is going on in their districts." After the meeting McClellan concluded that McAdoo did not have control of the police department and began to consider how to replace him.

The city's first subway line went into operation on October 27, 1904, with McClellan at the controls for the inaugural run. But until underground service was expanded to other parts of the city, the public relied on elevated trains and trolley cars running on streets that were congested with horse-drawn carriages, pedestrians, and ever increasing numbers of noisy automobiles.

During the Low administration (as described in chapter 2) the police had taken rudimentary steps to control traffic at selected intersections in Lower Manhattan, but it quickly became apparent that a completely new system of enforcement was needed for the burgeoning metropolis. To that end McAdoo established the Street Traffic Regulations Bureau. At first the public railed against him under the misguided assumption that the police department did not have the legal authority to limit the use of public thoroughfares. Judge Gaynor sided with the public and ruled that new regulations to control traffic were unconstitutional because they interfered with the personal liberty of individual citizens to go wherever they pleased.

While the city waited for the Court of Appeals to review Gaynor's decision, McClellan personally informed all the magistrates whose reappointments he controlled that if they failed to enforce the traffic laws, they would find themselves out of office when their terms expired. The not-so-subtle message had the desired effect. Convictions for traffic infractions started to rise.

The newspapers went on to ridicule McAdoo when he ordered the squadron of motorized traffic police to switch from blue caps to distinctive white caps. "Who would speed when they saw the white hats?" they wrote, failing to realize that McAdoo did not want his officers to arrest violators at every turn. He wanted compliance with the traffic laws. If the sight of the white hat slowed down a speeder, then as far as he was concerned, the mission was accomplished.

In early 1905 the New York Chamber of Commerce formed yet another bipartisan committee to determine how to correct defects in the structure of the police department. Both McClellan and McAdoo appeared before the nine-member committee to offer their thoughts, along with former chief of police McCullagh; former commissioners York, Partridge, and Greene; and representatives of the Patrolmen's Benevolent Association and the Roundsmen's Benevolent Association. Among the proposals to improve the department that came out of these sessions was that the rank of detective sergeant should be eliminated and that all future detectives should be selected from the uniformed patrol force based on merit. A reconstituted Detective Bureau should be placed under the command of a chief of detectives. The police commissioner should be given more leeway to penalize errant police officers. These recommendations and others would eventually come to pass but not during McAdoo's tenure.

McAdoo's previous naval experience led him to believe that he could rely on the roundsmen to keep the patrolmen under control, just as chief petty officers kept their shipmates in check at sea. To his disappointment McAdoo found the roundsmen completely lacking as supervisors. "If they [roundsmen] don't perform their duty faithfully, patrol is bound to be insufficient," he explained. He concluded that roundsmen were too friendly with their subordinates and as such often overlooked their breeches of duty. He was so frustrated by what he saw that he said the old system, where roundsmen paid politicians for their promotions, probably garnered better results because only men who truly wanted to be leaders were willing to pay exorbitant fees for the opportunity.

McAdoo decided that drastic measures had to be taken to rein in the force. With that in mind he reinstated the dreaded "shoofly" system that Chief McCullagh had abolished. He dispatched six roundsmen, wearing plainclothes instead of uniforms, directly out of Headquarters to spy on the patrol force. They were very successful at catching patrolmen off base, as evidenced by the sudden increase in the number of charges brought forward, but when McAdoo attempted to expand the unit in order to have a real impact on supervision, not a single volunteer offered to come forward.

After he left the force, McAdoo was invited back to give a lecture to a class of police recruits. He told them that he would have liked to have had an airship at his disposal to spy on patrolmen. Its spotlight, he said, would have come in handy at night to nab cops hiding out in dark allies, bakeries, and saloons.

On May 6, 1905, McAdoo and McClellan were joined by a host of dignitaries at the intersection of Centre and Grand Streets in Manhattan for the cornerstone-laying ceremony for the new Police Headquarters. As McClellan slathered a clump of wet mortar against the first five-ton block of Quincy granite lowered into place, he said wistfully, "May this building house a force of honest and honorable men."

In 1905 the state legislature extended the term for the mayor of New York from two years to four years. The prospect of four more years in office did not thrill McClellan. In fact he claimed in private that he would rather return to Washington but for the fact that he had unfinished business left to do.

The political infighting between McClellan and Charles Murphy had taken a toll on their relationship. McClellan ran for reelection with only tepid support from Tammany Hall. His main opponent was wealthy newspaper magnate William Randolph Hearst, who was running as an independent on the Municipal Ownership League ticket. The Republican nominee, William Ivins, was not expected to fare well, but it was thought that his presence in the race would siphon votes away from McClellan.

Hearst proved to be a formable candidate. He appealed to the "passions of prejudice and discontent" and promised constituents anything and everything. His newspapers denounced McClellan. Rather than defend himself against the scurrilous charges, McClellan touted his administration's most noteworthy accomplishments.

The contest was predicted to be close. The last thing McClellan needed was for McAdoo to blunder, yet that was what happened on Election Day. One of the primary functions the police department had when it oversaw elections was to secure the ballots until they were counted. Although the Board of Elections took over that responsibility so that it was no longer under police jurisdiction, it still required the department to safeguard the uncounted ballots.

For some inexplicable reason McAdoo permitted Hearst's campaign manager to remove a number of ballot boxes from police custody after the polls closed before they were counted. McAdoo explained that he turned the boxes over on orders from Judge Gaynor, who said the police had no legal authority to hold them. It turned out that neither he nor Gaynor was aware that the board had made prior arrangements for the police department to secure the ballots because the board did not have the facilities to do so, thereby rendering Gaynor's ruling invalid. As soon as McClellan found out what McAdoo had done, he dispatched his secretary to retrieve the missing ballots.

The next day McClellan was declared the victor by the slimmest of margins, but Hearst claimed that the ballots had been tampered with. Over the next two years his newspapers referred to McClellan as the "Fraud Mayor," as he pursued the matter in court, ultimately to no avail.

Before the start of his second term McClellan removed most of "Boss" Murphy's men from office. Among those he appointed in their place was an idealistic young attorney named John Purroy Mitchel, whom he chose as special counsel for the Office of the Commissioner of Accounts (later called the Department of Investigation). Mitchel would make a name for himself ferreting out corruption in all branches of city government, especially in the police department.

McClellan rewarded his secretary, John O'Brien, for rescuing the ballots by naming him fire commissioner. McAdoo, on the other hand, was told to tender his resignation. To wit he replied to the mayor, "I take pleasure in complying with your request." Many years later McClellan would write in his autobiography that McAdoo had meant well but was no man to command the police. In that regard he considered him a failure. Ironically he would say much worse about the man he chose to replace him.

For his next police commissioner McClellan wanted another outsider, but this time one with extensive military experience to restore order, just as General Greene had done for Mayor Low. He offered the job to retired brigadier general Theodore Bingham. Upon his acceptance Bingham told reporters, "If I stay honest, I'll raise hell," and that was exactly what he did for the next three and a half years, much to McClellan's chagrin.

Bingham was born in Connecticut in 1858. He was educated at West Point and served primarily as an army engineer and military attaché overseas during the early part of his soldiering career. He returned to Washington in

1897 to take charge of the nation's Parks Police, who tended to the capital's parks, monuments, and government buildings.

While serving in Congress, McClellan had struck up a friendship with President William McKinley, who as a teenager during the Civil War had served under McClellan's father, whom he greatly admired. McKinley regularly invited Congressman McClellan and his wife to the White House. It was during these visits that McClellan became acquainted with then Colonel Bingham, who, in addition to his duties with the Parks Police, also served as chamberlain of the White House.

Although extremely competent, Bingham had a tendency to be pompous and arrogant. In 1903 he was asked to leave his post after a dispute with the First Lady concerning plans to restore the White House. He was transferred to Buffalo to supervise an engineering project on the waterfront, where a seven-hundred-pound derrick crashed against his left knee. The injury necessitated the amputation of his left leg. He retired from the army in 1904 after being promoted to brigadier general.

An article in the *Army and Navy Journal* described Bingham as a strict disciplinarian, honest, fearless, impartial, and a resolute advocate of the "square deal." On his first day in office, while puffing on his ever-present pipe, Bingham announced to the newspapermen, "I'm here to save as much money for the city as possible."

Despite needing a cane and prosthetic leg to get around, Bingham strived to maintain his military bearing and expected the same from his new charges. One of his first directives instituted a more formal U.S. Army regulation salute for the uniformed patrol force.

He warned his inspectors that they would be absolutely responsible for the conduct of their subordinates or face the consequences. It was not an idle threat, as evidenced by the subsequent mass transfers that took place shortly after he was installed. Bingham intended to reorganize the department and wanted only men who were in agreement with him by his side.

In April 1906 Bingham's first deputy, Rhinelander Waldo, forever altered the uniform of New York City patrolmen when he ordered that the tall, distinct gray helmets be replaced on a trial basis during the summer months by a cap similar to what was already being worn by the Traffic Squad and ranking officers. It was rumored that he had gotten the idea while visiting police departments on the European continent. When asked for his thoughts about Waldo's change to the uniform, former first deputy Devery grumbled, "Wasn't American styles good enough for him? Why does he have to go to Germany and France for suggestions? Next thing you know he'll be makin' the reserves wear tuxedos while they're waitin' around the evenin's."

Patrolmen continued to wear the helmet for ceremonial occasions that required dress uniforms and during the winter months. It was not until several years later, when Waldo became police commissioner that the helmet was completely phased out.

McClellan had received great support from the police during his first run for office, and as a reward he implemented the three-platoon duty system. In June 1906, however, Bingham unilaterally restored the old two-platoon duty system, including the two-hour "Dog Watch" from 6 a.m. to 8 a.m. He claimed that the change was necessary to deal with the increased strain on the department to furnish sufficient patrol during the busy summer months, but most patrolmen believed that it had more to do with the fact that McClellan blamed members of the department for the ballot box debacle and wanted to punish them for not supporting his bid for reelection as strongly as they had during the first race. It became apparent to the Patrolmen's Benevolent Association that it would have to seek intervention from the state legislature to make the three-platoon duty schedule part of the law.

In his January 1907 police *Annual Report* to the mayor Bingham listed changes that he thought were necessary to provide the police commissioner more control over the force. For example, he recommended that the sole authority to promote or demote inspectors be given to the police commissioner so that they would, as he put it, "fear the head of the department instead of doing the bidding of politicians." He also recommended that the current Detective Bureau be abolished and that all of its members be returned to patrol so as to get rid of the "dead wood" and that a reorganized Detective Bureau be established in its place, one that was staffed by deserving patrolmen handpicked by him and headed by a new fourth deputy commissioner rather than a chief of detectives.

Bingham's proposals, along with several others submitted to the legislature by the Chamber of Commerce committee as a result of its interviews with

McClellan and McAdoo the previous year, became known as the "Bingham Bill." When it was enacted, the new law not only greatly expanded the power of the police commissioner, but it also dramatically altered the department's rank structure. The *New York Times* cautioned, "Commissioner Bingham has acquired the power he sought, and with it comes great responsibility."

Inspectors suddenly lost their civil service protection. Speculation began almost immediately as to which of the department's nineteen inspectors Bingham would reduce to captains and which captains would be elevated to take their place. When Bingham insisted on demoting a McClellan favorite, Inspector George McClusky, the mayor tried to intercede. According to an unidentified eavesdropper at Headquarters, Bingham told the mayor point blank, "If I can't run this police department like I want to, somebody else can come in and do it."

Not even the mayor could save McClusky. He lost command of the Detective Bureau and his rank, along with eight other inspectors. Bingham designated their replacements as "acting inspectors" to make it clear to all concerned that no inspector had permanent claim to the rank.

In conjunction with the department-wide reorganization, roundsmen were redesignated as sergeants at an annual salary of $1,500. Former sergeants and detective sergeants were promoted to the new rank of lieutenant and paid $2,000 per year. Lieutenants wore a single gilt bar on the collars of their blouses and a fire-gilded metal shield, with prominent identification numbers. Patrolmen deemed worthy by the police commissioner were designated either detective second grade, a rank that allowed them to work in plainclothes but paid no extra money, or detective first grade, a rank that paid the same rate as lieutenant. Like inspectors, detectives were subject to demotion at the whim of the police commissioner.

Bingham also got permission to add a fourth deputy to oversee the restructured Detective Bureau. He appointed Arthur Woods to the post. Woods established specialized units to deal with specific types of crime. He formed the department's first Homicide Squad, although under the law policemen were not permitted to gather clues at a crime scene until they received permission from the coroner (usually a person whose political connections were more important for securing the job than a bona fide medical background). It would not be until the law was amended in 1915 that police were allowed to investigate a crime scene before turning the body over to the coroner.

Woods was also credited with being the first person to utilize precinct maps in concert with different-colored thumb tacks to track and catalogue burglaries. Red tacks indicated nighttime break-ins, green tacks daytime thefts. Whenever a cluster of colored tacks appeared on one of his maps, Woods dispatched a detective to the neighborhood to begin an immediate investigation.

In July 1907 Patrolman Steven Walsh of the East Fifty-First Street station-house was tried for cowardice. It was the first such case in thirty years. Normally the third deputy commissioner presided over disciplinary hearings involving patrolmen assigned to Manhattan, but in this instance Bingham decided to try the case himself.

Patrolman Walsh had been alerted a week earlier that Frank Warner, who was wanted for murder, was holed up at a building on West Forty-Second Street. Upon entering the premises, Walsh encountered an employee who worked on the fifth floor and went with him up the stairs. As they reached the third-floor landing, Warner fired a shot down at them. According to the employee, Walsh reacted like he had been hit. The pair retreated into a tailor shop on the second floor, where Walsh asked the employee to check his wound. The employee told Walsh that he was not injured and urged him to give chase, but Walsh refused. He told the employee he was afraid that he would not be able to get a shot off because Warner had the advantage of high ground. By the time reinforcements arrived on the scene and captured Warner, he had murdered another person.

When Bingham announced his verdict the next morning, he said it was clear that Walsh had wilted. He dismissed him from the force but not before directing an inspector to strip him of his shield and collar brass. Then he ordered that the disgraced patrolman be ejected from the building. As Walsh was being dragged away, Bingham lamented, "My God, men, do not let this thing occur again while you and I are together." Ironically Bingham had terminated Walsh's brother from the force a year earlier for committing police brutality.

Two ill-considered comments by Bingham nearly resulted in his own dismissal during 1908. The first incident occurred in April, when Bingham spoke before the City Club. The host, George McAneny, praised Bingham's efforts to reorganize the NYPD. But instead of humbly accepting the compliments, Bingham complained that the bill named in his honor did not go far enough because captains still retained their civil service status. He told the audience, "I wish that about forty police captains would die overnight. They are no good." Bingham later apologized for his comments.

The second incident occurred after an article that Bingham had written appeared in the September 1908 issue of the *North American Review*. In it he declared that half the criminals in the city were Russian Jews and the worst offenders were their Hebrew sons, whom he described as natural pickpockets. McClellan called the comments utterly ridiculous and demanded the commissioner issue an immediate retraction. Bingham apologized once again, but this time he blamed his remarks on erroneous statistical information that had been supplied to him for the article. Although the Jewish community leaders forgave Bingham, the mayor later wrote that he wished he had taken the opportunity to get rid of him then as his aides recommended, rather than waiting until he finally had no choice.

Despite his biases many people sided with Bingham and felt that the police department needed to institute special measures to deal with the city's enormous immigrant population. Among them was Joe Petrosino, who as a result of the Bingham Bill had been promoted to lieutenant, thus becoming the first native-born Italian in any American police force to achieve the exulted rank.

Petrosino explained the dilemma facing the country: "The United States has become the garbage dump for all the criminality and banditry in Italy, and especially in Sicily and Calabria." During 1908 his unit investigated 469 cases of extortion attributed to the Black Hand. The investigations resulted in 285 arrests but only 45 convictions. According to Bingham, fear of the Black Hand had caused the "almost universal refusal of the victims to give the police any sort of assistance."

When Bingham secured private financing to help the police take on the Black Hand, the press speculated that at least part of the money came from Italian merchants fed up with being shaken down by gangsters. The commissioner and Petrosino discussed how best to utilize the funds. After some cajoling on Bingham's part, it was decided that Petrosino would undertake a secret mission to Sicily to gather background information about Black Hand members operating in New York. Bingham believed that this information would prove useful in deporting Italian malfeasants who had entered the United States under false pretenses. Unfortunately neither man knew that for a 500 lira bribe any Italians seeking to enter America could secure documents from corrupt government officials vouching for their good citizenship.

Petrosino's exploits had been fodder for the newspapers for nearly twenty-five years, so his unexplained absence was soon noticed by the press. When reporters inquired of his whereabouts, Bingham shrugged, "Why he may be on the ocean bound for Europe for all I know." This foolish slip of the tongue by Bingham would prove to be fatal for Petrosino. The reporters figured out where he was going, and once the news of his not-so-secret mission came out in the newspapers, the Black Hand dispatched its own assassin to hunt him down.

Petrosino arrived in Italy in February 1909. He visited his hometown of Padua in northern Italy for a few days before heading off to Sicily. He spent nearly a month on the island tracking down the backgrounds of criminals with whom he dealt back home. While his investigation was officially sanctioned by the Italian government and the local authorities were cordial, they were not particularly forthcoming with useful information. Thus Petrosino had to cultivate his own sources, just as he had done in Little Italy. But he was not on his own turf. In Sicily he was vulnerable.

Petrosino was gunned down in Palermo outside a café in Piazza Marina on the night of March 12, 1909. He was unarmed, a fact that gave credence to the theory that he had not expected trouble when he planned to meet with informants. The suspects escaped, and Petrosino became the first American police officer killed on foreign soil. In his possession was a postcard addressed to his wife with a handwritten message, "A kiss for you and my little girl, who has spent three months far from her daddy." It was signed with his lieutenant's badge number 285.

Bingham downplayed his role in Petrosino's demise. He sent two detectives overseas to conduct an investigation, but they never even made it to Sicily because the Italian consulate said it was too dangerous for them to travel there. On April 3, 1909, the authorities in Palermo arrested three men in connection with the murder, but all of them were eventually released because of insufficient evidence. Several others came forward over the years claiming to have information about Petrosino's assassination, but no one was ever prosecuted for the crime.

The same Italian businessmen who had paid for Petrosino's trip paid for his burial. The police estimated that 250,000 people lined the streets of Lower Manhattan to pay their respects as Petrosino's funeral cortege wound its way through the streets of Little Italy toward St. Patrick's Church on Mott Street. After the mass Petrosino's tearful widow wailed at his grave, "Joe, Joe, my Giuseppe, come back to me."

Bingham's reign as police commissioner came to an abrupt end ten weeks later. Policemen in Brooklyn had arrested a young hoodlum named George Duffy two years earlier. He was accused of being a "suspicious person." During the routine arrest process his picture was taken for the rogues' gallery. When the charge was dismissed, the police should have returned the photograph, as had been the practice in such cases. But that did not happen, so when Duffy subsequently found himself under arrest again, his attorney claimed that his client's rights had been violated because the police illegally possessed his picture when they showed it to victims of crimes. Duffy had the extreme good fortune to have his case find its way to Judge Gaynor's courtroom.

Gaynor berated the police department for its actions, even though a law mandating that the police return such photographs did not go into effect until September 1, 1907, two and a half months after Duffy's original arrest. But the public furor the case generated forced McClellan to intervene. He demanded that Bingham return Duffy's picture and that he discharge his personal secretary, Daniel Slattery, and Third Deputy Bert Hanson for their roles in the controversy. Bingham was also ordered to remove Inspector John Russell, who was in charge of the Brooklyn patrol force, so that a deputy commissioner could take charge of the borough's police affairs.

For his part Bingham was hesitant to act because he did not think the employees had done anything wrong. In fact, he stated, the use of "muggings" (as the pictures were called) to solve crimes was a practice that went back three decades. Bingham believed that the uproar was just a political subterfuge instigated by Tammany Hall to get rid of Inspector Russell, who had been hounding the illegal gambling resorts in Coney Island.

While he complied with McClellan's directives, in the end it was Bingham's hubris that had as much to do with his termination as any of his actions during the Duffy matter. He made the mistake of submitting his thoughts on the matter in writing to the mayor. The letter was not well received. McClellan wrote back, "For the insubordinate statement in your communication, I remove you from the office of police commissioner of the City of New York, to take effect forthwith."

The news was delivered to Bingham on July 1, as he sat in his office stoking his pipe. After he read McClellan's letter, Bingham informed the messenger, "Tell the mayor that I shall be out of here in twenty minutes."

A separate message was delivered to First Deputy William F. Baker, in which McClellan advised him that he was now police commissioner. This time around, however, McClellan decided all future decisions concerning the department would be vetted through him. In fact he said in his autobiography that during the last six months of his administration he was his own police commissioner in matters of import, with Baker acting as his assistant.

Baker was born in Pittsburgh in 1866 and moved to Brooklyn in 1885. He had served with distinction as president of the Civil Service Board until January 1908, when McClellan orchestrated an exchange of positions between him and First Deputy Commissioner Arthur O'Keefe. At the time, conjecture was that the mayor had made the move thinking it might bring about Bingham's resignation, but if that was the plan, it did not work.

McClellan rounded out Baker's executive staff by elevating Bingham's fourth deputy, Frederick Bugher, to first deputy. Although Baker claimed to be satisfied with the mayor's selection, the two men would soon become bitter enemies because Bugher's strict adherence to military protocols clashed with Baker's laissez-faire management style. Baker put him in charge of the Traffic Division.

Two weeks later Alfred Booraem, a thirty-four-year-old lawyer McClellan plucked from the Comptroller's Office, was appointed fourth deputy and placed in charge of the police in Brooklyn, thereby restoring civilian oversight to the borough.

It was thought that McClellan would direct Baker to ease up on the illegal resorts in Coney Island in order to secure Tammany Hall's support for a third term, but instead he declared that he had already given the city the best six years of his life and had no desire to give any more.

Once McClellan withdrew from the mayoral race, it became an open contest. There was speculation in the press that the Republicans would select Bingham as their nominee. Bingham took every opportunity to belittle the

Democrats, even going so far as to say that when he was police commissioner, he often felt like putting the mayor over his knee and giving him a good spanking. While such comments sold newspapers, they caused the Republican leaders to distance themselves from him. Instead they nominated Otto Bannard to run against the Tammany Hall candidate, Judge William Gaynor, and William Randolph Hearst, who was running as an independent.

On election night Bannard placed a distant third behind the winner, Judge Gaynor, and runner-up Hearst. Although the Democrats won the mayoral race, the Republican/Fusion Party claimed all of the other important contests, including president of the Board of Aldermen, which went to McClellan's youthful aide, John Purroy Mitchel.

During his final days in office McClellan busied himself pushing for the completion of several important civic projects that he had undertaken. These included the Queensborough and Manhattan Bridges, the Municipal Building, and the new Police Headquarters. The Headquarters was originally scheduled to open in September 1907, but modifications requested by Bingham, such as mounting Gatling guns in the parapets, along with cost overruns that totaled almost $350,000, had caused delays. Finally, at midnight on November 28, 1909, Baker threw a switch that transferred all of the telephone and telegraph service from 300 Mulberry Street to the department's new home at 240 Centre Street, referred to as the "Gold Dome," by the rank and file for its shiny copper cupola (eventually it would take on a patina hue).

The five-story fortress's thick granite walls were constructed to withstand siege, and in an emergency the building could quarter a thousand patrolmen. An elevated running track encircled the fourth floor gymnasium, where sixteen laps equaled a mile. The stage in the Lineup Room, where prisoners were paraded on a daily basis, was fitted with special bright lights that allowed detectives to eyeball the prisoners but prevented the prisoners from seeing the detectives in the audience. This was a vast improvement over an earlier proposal to have the detectives wear masks over their faces to conceal their identities.

With a new mayor taking office in a month, Baker assumed that he would be only a temporary caretaker of Police Headquarters. But mayor-elect Gaynor had other ideas. He asked Baker to stay on rather than beginning a protracted search for a suitable replacement. It was the first time that an incoming mayor kept an old police commissioner in office. But like most marriages of convenience, their relationship would end in a bitter divorce.

McClellan's six years as mayor soured him on public service. He knew that once he broke ranks with "Boss" Murphy, he metaphorically "died at age 45," as far as politics were concerned. After his term expired, he and his wife voyaged to Europe, where they spent the next nine months touring the continent. He returned to New York and joined a law firm for a short time but quit when he found out that Murphy had blackballed him. When an opportunity at Princeton University opened up for him to become a professor, McClellan jumped at the chance. During World War I he took a sabbatical to join the army at the advanced age of fifty-one. He was commissioned a major and served in France in an ordinance unit. By the end of the war McClellan had achieved the rank of colonel. He returned to Princeton, lectured, and wrote books until he retired in 1930.

As far as his relationship with his police commissioners, much like his father, McClellan was by temperament unsuited to aggressive, offensive generalship. With both McAdoo and Bingham he had waited too long to act, but he found solace in the wisdom of his father's words: "The deserving often fail." In time much of the bad blood between McClellan and Tammany Hall was forgotten, and he enjoyed his status as a well-respected elder statesman in the years before his death in 1940.

McClellan's first police commissioner, William McAdoo, wrote a book about his experience titled *Guarding a Great City*, in which he told his side of the story. In 1910 Mayor Gaynor appointed McAdoo chief magistrate for the City of New York. He served in that capacity for twenty years until his sudden death in June 1930 at age seventy-six.

Although McAdoo left the department under a cloud, he never lost his affection for the men of the force and often returned to the School of Instruction to tutor recruits on how to give proper court testimony. He also used his clout to oversee the formation of the city's first Traffic Court, which heard cases involving motor vehicles.

A true testimony to McAdoo's unwavering honesty was that in his fifty years of public service he had been in a position to accumulate great personal wealth, but he always adhered to the righteous path. At the time of his death he left his widow and daughter a meager estate of but $5,000. Perhaps his greatest contribution to the police department were views that future police commissioner Lewis Valentine took to heart: "When the best friends of a police administration are the enemies of the public, when its most ardent advocates are the breakers of the law, when its praises are chiefly sung by beneficiaries of its infidelity or indifference to the obligations of its oath of office, then, indeed, the thistles and thorns of vice and crime have overgrown and overthrown the vines of civic virtue; the orchard is hidden and strangled by deep, impenetrable thickets of thorns, long breathing of the exudations of which beget lethargy, coma, and a stifling of the public conscience."

As for Bingham, he busied himself penning police-related articles concerning patrol strategies, organized crime, and the alleged third degree. He took turns as both the chief engineer of the Bureau of Highways and consultant to the Bridge Department. Bingham sued Mayor Gaynor for slander over the Duffy affair. After Gaynor wrote him an apology, he dropped the lawsuit.

There was talk in 1915 that Bingham would return to the police commissionership, but that never materialized. He was reactivated during World War I and served as an army engineer in command of the Second Engineering District in New York and later as chief engineer at Governor's Island. He died at his summer home in Nova Scotia at the age of seventy-six in September 1934. Upon news of his passing, Police Commissioner John O'Ryan acknowledged that even though many years had passed since Bingham had left office, his ideals had left a distinct impression upon the men of the department.

4

POLITICIANS TAKE
ADVANTAGE

Periodically men come to power who on first blush defy explanation. As a result they are later regarded as odd quirks in what some would call the normal course of political events. The Greater City of New York's fourth mayor, William J. Gaynor, was such a man. Few men who occupied public office had less regard for political convention than he. What is even more remarkable is that he was elected to office on a Tammany slate, although admittedly it was during one of those periods when in order to retain power the Democrats were forced to place a reformer at the head of their ticket.

Gaynor was born in upstate New York on his family's Mohawk Valley farm in 1851. As a youngster he demonstrated an aptitude more befitting the pursuit of intellectual than physical labor, so his Irish Catholic parents sent him to study in a Christian Brothers seminary in Utica. But Gaynor decided that he was not suited for the priesthood and left the order to study law. Good fortune landed him in the practice of former New York governor Horatio Seymour. The following year Gaynor left to join the staff of Judge Ward Hunt, a man who would later sit on the Supreme Court. His early association with these two prominent Democrats kindled an interest in politics.

After admission to the bar and a brief tryst with a Boston law firm, Gaynor relocated to Brooklyn in 1873. At that time Brooklyn was a sleepy community of private homes on tree-lined streets that had more in common with rural Long Island than bustling Manhattan. Within ten years Gaynor was one of Brooklyn's most successful lawyers, as well as a prominent proponent of political reform. Despite his Democratic leanings, Gaynor accepted a nomination and subsequent appointment as a State Supreme Court justice in 1893 as a Republican. In reality political affiliation mattered little to him since he let his conscience be his guide.

As a magistrate, Gaynor frequently criticized the manner in which the police treated ordinary citizens. He was said to have derived great satisfaction from berating patrolmen who appeared in his court, even going so far as to denounce the entire department as a "bunch of autocrats." When a young thug named Duffy was arrested for disorderly conduct, Gaynor's public attack on the NYPD's practice of fingerprinting and photographing suspects charged with minor infractions led to Mayor McClellan's dismissal of Police Commissioner Bingham. (Ironically when the same hoodlum was arrested after Gaynor became mayor, Duffy's pleas for leniency a second time fell on deaf ears.)

The notoriety Gaynor achieved from the Duffy incident brought him to the attention of Tammany Hall's Charles Murphy, who was deeply concerned about the prospects of a Republican/Fusionist administration regaining the mayoralty when McClellan's term ended. To keep the reformers at bay "Boss" Murphy proposed the white-bearded Justice Gaynor as Tammany's candidate for mayor. It was a shrewd selection since the Fusionists were seriously considering Gaynor themselves. But Murphy was certain that the judge would refuse their offer if Tammany Hall dangled its political carrot first. Murphy was right, not because Gaynor felt a particular kinship toward Tammany Hall but because at the advanced age of sixty-one, he had to run with the party that gave him the best chance to win.

Unlike in previous mayoral campaigns, the issue of police corruption took a back seat to individual personalities. The Fusion Party nominated a bland but politically correct banker, Otto T. Bannard, as its standard bearer, while William Randolph Hearst ran once again as an independent, utilizing his great personal fortune and publishing empire to present his case. Throughout the contest Gaynor and Hearst traded barbs, while Bannard did his best to steer clear of the fray. Gaynor's reputation, though popular with the people, was lambasted by the press, much of which Hearst controlled. Of Gaynor's nomination, the newspaper editor of the *Sun* commented, "A worse man than Judge Gaynor might have been chosen, but it would have entailed a good deal of trouble to find him."

But Gaynor attracted the common man with his "the best government is the least government" rhetoric. Hearst's attempts to ridicule him with political cartoons and derogatory articles failed to overcome Gaynor's colorful personality and the resourcefulness of Tammany Hall. The morning after

Gaynor won the election, the *Sun* declared, "Judge Gaynor [is] certainly the most unfit candidate ever offered for the mayoralty," even though he was elected by an impressive plurality.

While the voters obviously preferred Judge Gaynor, they cared little for the other candidates on the Tammany slate. Fusionist John Purroy Mitchel was elected president of the Board of Aldermen and Charles Whitman, also a Fusionist, was elected district attorney for Manhattan. Both men would rise to political prominence during Gaynor's term as a result of their direct involvement with the NYPD.

Although Gaynor made it clear to Murphy in the weeks preceding his inauguration that he alone would decide who would be police commissioner, the Tammany chieftain was not overly concerned. Graft in the police department was such that Murphy assumed no public servant, elected or appointed, could rein it in. It's doubtful that Gaynor felt the same way, especially in light of his role in Police Commissioner Bingham's demise. Nevertheless, he stunned the political establishment when he announced that he intended to retain the incumbent, William Baker, instead of naming a successor. It soon became apparent that the fact that Gaynor had kept him on in no way meant that he had full confidence in Baker's abilities to lead the department. Their brief partnership would become one of the more bizarre in the history of the department.

In the early days of the new administration two mounted patrolmen, Charles Cunningham and Thomas Keenan, from the Westchester Precinct in the Bronx, arrested Ernest Olpp, president of the Westchester Liquor Dealers Association, for violating the state's excise law as it related to the sale of alcohol on Sundays. Shortly afterward Baker reassigned the pair to a precinct in Lower Manhattan. The newspapers inferred that the transfers were done purely for political reasons, but the reporters failed to mention that the officers were on their day off when they decided to make a special effort to enforce the law and that both of them had been accused of "accepting" money from bartenders in the past.

At their department trial Cunningham and Keenan were found guilty of "inappropriately borrowing money" from saloonkeepers. They were subsequently dismissed from the force, though many of their colleagues believed they had been sacrificed in order to keep the graft system in place for the benefit of politicians and high-ranking officers. When asked for his comments regarding their removal, Mayor Gaynor said he approved of it because in enforcing the law on their day off, the officers were doing so without the knowledge of their supervisors and not necessarily with the interests of the city or the department in mind. This breach of the chain of command, he felt, more than anything warranted their termination. He refused to consider whether or not they were truly guilty of the charges levied against them.

The enforcement of the excise law had been a thorny issue for every administration, and each mayor had taken a different approach, ranging from ordering the police to ignore its provisions to ordering the police to strictly enforce them. Gaynor felt the system he had inherited, in which plainclothesmen covertly entered premises suspected of illegally selling liquor, observed the violations, and then identified themselves to management, only served to promulgate acts of corruption because it gave both parties an opportunity to work out a financial arrangement in the back room.

Gaynor discussed the practice with Baker. As a result of their conversation, Baker issued General Order No. 17 in April 1910. In it he put the force on notice that he would dismiss any officer who, after making his observations, identified himself to the saloonkeeper. Instead the officer was to leave the premises and turn his information over to the district attorney. If the evidence was sufficient, the district attorney would obtain a warrant, and only then would the department act to enforce the law.

But Gaynor realized that as long as there were plainclothesmen in the department, they would find ways to circumvent Baker's order the same way they had done in the past. He ordered Baker permanently to remove all of them, just as Greene had done in the case of the wardsmen in 1903. That ouster had been short-lived because Mayor McClellan reinstated the wardsmen as soon as he took office in 1904.

Baker, however, believed that plainclothesmen were necessary to enforce the excise law, even if some of them were on the take. He waited several weeks before reassigning the entire 203-man plainclothes force to uniformed patrol. Without the plainclothesmen, Gaynor told Baker to rely on the language of the law to enforce it.

According to the statute, the windows of all taverns were supposed to have unobstructed views so that officers on the street could personally observe goings-on inside. This provision would prove crucial to the enforcement of the excise law by the police during the Gaynor administration, but one cynical precinct commander remarked, "They can't hold us responsible any more for anything we can't see on the surface. How are we supposed to get after anybody who takes the precaution to shut his doors and pull his window blinds down?"

Meanwhile, the former plainclothesmen were confident that they would soon be back because of a loophole in department regulations called "Special Orders" that permitted captains and inspectors to detail any officer to plainclothes duty for twenty-four to forty-eight hours at a time without requesting permission from the police commissioner. As it turned out, that is exactly what happened despite Gaynor's edict to the contrary.

Baker was never considered a strong disciplinarian, so when the newspapers began publishing sensational stories about drunken patrolmen who abused their authority, Gaynor assumed that the reports were true. Baker attributed the spate of police assaults to the class of men being hired. He said the $800 first-year salary did not attract the type of men with the knowledge needed to enforce the law or provide first aid.

In the past the mayor's staff had routinely referred matters of police misconduct directly to the police commissioner for investigation, but Gaynor decided to sidestep the police department entirely. He instructed Baker to take a vacation and then had the complaints that his staff received concerning police transgressions forwarded to the commissioner of accounts, Raymond B. Fosdick, instead. Under the City Charter Fosdick's office had the power to investigate reports of misconduct by any city employee or department, including the police. Fosdick substantiated most of the complaints made against the department in a scathing report to the mayor that was published in the newspapers. Only the *New York Times* came to the aide of the beleaguered patrolmen, declaring that "Many of the tales told about it [the third degree] are gross exaggerations" and that "Patrolmen need their clubs at night, especially in bad neighborhoods, for self-defense."

When he read the report, Baker could barely contain his anger at the mayor for keeping him in the dark. "There has been so much 'roasting' of policemen who have had to use force in making arrests," he said, "that many of the men would rather suffer a beating than resort to their sticks even in self-defense. This is all wrong. A policeman should not hesitate to use his weapons to protect himself from assault by vicious gang members."

Rather than dismiss Baker for insubordination, Gaynor simply ordered him to calm down and take another vacation. With Baker sequestered for the summer in New Hampshire, Gaynor started to funnel his orders for the police department through First Deputy Bugher, who was only too happy to comply because he and the police commissioner had been at odds ever since Baker had taken away his spacious office and relocated him into a room he described as not much bigger than a broom closet. Baker had called Bugher's new office more than adequate for a man who was as "physically and mentally small" as he was.

Among the changes that Gaynor directed Bugher to make was to abolish the Homicide Squad. The experiment to create the squad by Fourth Deputy Commissioner Arthur Woods was deemed a failure because several murders were unsolved. Under the new arrangement homicide investigations would no longer be handled by specialists working out of the Central Office at Headquarters but by detectives in the precinct where the murders had taken place.

Among the new laws passed in 1910 that changed the way the department did business was one that guaranteed prisoners three free telephone calls so that they would not have to pay "fees" to patrolmen and desk officers to notify friends or family of their whereabouts. The law eliminated what had been a lucrative source of revenue for arresting officers.

Another provision in the law allowed properly identified persons accused of minor offenses to appear in court on a later date rather than immediately following their arrest. The police issued special "police identification cards" to individuals who permitted the department to verify their identity beforehand. The new cards proved to be particularly popular with suffragettes, who were subjected to arrest on a regular basis while advocating for women's right to vote.

The constant bickering with Baker had taken a toll on Gaynor's mental health. He was looking forward to his vacation, an end-of-summer voyage across the Atlantic aboard the German ocean liner *Kaiser Wilhelm der Grosse*. On August 9, 1910, as he chatted with fellow passengers on the deck shortly before the steamer set sail, a fifty-eight-year-old Irishman snuck aboard and slinked along the ship's rail unnoticed. When he reached Gaynor, he took out a revolver, pointed at the back of the mayor's head, and fired. The bullet lodged in Gaynor's throat and sent a spray of blood onto the startled passengers. Street Cleaning Commissioner William "Big Bill" Edwards, a former Princeton University football player on board to see Gaynor off, wrestled the would-be assassin onto the ground before he could discharge a second round.

It turned out that the shooter, later identified as James J. Gallagher, had been discharged from his municipal job as a night watchman with the Docks Department and blamed Gaynor for his misfortune. In his confession Gallagher wrote that the mayor had "deprived him of his bread and butter—not porterhouse steaks."

Gaynor was removed to St. Mary's Hospital in Hoboken. There doctors using the latest medical marvel, the X-ray machine, determined that the wound, while serious, was not life threatening. The surgeons opted to leave the slug in the mayor's neck rather than risk further damage by removing it. Although it was a prudent medical decision, Gaynor's voice would never again rise above a hoarse whisper. He remained in the hospital for three weeks before departing for his summer home on Long Island to complete his recovery.

Board of Aldermen president John Purroy Mitchel became acting mayor during Gaynor's convalescence. Mitchel directed his former colleague, Commissioner of Accounts Fosdick, to gather as much information as possible about illicit gambling in Coney Island. Mitchel then published the findings in a hastily prepared exposé that accused the police of permitting unabated vice in Coney Island.

When Baker returned from his vacation (he had briefly interrupted it when Gaynor was shot), he chastised Mitchel for interfering with police business. Mitchel responded by personally ordering the commanding officer of the Coney Island precinct, Inspector John O'Bryan, to raid one of the gambling establishments identified in Fosdick's report.

O'Bryan inadvertently found himself caught in the middle. Baker suspended him, not because he had obeyed Mitchel without informing him but because he had allowed illegal gambling in his precinct. Charges were preferred against him, and he was immediately demoted. At a departmental trial eight months later, O'Bryan was found guilty of failing to suppress gambling within his command and dismissed from the department, even though no gambling indictment against the establishment was ever handed down by the Brooklyn district attorney.

As open hostility between Baker and Mitchel continued to fester, Gaynor refused to side with either one of them while he was recuperating. Mitchel took advantage of the mayor's condition to raise his own political standing. He once again pressed Fosdick to identify locations, this time in Manhattan, suspected of harboring vice operations. Mitchel presented Fosdick's list to Baker, believing that his policemen would gather additional evidence against the establishments needed by the district attorney to present cases to a grand jury. But Baker had no desire to cooperate with Mitchel, so he merely mailed a notice to each landlord advising him that possible unlawful activity was taking place on his premises and considered the matter closed.

When Gaynor returned to work in October, he found his office flooded with complaints from the owners of the properties on Fosdick's list. It turned out that the list was faulty because it included a U.S. Army building, the Customs House, and a building that had been torn down years before to make room for Pennsylvania Station.

Mitchel refused to accept any responsibility for the accuracy of the information that he supplied to Baker and blamed the commissioner for failing to verify the allegations of illegal activities at the locations before mailing the notices. Gaynor could barely contain his anger with both of them. First Deputy Bugher, sensing that this might be an opportunity for him to replace Baker, tendered a self-serving resignation letter in which he claimed that the limitations of his power as first deputy made it impossible to take any responsibility for the condition of the department under its present head. After reading the letter, Gaynor said that anyone could sit at a desk and be a marionette. He accepted Bugher's resignation. Bugher realized too late that he had overplayed his hand, but it would not be the last time that he made such a foolish blunder.

Baker realized that he had no future with the department. He submitted his own resignation the next day, October 20, 1910, and told reporters that he was "glad to get out." Second Deputy Charles Kirby, who had been spearheading the latest reorganization of the Detective Bureau, became the third victim of the feud between Baker and Mitchel. He was terminated after refusing to resign. He called it "a rotten deal."

For his next police commissioner Gaynor tapped a little known but highly regarded thirty-eight-year-old Brooklyn lawyer named James C. Cropsey. Although the new appointee had very little police experience, Gaynor had admired the manner in which he conducted himself in the courtroom. And while Gaynor barely knew him on a personal level, he firmly believed Cropsey to be a "straight shooter," just the kind of person he was looking for to run the police department.

Cropsey was born in Brooklyn in 1873 to a wealthy family with Dutch ties. He graduated from Columbia Law School in 1893 and began to make a name for himself handling negligence cases. At first the slim, balding Cropsey was reluctant to take the police post because his law practice reportedly netted him $40,000 a year, five times the police commissioner's salary. But Gaynor appealed to his sense of honor by offering him the opportunity to do something important for the community. "In entrusting the Police Department to you," Gaynor said, "let me say that, although I can devote only a little time to it now and then, I shall always be glad to confer with you about the policies and general management of the department, but for the enforcement of the outward order and decency first and next for the detection of the secret illegal places, I shall hold you responsible."

Despite his obvious respect for Cropsey, Gaynor was shrewd enough to realize that his new department head was a novice when it came to police matters. With that in mind he personally selected the two men who were to serve as Cropsey's top deputies. Clement J. Driscoll was reassigned from his position as commissioner of weights and measures to become first deputy. The thirty-year-old Driscoll had a newspaper background and was expected to tackle the city's vice issues with vim and vigor. To help get through the long days that he anticipated putting in, Driscoll moved a cot into his office at Headquarters and spent his first midnight on the job touring the Tenderloin with Chief Inspector Max Schmittberger.

Gaynor persuaded William J. Flynn to take the job of second deputy commissioner. Flynn brought with him ten years of top-level law enforcement experience as director of the New York branch of the Secret Service. His mission was to continue the reorganization of the Detective Bureau started by Police Commissioner Baker and Deputy Kirby. Flynn planned to accomplish this by putting into practice basic Secret Service tenets: hide your evidence-gathering mechanisms and solve crimes not through the efforts of one clever detective but by amassing as much information as possible and analyzing it thoroughly.

Despite high hopes it turned out the trio was doomed from the start. Cropsey was a man of strong personal values who preferred an honest department over an efficient one. As a result he found himself at odds with his subordinates, who had come on board with specific ideas in mind.

Within a short time Flynn had succeeded in transforming the Detective Bureau by modeling it after Scotland Yard and his own Secret Service. He dumped 150 old-time detectives, whom he considered "dead wood," and replaced them with patrolmen he believed to be super ambitious. But what made the transfers so unusual was Flynn's desire to keep the names of the new detectives a secret from everyone, including Cropsey. Only in this way, he believed, could the new men obtain the best possible information about criminal activity. Then Flynn divided the city into ten detective districts, each commanded by a lieutenant detailed as an acting captain. He staffed the local precincts with nearly five hundred detectives, leaving only a small cadre of men to handle special cases at the Central Office at Headquarters and the Brooklyn office.

Flynn made arrangements with Gaynor to have all of the detectives placed under his direct command and for the Detective Bureau to be granted total autonomy from the rest of the department. Reports of crimes were forwarded from the Central Office to district supervisors, who assigned the cases to precinct detectives. In order for him to better monitor their activities, Flynn required all the detectives to submit a daily activity report of their progress on each of their assigned cases to him for review. Flynn then announced a plan to rotate detectives from one precinct to another every few months so that they could stay fresh and become familiar with all areas of the city.

Flynn's measures were put to the test when the notorious Black Hand kidnapped a young boy and held him for ransom. For the first time in department history detectives apprehended the kidnappers and returned the boy unharmed to his parents—something even the legendary Lieutenant Petrosino had been unable to do. But in keeping with his ideology of complete secrecy, Flynn refused to divulge the methods he had employed to recover the boy.

If Flynn was enjoying success, just the opposite could be said for First Deputy Driscoll. He had made the mistake of ordering a raid on the Hesper Club, a notorious gambling establishment controlled by Tammany Hall politician "Big Tim" Sullivan. The two detectives who coordinated the raid at Driscoll's behest, Edward Cody and John Murphy, found themselves caught up in the same political muck that had claimed Inspector O'Bryan. They were immediately transferred out of the Vice Squad. Within days the entire 150 man unit was taken away from Driscoll and placed under Flynn's control, prompting speculation that Driscoll's departure was imminent. A wise but anonymous source at Headquarters observed, "It's this sort of thing that keeps the patrolmen from doing their jobs. Graft goes higher than the man on the streets."

Cropsey realized the truth in this sentiment. If he was to accomplish any of his goals, he would need his ranking officers to set an example. Over the years a practice had evolved wherein precinct and district commanders were permitted to select their own replacements when they were on vacation. It was common for them to appoint a subordinate whose sole function was to tend to the commanders' special interests while they were away.

Cropsey stopped the practice. Commanders could no longer simply inform Headquarters who would be taking over during their absence, nor would they be permitted to even suggest names of replacements. Since all future substitute commanders would be controlled by Headquarters personnel, Cropsey believed that he had removed at least one link from the department's long chain of graft.

During Cropsey's first four months in office he was credited with unprecedented advances in the department, yet on a personal level he was very unhappy. He no longer spoke to Second Deputy Flynn because the latter refused to divulge the details of his covert investigations. Whenever Cropsey pressed him for information, Flynn inevitably flaunted the letter from Gaynor that granted him complete control over the Detective Bureau.

When a crime wave hit the city in March 1911, Cropsey finally had the opportunity he had been waiting for to question Flynn's methods after a magistrate accused his detectives of making false arrests of pickpockets based on their knowledge of the suspects' past criminal histories rather than observing them during the commission of crimes. As a result of the disclosure, Flynn's reputation suddenly began to lose some of its luster. A month later he submitted his resignation. It languished on Gaynor's desk for ten days. Finally Flynn just quit, leaving the mayor to learn the news in the morning papers. His stay in the police department had lasted little more than six months. When he walked out the door he said, "I came here to do detective work, pure and simple. I found that a lot of people were working against me. I was being saddled with a lot of extraneous matter. This greatly hampered me."

Flynn's supporters urged the mayor to dump Cropsey and name Flynn police commissioner, but Flynn eliminated himself from contention when he criticized Gaynor's restriction on patrolmen's uses of the baton. "There's no doubt," he said, "that there's a whole lot of law and order in the end of a nightstick." Flynn was not out of work very long. He returned to the Secret Service and became its director.

Cropsey himself stayed around just long enough to swear in Flynn's replacement. The department's new second deputy, George Dougherty, came from the Pinkerton Agency.

Cropsey departed on May 23, 1911, after Gaynor had questioned his latest appointments to the force. Cropsey had failed to follow the exact numerical order of the civil service list when hiring new recruits. He claimed that it had been his intent to keep out of the department, as far as possible, improper men by utilizing his managerial prerogative under the civil service "one-in-three rule."

Gaynor could care less what Cropsey's reasons were; he knew only that Cropsey had disregarded his administration's policy and for that, he had to go. Cropsey's seven-month ordeal had left him exhausted. As he fled Headquarters, he told reporters that he was very tired and only wished to rest.

In selecting his third police commissioner, Gaynor decided not to take any more chances. The last thing he wanted was more conflicts with his head of police. The next commissioner had to be willing to carry out his programs without question. He quickly settled on Fire Commissioner Rhinelander Waldo, who had been the first deputy under Police Commissioner Bingham. In addition, as fire commissioner, Waldo had expertly handled the investigation into the tragic Triangle Shirtwaist Factory fire that had cost 146 garment workers their lives. But most important, Waldo had strictly complied with the mayor's policy when he hired firemen off the civil service list. Gaynor credited him with doing away with graft and favoritism in the Fire Department and implored him to do the same for the police.

Rhinelander Waldo was born in 1877 to a wealthy and prominent New York family with ties to the Knickerbocker fortune. He had graduated from Columbia University with a degree in engineering in 1893 and had then enrolled in West Point to pursue a military career. As a young lieutenant attached to the Seventh Infantry, he served in the Philippines, where he saw extensive action against insurrectionists. He also got his first taste of police work as a captain attached to the Philippine constabulary. Waldo resigned from the army in 1905 as a major. Once back in New York, abetted by his family connections, brash self-confidence, a strong education, and his life experiences, he had the courage to seek an audience with the newly installed police commissioner, Theodore Bingham.

Bingham was so impressed with Waldo that he practically named him first deputy commissioner on the spot. Waldo remained at that post for just one year but took advantage of the opportunity to travel and study the police departments of Europe's largest cities. In the years between leaving the department and becoming the city's fire commissioner, Waldo organized a police force to patrol and protect the city's Catskill reservoir system. One other factor distinguished Waldo from either of his predecessors: the mayor genuinely liked him and made no qualms about it. For Waldo the feeling was mutual.

One of Waldo's early priorities was to reestablish the three-platoon duty system. In actuality his reason for this priority had more to do with a plan that he believed would drastically reduce crime rather than a desire to curry favor with the patrol force.

Waldo unveiled the "Stationary Post Plan" in June 1911 as a pilot project in a small, crime-ridden section of northern Manhattan. A series of fixed posts, also called "fixers," were spaced at intersections every four blocks along the avenues. Half the patrolmen on duty in the precinct between 11 p.m. and 7 a.m. were assigned to the fixed posts. They were required to remain in the middle of the intersections so they could be seen at all times under the bright glare of the electric street lamps. If they needed help from their fellow patrolmen, they could either rap their batons on the pavement three times or blow their whistles three times. The other half of the platoon walked intersecting beats, and these patrolmen were supposed to exchange places with their counterparts every two hours, but that did not always happen. One beleaguered old-timer grumbled, "Bill Devery never invented anything like this, an' I'll tell you that the men would do more for Bill Devery in a minute than they'd ever do for Waldo in a lifetime."

The program was under perpetual attack by the patrol force from the start, but Waldo refused to give in because in the areas that were under constant night watch burglaries declined by 19 percent, and assaults and robberies declined by 51 percent. But he continued to refine the plan, first by changing the hours, making them from 10 p.m. to 6 a.m. Then he allowed the patrolmen to move freely about the intersection so long as they stayed within the confines of the four corners. Later he beefed up the manpower in the precincts where the fixed posts were being utilized to ensure that the men were properly relieved.

While members of the force detested the fixed-post system, it soon became a source of income for ambitious neighborhood youths. Patrolmen hired youngsters to do errands for them, such as getting their raingear from the stationhouses during storms or bringing sandwiches and coffee to their posts in the middle of the night, when they were stranded without relief. The most important job the boys did was to "lay chickie" for patrolmen who were "in the coop"—police vernacular for a place that the cops ducked into for a nap or a nip. The boys, nicknamed "buffs" by the bluecoats, became their eyes and ears, constantly scouring the streets for sergeants and shooflies. But they had to be fast because Waldo had put his sergeants on bicycles to improve supervision. It was said that a good "buff" could make ten cents a day if he did his job well.

On June 28, 1911, Samuel J. Battle became the first black patrolman appointed to the NYPD since the merger in 1898. A handful of black patrolmen had come over with the old Brooklyn Police Department, including Battle's brother in-law, Moses Cobb. Although Battle scored an eighty-four on the police entrance exam, Cropsey had passed him over because he had a "murmuring heart." In most instances Battle's medical condition would have precluded him from joining the force, but Waldo was concerned only with his position on the civil service list.

Battle's early days in the department were far from tranquil. He was shunned by his fellow officers, and there was a debate as to where he should be assigned once he completed his training. It was decided that the best place for him was a foot post in a part of the city where his own "race abounds." Curiosity seekers traveled up to Harlem to see the consolidated department's first colored policeman walking a beat. His commanding officer described him as a "good sensible Negro who seems to know what he bargained for in taking a place on the force."

Eventually, however, the silent treatment got to him. Battle was fined two days' pay for being AWOL. But Waldo had made it his business to keep an eye on him and decided that eight months of abuse was enough for any man. He transferred him to the first deputy's office, where he embarked on a commendable career as an undercover officer in the city's "colored neighborhoods."

In January 1912 robbers began to use automobiles as getaway cars. For a while it appeared that the police would be unable to stop them, despite the assignment of hundreds of detectives to the cases. The most notorious heist, the Trinity Place Robbery, took place in Lower Manhattan and involved a pair of thieves who forced their way into a taxicab and robbed the driver and guard of $25,000 before speeding off.

The police brought the cabbie in for questioning. He vehemently denied his involvement in the theft. Despite his protestations detectives were able to connect two possible suspects to the driver, but after that the trail went cold. The former Pinkerton man, First Deputy Dougherty, decided to try a novel tactic. He brought police matron Isabella Goodwin into the investigation.

Goodwin had become a matron after the death of her husband, who had been a roundsman seventeen years earlier. On occasion she had been detailed to perform undercover work when a female was required. Her specialty was exposing fortunetellers. Of one particular clairvoyant Goodwin quipped, "He could tell me the most wonderful things about my past and look into my future—all for two dollars of course, but he couldn't get the slightest inkling from his physiological powers that I was a detective."

The police believed that two suspects from the Trinity Place Robbery frequented a disorderly house run by a woman known as "Swede" Annie Hall. Dougherty had Goodwin apply for the position of domestic servant at Mistress Hall's house. Within a matter of weeks Goodwin had won her employer over and secured enough evidence against the suspects, subsequently identified as Edwin Kinsman and Jesse Albrozo, as well as the cabbie, to arrest all three for the crime. As for "Swede" Annie Hall, her loose lips earned her a short sentence at the House of Detention.

In recognition of her extraordinary efforts, Waldo promoted Goodwin from matron to detective first grade. When interviewed about becoming the department's first female detective, she said, "Despite my peculiar work, I try not to neglect my home. A woman's first duty is to her family, and I have always tried to remember that."

During his previous stint as first deputy, Waldo had noticed that while there was often a public furor when patrolmen were caught abusing ordinary citizens, just the opposite was true when excessive force was used on criminals. In fact he sensed that law-abiding citizens enjoyed it when crooks got what was coming to them. With this in mind he formed a trio of special units to prevent crime, break up gangs, disperse corner loafers, suppress ferryboat hoodlums, and discourage car rowdies. In reality officers of these three units meted out on-the-site punishment to all persons deemed worthy of their special attention. As a result the press dubbed these units the "Strong-Arm Squad."

Magistrates refused to discourage the squad's special brand of street justice so long as certain rules were followed. First, the department had to receive a legitimate complaint concerning vice activity or bawdy behavior at a particular location. Then one of the three squads was dispatched to verify the charge and gather additional evidence through discreet observation. Its findings were relayed directly to Waldo, who alone decided if the unit's unique skills were warranted. Only if and when he gave the go-ahead did members of the unit spring into action, swinging fists and anything they could hold in their hands. Small jobs were handled by just one or two men, but big jobs, such as taking down an illegal casino, required all three squads plus reserves.

The assignment was not without its perils. The hoods seldom went easily and were not afraid to use lethal methods of their own against the police. A favorite tactic of the criminals was to pour boiling water off roofs onto squad members as they barged through casino and brothel doors.

The person most associated with the Strong-Arm Squad was Lieutenant Charles Becker, even though he shared his duties with Lieutenant Daniel "Honest Dan" Costigan, New York's first traffic cop. Initially Lieutenant Becker was praised for his efforts to combat vice, but public opinion changed when he became involved in one of the department's all-time-worst scandals.

Before the summer of 1912 Waldo had received a number of anonymous reports alleging that Lieutenant Becker was dirty and that he had accepted money in exchange for providing police protection to the well-known gambler Herman Rosenthal. Waldo confronted Becker directly. Becker denied the charge, and to prove his honesty he conducted a raid on a betting parlor known to be operated by Rosenthal's nephew. The elder Rosenthal was so upset by Becker's betrayal that he paid a visit to District Attorney Whitman and implicated Becker in a department-wide system of shakedowns and payoffs.

Whitman initially put little faith into the story of a gambler with an axe to grind against the police department, but when Rosenthal told his tale to the newspapers, the spectacular headlines that resulted backed the district attorney into a corner. Whitman agreed to convene a grand jury with Herman Rosenthal slated to be the star witness.

Despite the allegations Gaynor steadfastly supported Waldo's decision to allow Becker to remain in charge of the Strong-Arm Squad. "Don't bend a single bit to the clamor and especially the clamor chiefly created by hired press agents of the gamblers, with whom you are at war, and those corrupt newspapers which have been all along and are now at the service of such gamblers against you. Rest assured that the Mayor will stand with you against the corrupt scamps now trying to defame you," he said.

Heeding the mayor's advice turned out to be Waldo's biggest mistake because it gave Becker the time he needed to silence the gambler before he testified. During the course of his work with the Strong-Arm Squad, Becker had become acquainted with a low-level hood known as "Billiard Ball Jack" Rose. It later came out that Rose sometimes acted as an intermediary between Becker and those from whom he extorted money.

At Becker's behest Rose recruited four gunmen—Jacob Seidenscheiner (a.k.a. "Whitey Lewis"), Lefty Louis Rosenberg, "Dago" Frank Cirofici, and Harry "Gyp the Blood" Horowitz—to murder Rosenthal for $500 apiece, payable in advance. But Becker had just bought a parcel of real estate in the Bronx, and although it was not true, he claimed that he did not have enough cash to finance the hit, so he imposed a levy on pool hall owner Bridgey Webber to pay for it.

Rosenthal's grand jury appearance was scheduled for July 16, 1912. The press leaked news that he would name at least thirty cops who were on the take. With time to silence Rosenthal running dangerously short, Becker gave Rose an ultimatum: either kill the gambler before he testified or suffer the consequences. As fate would have it, Rose learned that evening that Rosenthal was camped out in the lobby of his favorite haunt, the Metropole Hotel on Forty-Third Street near Broadway. He dispatched the four hired guns to finish him off.

Rosenthal spent most of that night in the dining room of the hotel, castigating the police to anyone who would listen. Finally at two in the morning he got up to leave. As he stepped into the street, the four gunmen riddled his body with bullets and made a clean getaway in a gray Packard touring sedan. Eyewitnesses alleged that patrolmen in the vicinity failed to pursue them. Fortunately a number of citizens noted the vehicle's license plate number and came forward with the information. Two hours after the shooting the police had the driver of the getaway car in custody.

Becker's name was immediately connected to the hit. This time Waldo did not hesitate to relieve him of his command. He transferred Becker to desk duty at the Bathgate Avenue stationhouse in the Bronx.

Before long Rose was in custody and singing like the proverbial canary to the district attorney. He claimed that Lieutenant Becker was the mastermind behind the hit. On July 29 two private detectives hired by Whitman arrested Becker while he was on desk duty at his precinct. The next day Becker entered a plea of not guilty to first-degree murder and was remanded to the Tombs Prison, where he awaited trial in the same cell in which William Magear Tweed, the corrupt former leader of Tammany Hall, had languished during his final days on earth while waiting to answer for his many sins.

In the meantime Becker's entire nineteen-year police career was put under a microscope by the press. The lurid stories bordered on libel, but there was nothing Becker could do about them because Whitman provided Herbert Swope of the *World* with exclusive daily updates, in return for the reporter's printing incriminating material to sway public opinion without question. One intrepid reporter managed to get hold of Becker's bank statements, which he claimed showed deposits in excess of $50,000. In reality Becker had only $29,000 in the bank, but that was still a huge amount of money in comparison to his police salary. (The reporter never bothered to correct his mistake, even after it was pointed out to him.)

Becker's alleged criminal activities created the impression that most of the men on the force were no better than thieves themselves. When a patrolman stationed in front of the Metropole Hotel told a group of loiterers to move on, one of the vagrants cracked, "Why? Are you getting ready for a murder?"

Waldo did as much damage control as possible. He admitted that there were a small number of grafters on the force and pointed out that if Becker was guilty, it proved that not even a powerful lieutenant could deliver on a promise of immunity from the police in exchange for payoffs. But no matter how he rationalized the situation, neither Waldo nor Gaynor could stop the Board of Aldermen from conducting its own inquiry into police corruption.

The investigation became known as the Curran Committee, for its chairman, Alderman Henry H. Curran. During the course of the hearings the committee, like those before it, uncovered a vast network of police graft, not only in gambling, but also in prostitution. The committee estimated that annual payoffs to the force were in excess of $2.4 million. It blamed all of the department's woes on Waldo and called for him to resign, but Gaynor would not hear of it.

Becker's trial took place in October 1912, with Justice John W. Goff, a noted proponent of police reform, presiding. The sixty-four-year-old magistrate had established his reputation during the Lexow Committee hearings as chief counsel for the panel of investigators. He was known to detest former police chief Alexander "Clubber" Williams, whose career he helped bring to an abrupt end. "Clubber" happened to be a very close friend of Becker's and was present at his trial to offer moral support, but his presence biased Goff more against Becker than any of the evidence leveled against him by the district attorney.

Much of Whitman's case was built on the fact that Becker had a bank account and property holdings far in excess of what a man of his station in life could expect, along with the confessions of Bridgey Webber and Jack

Rose, who had been given immunity in exchange for their cooperation. Becker's defense introduced evidence that Rosenthal was upset because the raids against his establishments were hurting business. The easiest way to get rid of Becker was to implicate him as a corrupt cop. Becker's attorneys claimed that Rosenthal's threats to tell all would have been more detrimental to many of New York's big-time gamblers than to Becker. That gave any one of them a motive even more powerful than Becker's.

In total ninety-eight witnesses testified for the prosecution and defense, but Becker did not take the stand. This decision to remain silent was later attributed to his desire to protect the politicians with whom he had allied himself during his career, in particular Tammany Hall's "Big Tim" Sullivan, the same state legislator whose influence had caused First Deputy Driscoll's demise over the raid of his "protected" establishment. Ironically Sullivan was also quite friendly with the murder victim, Herman Rosenthal.

During the trial the press focused much attention on Becker's devoted young (third) wife, Helen. She became a celebrity in her own right, and at times the newspapers even managed to show her compassion. But her popularity was not enough to keep the jury from finding Becker guilty of first-degree murder after only four hours of deliberation. Becker was sentenced to death. He collapsed as the verdict was read. The entire proceeding, from murder to conviction, had taken three months.

Becker's counsel filed an appeal based on Judge Goff's obvious bias. A second trial took place in 1914. It was presided over by Judge Samuel Seabury, who years later would be instrumental in forcing Mayor Jimmy Walker out of office and getting Fiorello LaGuardia elected mayor. The jury upheld the original verdict. In 1915 Becker became the first police officer in America put to death by the electric chair. As for the four gunmen, their attempts to strike deals with the district attorney fell on deaf ears. They were executed but with much less fanfare than their accomplice.

District Attorney Whitman went on to become Governor Whitman and signed off on Becker's death warrant. Becker's widow attempted to attach a silver plate to her husband's coffin bearing an inscription that he had been murdered by Whitman in order to propel himself into higher office. She reluctantly allowed the head of the Detective Bureau, Inspector Joseph Faurot, to take possession of the plate after he convinced her that Whitman could sue her for libel.

In September 1913 Gaynor boarded the steamer *Baltic* for a two-week transatlantic voyage to England. With the mayoral election only eight weeks away, the cruise caught his supporters by surprise. Gaynor had severed his ties with Tammany Hall and was running as an independent against Democrat Edward E. McCall and the Fusion Party standard bearer, former president of the Board of Aldermen, John Purroy Mitchel, who had resigned from office to start his campaign.

Most New Yorkers did not know that the mayor's health had been steadily deteriorating since the beginning of the year. He barely spoke above a whisper and was often subjected to debilitating coughing fits. Gaynor hoped the ocean air would revitalize him in time for the mayoral race. But his name never appeared on the ballot. Gaynor died at sea on September 10, 1913, while reading on the deck of the ship.

Adolph L. Kline, interim president of the Board of Aldermen, was immediately called to City Hall. Although he had been acting mayor during Gaynor's scheduled absence, under the City Charter he automatically became mayor upon the death of the elected mayor.

The fifty-five-year-old Kline was a hard-line Republican. He was born in New Jersey but had lived in Brooklyn since 1875. In 1876 he enlisted in the army. During his career he rose to the rank of colonel and saw action on the front line during the Spanish-American War. After the war he dabbled in politics and became an alderman in 1904. He lost a bid for reelection two years later but returned to the board in 1911. When Mitchel resigned to begin his mayoral campaign, Kline succeeded him as president.

News of Gaynor's death reached Waldo as he was reviewing police recruits during a training session at the Twelfth Regiment Armory. Tears streamed down his cheeks as he cried, "The mayor is dead. The mayor is dead."

Speaking for the first time as mayor, Kline made it known that he did not contemplate any changes in city government. Those who had been looking for Kline to oust Waldo were disappointed, but he realized that little could be gained by changing police commissioners at this late stage of the term.

Gaynor's remains were returned to New York via the RMS *Lusitania*. City Hall was adorned with black bunting, and his body was placed inside for public view. The line of mourners waiting to get a glimpse of the dead mayor stretched all the way up from the Battery to the steps of City Hall. On the day of his funeral it was estimated that half a million people crowded the streets to watch the procession to Trinity Church. In recognition of Gaynor's political contributions, former president William H. Taft led the procession of honorary pallbearers, along with former mayors Seth Low and George McClellan. It was reported that the nation had not seen such a spectacle since President Lincoln's funeral.

Gaynor's friends and enemies called a truce for the occasion. He was eulogized as a man of courage and independence and fondly remembered for the reform measures he had instituted in the NYPD. In short his view of the role the police played in society was simple: "Preserve outward order and decency." That, they said, was what he had tried to have the bluecoats do.

Waldo finished out the year lavishing attention on his last recruit class. His personal scrutiny ensured that the recruits received the best training of any police class up to that point. He increased classroom instruction from thirty days to six weeks and brought in former police commissioner (and now chief magistrate) William McAdoo to conduct mock trials to improve the recruits' courtroom testimony. When the recruits graduated that October, Waldo transferred every single officer out of the Fourth District, which included the infamous Tenderloin Precinct, where Herman Rosenthal had been murdered, and replaced them with the rookie class. He also replaced the district's ninety supervisors with new promotees, one of whom was a future police commissioner, Sergeant Lewis Valentine.

That November Fusion Party candidate John Purroy Mitchel became the youngest man in city history to win the mayoralty. Waldo continued to carry out his duties, part of which included making better use of improved technology. For example, he announced the start of a pilot project to mount newly designed signal boxes on poles at selected sites in Upper Manhattan. If the desk officer wanted to get in touch with a particular patrolman on his foot post, he merely pushed a button at the stationhouse to activate either a green electric light or bell to signal the officer to come to the box and use the phone inside to call the precinct for instructions. This new system would mean the end of Waldo's dreaded fixed posts because for the first time there was a reliable method of two-way communication between foot cops and the stationhouse supervisors.

Although Mitchel had said that the position of police commissioner would receive his most careful consideration, it appeared during the transition period that nobody wanted the job. As late as Christmas Eve there was still speculation that Waldo would remain in office, but rather than wait for Mitchel to make up his mind, Waldo directed his deputy commissioners to submit their resignations to him. Then he tendered his own resignation to Mayor Kline on December 29, to become effective at midnight on December 31. Waldo explained that it was his desire to leave his replacement unburdened by his political appointments so that the next police commissioner could decide for himself who merited each position. He placed Chief Inspector Schmittberger temporarily in charge until his successor was named.

For the first time since 1898 the NYPD was without civilian oversight. This infuriated outgoing mayor Adolf Kline so much that he scribbled a note to Waldo informing him that he had been officially removed from office effective as of 11:08 a.m., December 31. Waldo wrote back that this was a "peevish act" since he had already tendered his resignation. Waldo later sued to have the record amended to read that he had not been removed from office but had resigned. In either case Kline and mayor-elect Mitchel agreed that Waldo's first deputy, Douglas McKay, would become acting police commissioner until a permanent replacement could be named.

Waldo left the department with these final thoughts: "Let the same amount of energy be expended in the prosecution of criminals that is expended very properly on the investigation of the police." History remembers Waldo more for his devotion to Gaynor and the mayor's reciprocal feelings for him than for his many accomplishments. As a result the portrait of his administration has been unfairly colored. He was an innovator who was willing to defy convention in order to deliver improved police services to the citizens of New York. He welcomed women into the ranks of detective and ensured the department's first black officer got a fair shake. As commissioner, he studied problems and proposed solutions. He unflinchingly faced any criticism that was leveled against him. In part the Lieutenant Becker affair occurred because he had defied the Tammany Hall politicians who wanted their paid protection racket to continue unabated by the police. Waldo, whose own integrity was beyond reproach, could not be bought. Unfortunately the same could not be said for the commander of the Strong-Arm Squad, Lieutenant Becker.

After retirement Waldo remained active in politics. Although he never held another public office, he served as one of Police Commissioner Richard Enright's honorary deputy commissioners. He was just fifty years old when he died in 1927 from pneumonia, attributed to his earlier military service in the Philippines.

Waldo's predecessor, James Cropsey, fared much better in his post-police career. In 1911 he ran successfully as a Republican to become district attorney for Brooklyn. In 1916 the governor appointed him to fill an unexpired term as State Supreme Court justice, and he went on to win election for judge twice. His name was often bandied about as a candidate for mayor and governor, but he chose to remain on the bench. Cropsey died of a glandular ailment at age sixty-four in 1937, leaving behind a widow but no children.

Three years after he left the police department William Baker bought the Philadelphia Phillies baseball club. His team won the national league pennant in 1915, thanks to the pitching of Hall of Famer Grover Cleveland Alexander, who won thirty-one games that season. The Phillies lost in the World Series to the Boston Red Sox in five games and never again made it to the series under Baker's ownership, mainly because he regularly sold off his best talent and pocketed the money for himself. When he died in 1930, he was remembered more for his tight-fisted baseball acumen than his run-ins with Mayor Gaynor during his short time in charge of the NYPD.

Adolph Kline, the forgotten mayor of New York, was rewarded by Mitchel with a patronage appointment as tax commissioner. He was elected to Congress in 1920 and died in October 1930.

Although Gaynor and Waldo had tried their best to reform the police department, it nevertheless lost much of its luster under the ever more scrutinizing eye of the public. But at least the department's dirty little secrets were out in the open for all to see, and, if nothing else, the police force inherited by their successors was the better for it.

5

BECOMING A FORCE
FOR SOCIAL REFORM

John Purroy Mitchel was born in the Fordham section of the Bronx in 1879. Thirty-four years later he was the youngest person ever elected mayor of New York, and his lanky build made him appear even younger. Because of his age, he was sometimes called the "Boy Mayor." It was not necessarily a term of endearment, but few before him or after him came into office more qualified to run New York City.

He was the grandson of John Mitchel, a famous Irish journalist and hero of Ireland's struggle for independence from England. John had been exiled to Tasmania for his scathing essays against English treatment of Irishmen but later escaped to America and settled in Richmond, Virginia, where he edited a newspaper. His three sons fought in the Civil War for the Confederacy. James Mitchel, the mayor's father, rose to the rank of captain and was the only brother to survive the conflict, although it cost him an arm. After the war James moved to New York and married a girl from the Bronx, Mary Purroy, whose family was descended from Spanish nobility. She was also the sister of the county clerk, Henry Purroy, a well-connected Democrat. After the marriage James became a well-respected fire marshal in the city, but his meticulous arson investigations sometimes ruffled feathers. As a result when his brother-in-law fell out of favor with Tammany Hall, he also ended up losing his job.

Mitchel's parents believed in education. Their son attended Catholic preparatory school at Fordham, Columbia University, and New York Law School. After admission to the bar in 1902, he joined a small law firm, and while he enjoyed legal work, his parents convinced him that he was destined for bigger things.

Mayor McClellan was starting his second term in 1906 and had had a falling out with Tammany Hall. He was seeking to hire young, ambitious, incorruptible men looking to make a reputation for themselves. Mitchel heeded the call to public service and secured an appointment to the Office of the Commissioner of Accounts.

Over the next three years Mitchel's investigations into municipal corruption brought down four borough presidents, a fire commissioner, the aqueducts commissioner, the appraiser of real estate, and a Night Court magistrate. As a reward for his excellent work McClellan promoted Mitchel to commissioner of accounts.

In 1909 Mitchel was drafted by the Fusion Party to run for president of the Board of Aldermen, the second most powerful political office in New York City. With the exception of Democrat William J. Gaynor, who was elected mayor, Fusionists swept every other important contest in the city.

The City Charter stipulated that if the mayor became incapacitated, the president of the Board of Aldermen would become acting mayor. As discussed (see chapter 4), in August 1910, after just eight months in office, Mayor Gaynor was shot in the neck by a disgruntled civil servant. Mitchel took charge of city government while Gaynor recovered from the assassination attempt. Mitchel seized the opportunity to advance his political career by ordering a controversial investigation into illegal resorts operating in Coney Island. By the time the smoke cleared, the precinct commander and Police Commissioner William Baker both lost their jobs, but the praise Mitchel received only enhanced his reputation.

Mitchel's fellow Fusionists thought his honesty and popularity made him an ideal candidate for mayor in the 1913 election. During the campaign he promised to eliminate police corruption and improve the economic efficiency of city government. Law and order and prudent money management carried the day. Mitchel easily defeated Democrat Edward McCall, although the outcome might have been different had the popular incumbent, Mayor Gaynor, who was expected to run again, not died two months before the election. After Tammany Hall's Charles Murphy conceded the race, Mitchel announced, "I have but one ambition, that is, to make New York the best-governed municipality in America."

For the head of the police department, Mitchel believed that the candidate, as he put it, "must have a good working knowledge of business systems, be essentially human with an understanding of the men and people of the city, give individual police full measure of respect, and inspire in him respect for his job." He had one particular person in mind, Colonel George Goethals, the chief army engineer overseeing construction of the Panama Canal. Mitchel spent a great deal of time between the election and his swearing-in trying to convince Goethals to accept the post, but the colonel would agree only if he had absolute power to terminate police officers for acts of misconduct. Without such authority he wanted no part of the job. To meet Goethals's demand would require that the state legislature amend the law, but the rank and file vehemently opposed such legislation because they believed that it would put too much control in one man's hands. Mitchel became so preoccupied with pushing for the so-called "Goethals Bill" that he did not consider an alternative candidate in the event the measure was defeated.

In the meantime, just two days before Mitchel was to be sworn in, Police Commissioner Rhinelander Waldo tendered his resignation to Mayor Adolph Kline. Since there was no time for Kline to name an interim replacement before his term ended, he deferred the decision to the incoming mayor. Mitchel told Kline to appoint First Deputy Douglas McKay as acting police commissioner until he appointed his own candidate.

Douglas McKay was born in New York City in 1879, the same year as Mitchel, and was a graduate of West Point. His association with law enforcement began in 1907, when he resigned his army commission to become second in command of the Aqueduct Police Force under Rhinelander Waldo. Police work in the rural watershed area at that time was dangerous business. McKay soon learned that an officer had to be quick with his hands to survive. His experiences rousting backwoods troublemakers forged a lifelong philosophy that a policeman should not have to spend a lot of time convincing a man that the "climate is unhealthy" in order to get him to move on to greener pastures.

When Gaynor had appointed Waldo police commissioner, Waldo had brought McKay along as first deputy. McKay served in that capacity until Waldo's controversial departure opened the door for him to become, at age thirty-four, the youngest police commissioner in city history. McKay wasted little time proving to Mitchel that he was up to the job so that he might keep it. Within twenty-four hours of taking over he had most of the

Headquarters staff back in place and had convinced George Dougherty to return temporarily as second deputy commissioner.

On January 5, 1914, McKay reinstated the Strong-Arm Squad. But rather than target the gamblers who enjoyed the support of crooked politicians, he directed the squad's forty plainclothesmen to strictly enforce only Paragraph 10 of the Penal Code, the statute that allowed police officers to arrest on sight gangsters, vagrants, and other persons known to have been convicted of pickpocketing, theft, or burglary anytime they were observed loitering in a public place. The roundups began immediately, and although nearly every case was dismissed for lack of evidence, the harassment tactics seemed to work. Reports soon started coming in from the surrounding counties that New York City's known "dips" (pickpockets) were being arrested by other jurisdictions.

Although McKay had given the Strong-Arm Squad a different mission, it did not mean that gangsters were free to do as they pleased. He set the entire patrol force on them. When the officers complained that rules implemented by Gaynor restricting their use of nightsticks were still in effect and thus made it dangerous for them to confront crooks, McKay vowed that no policeman would be brought up on charges for using his club on any suspect who could not prove good character. When asked for his thoughts regarding McKay's promise, Mitchel said that he certainly had no problem with the police using their clubs on known criminals, but privately he expressed concern that McKay's zealous enforcement methods would become a liability.

When Second Deputy Dougherty resigned after a month to return to his private detective business, McKay appointed Robert Rubin, a former assistant district attorney who had assisted in the prosecution of Lieutenant Charles Becker, to help him reorganize the Detective Bureau. Their first order of business was to restore the daily lineup that Mayor Gaynor had Waldo abolish. McKay told reporters that he thought it was necessary to provide "green" detectives with the opportunity to acquaint themselves with professional thieves.

Lieutenant Daniel "Honest Dan" Costigan had not been tainted by the Strong-Arm Squad scandal that had taken down Lieutenant Becker, even though he had shared duties with Lieutenant Becker (see chapter 4). Instead he became a trusted confidant of Waldo's and then of McKay's. When McKay got an anonymous report that Inspector James Gillen, commanding officer of the Tenderloin, was doing nothing about the disorderly houses in his precinct, he relied on Costigan to conduct an investigation. Costigan determined that Inspector Gillen had forwarded inaccurate reports to Headquarters falsely claiming to have the situation under control when in fact just the opposite was true.

Armed with this damning information, McKay paid a surprise visit to the West Thirtieth Street stationhouse. Upon arrival he wrote a notation in the desk blotter suspending Gillen and demoting him to captain pending the outcome of his department trial. Then he banished Gillen's entire staff to distant corners of the city. The following morning he warned all seventeen inspectors that he would hold them personally responsible for the moral conditions in their districts, and if their oversight was found to be lax, they too would be subject to discipline and dismissal.

Although Mitchel publicly praised McKay's efforts to combat vice and crime, behind the scenes he continued to lobby for passage of the Goethals Bill. It became apparent by the end of March 1914 that the bill would be defeated. McKay approached the mayor and asked if he intended to keep him on. When Mitchel refused to commit to him, McKay penned his letter of resignation. In it he wrote, "I feel very strongly that the discipline of the department requires you to appoint a Commissioner whom you expect to retain and support during the rest of your administration." Mitchel accepted his resignation but acknowledged that McKay had accepted the appointment at a time of crisis and had administered the department effectively under trying conditions.

While it was true that he thought that McKay was an efficient administrator, Mitchel was looking for someone who saw the police department as more than an organization that simply apprehended criminals. He wanted a visionary to create a department that interacted with society to prevent crime.

Shortly after eleven in the morning on April 8, 1914, Mitchel turned over control of the NYPD to his confidential secretary and close personal friend,

Arthur Woods. The mayor stated emphatically that Woods would last until the end of his administration; reporters noted at the time that such a tenure would make Woods the longest-serving police commissioner in the history of the department.

Woods was born in Boston in 1870. He graduated from Harvard and studied overseas at the University of Berlin. When he returned, he taught English at the exclusive Groton School in Massachusetts. Among his students was future president Franklin Delano Roosevelt. Woods left the teaching profession in 1905 and came to New York, where he worked as a newspaper reporter for the *New York Evening Sun*. His stories about the police department caught Police Commissioner Bingham's eye. Bingham made him fourth deputy commissioner, a position Woods held from 1907 to 1909. In that capacity he oversaw the reorganization of the Detective Bureau, formed the department's first Homicide Squad, and traveled extensively throughout Europe studying the crime-control strategies of its largest cities. Along the way he became a close friend and trusted confidant of Mitchel's. As for his reason to appoint Woods, Mitchel told the *New York Times*, "His ideas, more closely approximate my own than those of any other available men I have considered." He failed to mention his concerted effort to secure the services of Colonel Goethals.

After the swearing-in ceremony at City Hall Woods walked to Police Headquarters, where McKay was waiting. As the two men shook hands, McKay said that he wished him all the good luck in the world.

Since becoming mayor, Mitchel was afraid that a disgruntled employee might one day try to kill him, just as one had tried to kill Mayor Gaynor. Rather than take any chances, he paid a dollar to the police department for a license to carry his own pistol. It proved to be a wise precaution because on April 20, 1914, a mentally unstable seventy-one-year-old male, subsequently identified as Michael Mahoney, shot at him as he sat in an automobile with Police Commissioner Woods and corporation counsel Frank Polk in the City Hall parking lot.

Woods lunged at the deranged man and grabbed hold of his pistol, diverting the shot. The would-be assassin managed to get off a second round. It too missed the mayor but struck Polk in the jaw before Woods overpowered him. Mitchel kept the shooter covered until help arrived.

Polk survived but lost two teeth. Mahoney confessed that he was upset at the way Mitchel was running the city and in particular his appointment of a woman to run the city jails. A three-man panel of psychiatric experts concluded that Mahoney was insane and had him institutionalized.

Woods was not a fan of Waldo's fixed-post system. He thought it required too many men who covered far too little territory. In place of the fixed-post system he created a system of "block posts." Patrolmen were free to roam the streets within their assigned territory in order to familiarize themselves with the people and conditions on their beat. The officers were required, however, to remain within eyesight of the new green signal boxes that were being installed throughout the city by the telephone company. The signal boxes allowed for two-way communication with the stationhouses. Each box also had a built-in "citizen call button," which, when pressed, activated a flashing green light to alert patrolmen of crimes in progress. The public had a nickname for the signal light: the "blinking Irishman."

In the outer boroughs, where the precincts covered much larger and more sparsely populated areas, Woods experimented with a system of police substations. In reality these were little more than small wooden shacks equipped with telephones and potbelly stoves. They were staffed around the clock by two police officers who alternated between patrolling the area on a bicycle and remaining within twenty feet of the substation to answer the telephone. Flyers were distributed throughout the rural precincts advising citizens to report to the substations in person or contact the patrolmen assigned there by telephone when seeking police assistance.

In June 1914 Woods began his overhaul of the Detective Bureau, building on plans laid out by McKay and Second Deputy Robert Rubin. Woods believed that the civil service testing process used to promote sergeants, lieutenants, and captains served only to encourage mediocrity. He decided that as long as he was police commissioner, the merit system would be the primary method used to identify the best candidates for promotion to detective. Such a method would focus on the number of arrests and convictions each patrolman made.

In addition, Woods reestablished the Homicide Squad that had been disbanded by Waldo at Mayor Gaynor's direction and formed several new specialty squads to deal with burglars, mendicants, drug addicts, pickpockets, and pawnshops. He also created the Criminal Identification Bureau to warehouse a new rogues' gallery after Waldo had had most of the old mug shots destroyed, again at Mayor Gaynor's behest.

In order to staff these new units Woods reduced the number of detective districts—also known as branches—from seventeen to nine. The detectives who remained in the consolidated branches complained because they were forced to pick up the workload of those transferred to the specialty squads. Their grumbling fell on deaf ears because Woods believed that by zeroing in on specific types of crimes, detectives would be better able to prevent their commission; he thereby aligned the department's mission with Mitchel's vision. In his annual report to the mayor, Woods cited a 35 percent drop in reported crimes by pickpockets to validate his use of specialists.

In the autumn of 1914 Woods asked Captain John Sweeny to organize a "junior police" program in an attempt to stem the rise in juvenile delinquency. Each boy who enlisted in the program was given his own replica police shield—but only after providing a fifteen cent deposit. Once the boy had a shield, he became a junior patrolman, but he could advance up the ladder all the way to chief. The boys attended meetings and took part in recreational activities in empty city lots that were converted into playgrounds. The idea was to keep boys on the straight and narrow, but some of them got into trouble because they thought the badge gave them the authority to mete out punishment to juvenile lawbreakers. The program lasted until Captain Sweeny retired in 1917. Another decade would pass before the department attempted to sponsor another youth program.

In keeping with Mitchel's philosophy that the police department should share information with other agencies for the betterment of the entire city, Woods replaced the patrolmen's memorandum books with preprinted forms. On these forms patrolmen were required to note conditions not requiring immediate police intervention with a series of check marks and short descriptive narratives. The forms were then turned over to the desk lieutenant, who collated the information and forwarded it to the city departments concerned: health, education, fire, housing, and so on.

If action was taken by any city agency as a result of the information supplied by a particular officer, a letter of commendation was placed in his personnel file. The system allowed precinct commanders to measure and compare an individual patrolman's actions and observations against those of his peers. Despite the program's many positive applications, patrolmen complying with Woods's order often purposely entered erroneous information on the forms, once again demonstrating to the brass how resistant police officers were to change, even when the change was perceived to be beneficial.

By January 1915 much of the goodwill that Woods had established early on with the force had dissipated as a result of his constant tinkering. The uniformed associations hired William B. Ellison Esq. to discuss the matter with Woods, but Woods refused to meet with him and instead offered to make his case with each of the organizations' leaders. Lieutenant Richard Enright, president of the Lieutenants Benevolent Association, was the only one who declined the invitation. He said that during his twenty-year career the department had already been reorganized sixteen times, and as far as he was concerned there was no need to do it again. Woods rewarded Enright for his candor by passing him over for promotion, but Enright would have the last laugh when he became police commissioner and undid most of Woods's special programs.

A great war was under way in Europe. In New York City sympathizers on both sides of the conflict were busy conspiring against the United States. Every week a large group of anarchists rallied in Union Square Park to denounce the policies of the federal government. Confrontations between the anarchists and uniformed patrolmen who were there to keep the peace were often violent. Woods began to use plainclothesmen to discreetly monitor the anarchists' activities from within.

The strategy paid off in March 1915, when the department uncovered a plot by a group of Italian anarchists to blow up St. Patrick's Cathedral. It was a big break for the police since a bomb had exploded in the cathedral six months before and the case was still unsolved. This time, however, the zealots were unaware that a young Italian detective named Emilio Polignani had infiltrated their ranks and alerted his superiors at Police Headquarters of the plan.

The perpetrators, subsequently identified as Frank Arbano and Charles Carbone, entered the cathedral just as the Sunday morning mass was about to begin. They took their place in the pews, completely unaware that they were being watched by a team of undercover officers in disguise. As the parishioners knelt in prayer, one of the plotters removed a crude bomb from his overcoat, placed it on the floor, and then used a cigar to light the fuse. As the would-be bomber hurried off with his partner, one of the plainclothes policeman slipped into the pew and snuffed out the smoldering fuse before it could detonate the dynamite. Both suspects were apprehended without further incident by the undercover officers and were later sentenced to twelve years in jail.

Woods praised his men's heroics as "a piece of real detective work." Mayor Mitchel was similarly pleased because it demonstrated what he considered the police department's most important function: the prevention of crime.

One of the reasons anarchists used dynamite in their crude explosive devices was that anyone could buy the highly volatile compound. In preparation for his one-man terror campaign, anarchist Eric Muenter, a.k.a. Frank Holt, purchased 120 pounds of dynamite from a company in Queens and had it delivered to his home on Long Island, no questions asked. Before becoming involved in the anarchist movement, Eric Muenter had been a German-language professor at Harvard University. He disappeared from the campus shortly after the death of his wife in 1906. He had good reason to flee. The autopsy revealed that he had poisoned her with arsenic.

While in hiding, Muenter changed his name to Frank Holt and continued to teach German at a college in Texas. After living for several years under a false identity, Holt moved to Long Island, determined to do whatever he could to prevent the United States from entering the war against his beloved Germany.

Holt's crime spree began on July 2, 1915, when he took the train from New York to Washington DC. Shortly before midnight he walked into the U.S. Capitol and left a bomb with three sticks of dynamite in the empty Senate chamber. He lit the fuse and fled. Although the blast caused substantial damage to the Capitol's north wing, there were no injuries. The post-explosion investigation cited budget cuts as the reason for the lack of security that had allowed Holt to enter the Capitol undetected.

Holt returned home by train. The next day he journeyed to the Long Island estate of John Pierpont Morgan Jr., armed with a pair of pistols. He intended to murder Morgan because his company was the primary supplier of munitions to Britain and France in their fight against Germany. The arrangement was quite lucrative for Morgan.

Holt's assassination attempt on Morgan was thwarted by the British ambassador, Sir Cecil Spring-Rice, who happened to be present at Morgan's home, most likely discussing the terms of their business deal. Holt managed to get two shots off before he was subdued by the ambassador and two servants. The bullets struck Morgan in the thigh and abdomen but were not life threatening. A stick of dynamite found in Holt's pocket was later matched to the explosive used in the Capitol bombing.

Woods, who was engaged to Morgan's niece, rushed to the scene to take charge of the investigation. While he was at the estate, a bomb exploded in the basement of Police Headquarters. The blast sent smoke billowing out through the shattered windows. A heavy wooden door was reportedly turned into matchsticks and a concrete staircase became a crater. Miraculously no one was injured.

When Woods returned to his office that night, rumor had it that Headquarters had been targeted because of his association with the millionaire. After surveying the damage, Woods would comment only that "an explosion at the very heart of and center of the police department is a bad thing for us."

Any hopes that Morgan's would-be assassin would admit to planting the bomb at Headquarters were dashed when he committed suicide in the Nassau County Jail before he was questioned. Although there were allegations that Holt did not go to the grave voluntarily, nobody seemed to care very much about what had happened in the county lockup that night.

District Attorney Whitman had used the notoriety he achieved prosecuting Lieutenant Becker to propel himself to the governorship. When his replacement, Edward Swann, took over as district attorney in January 1916, one of the first things he did was to launch his own investigation into police misconduct. It seemed that Becker's death sentence had had little impact on corruption. Swann charged twelve patrolmen, two lieutenants, and an inspector with taking $45,000 in protection money from twenty separate disorderly houses in the Tenderloin district.

Swann claimed that the financial arrangement was very beneficial to the police officers involved in the scheme. In addition to the regular monthly "fees," the officers also received 25 percent of each disorderly house's profits, while the brothels that did not go along with the program were put out of business, thereby making the ones that cooperated even more profitable for the police. After his police career Woods lamented, "The public hires policemen to enforce the law; the crooks hire them not to."

Mitchel, by nature, tended to be suspicious of everybody, so when he heard rumors that the money the city paid to outside entities to care for "feeble-minded" children was not being spent properly, he ordered his charities commissioner, James Kingsbury, to look into the matter. For the most part the caregivers in question were affiliated with religious organizations, with the vast majority of underprivileged children enrolled in programs run by the Catholic Church. When Kingsbury reported back that he was unable to account for $700,000, Mitchel ordered Woods to conduct a full-scale investigation.

Kingsbury told Woods that he had identified two prominent Catholic priests as possibly having knowledge of the whereabouts of the missing monies. Woods decided that the best way to gather evidence against the priests was to tap their telephones. In those days the police commissioner would simply submit a form letter to the New York Telephone Company that read, "I have reason to believe that the following telephone is being used for criminal purposes and respectfully request the cooperation of your company in detecting the matter." Woods did not think anything of it because the police had been using wiretaps since Theodore Roosevelt had served as president of the defunct Police Board.

Although detectives monitoring the conversations testified that they uncovered minor wrongdoing on the part of the priests, it came out during cross-examination that they had not only listened to the priests' conversations, but had also tapped into the phone lines of union labor leaders and a prominent law firm. It was further revealed that since he had become police commissioner, Woods had requested several hundred phone taps involving all sorts of people suspected of criminal behavior.

The disclosure forced the state legislature to conduct a review of the department's wiretapping policy. Woods explained that he had authorized the wiretaps of certain union leaders because their members had been involved in several violent strikes. Regarding the recorded telephone conversations of the law firm, he said that they concerned the sale of munitions to

Great Britain and France by J. P. Morgan and had national security implications for the United States and that he had shared the information with the federal government. It was his distinct opinion that law-abiding citizens did not have to be concerned that the police would wiretap their telephones.

The priests were found not guilty, but Mitchel refused to drop the matter. He insisted that the two priests had committed perjury because their testimony on the witness stand contradicted what they had said on the telephone. His viewpoint infuriated Catholics across the city. An unintended consequence of being a straight shooter is that sometimes one can be punished for advocating high moral standards. Mitchel would learn this firsthand when he ran for reelection.

In the meantime Woods tried to generate some good publicity for the department by directing captains to solicit money and merchandise from businesses and wealthy citizens in their precincts in order to provide a "real Christmas" to the destitute children of New York. Since there was always a chance that the captains would misappropriate the donations for their own benefit, Woods informed them that he would hold them personally responsible for any goods or money that went missing.

Nearly $20,000 in cash and a wide variety of goods were donated to the cause. Patrolmen in fifty-one precincts put up Christmas trees in their stationhouses. Santa Clauses in blue police uniforms provided thousands of youngsters with gifts of clothing, toys, candy, and refreshments, along with games, movies, and magic shows. When questioned by reporters as to why the police were going to such trouble, an anonymous official at Headquarters explained that making the neighborhood poor happy was part of a policemen's duty.

Ruth Cruger, age eighteen, was last seen on February 13, 1917, leaving her residence on Claremont Avenue in Manhattan. She was going to pick up a pair of ice skates that she had dropped off to get sharpened at a motorcycle repair shop on West 127th Street. When she failed to return home that evening, her father notified the police that his daughter was missing. The officers took the information but, as was their practice, waited twenty-four hours before acting on the complaint.

The motorcycle repair shop owner, an Italian immigrant named Alfred Cocchi, told the police that Ruth had indeed picked up her ice skates and left in good health. He said that he did not know where she went after that. Since Cocchi was the last person to see Ruth, the police performed a perfunctory search of his garage and turned up nothing. When Cocchi left town suddenly the next day, the detectives assigned to the case did not consider it suspicious because several patrolmen assigned to the Motorcycle Squad vouched for him.

The police thought that Ruth had either left home of her own accord or had been abducted by white slavers who had shipped her off to Cuba, although there was no evidence to suggest either theory was true. Her father asked District Attorney Swann to initiate his own investigation. Swann agreed to bring in Cocchi's wife for questioning. After meeting with her, he reported that he expected both her husband and Mr. Cruger's daughter to show up very soon. His optimism proved to be wishful thinking.

It was not until June, after Mrs. Grace Humiston, a lawyer and crusader against white slavery, got involved in the case that Ruth's disappearance was finally solved. Mrs. Humiston's persistent badgering irked the detectives assigned to the case but gained the ear of Commissioner Woods. Although the vast majority of missing girls returned home of their own volition, Woods acquiesced to Mrs. Humiston's request to have Cocchi's shop searched one more time and to allow her to personally take part. The detectives discovered Ruth's body rotting away in a pit under the floor of Cocchi's garage, still wearing the clothes she had had on the day she vanished. Solving the crime under these circumstances proved extremely embarrassing to Woods because he had spent so much time making sure that only the department's best officers became detectives. To make matters worse, Cocchi turned up in Italy and under international law could not be extradited.

Mr. Cruger was so upset by the ineptitude of the police commissioner that he demanded Mitchel fire Woods for "stupidity." In defense of Woods, Mitchel said, "Sound judgment cannot be predicated upon an isolated act or omission, unfortunate and deeply regrettable as that omission may have been."

But a grand jury looking into the matter revealed that what had happened went well beyond mere incompetence on the part of Woods. It turned out that Cocchi had developed a cozy relationship with the same policemen who had vouched for him, a fact that explained why detectives had failed to consider him a suspect from the start. It was revealed that whenever these particular motorcycle patrolmen issued a summons to a driver for a traffic infraction, they directed the violator to go directly to Cocchi's shop to "settle up." That way the fines, from which Cocchi received a cut, could go directly into their pockets instead of the city treasury. Four members of the Motorcycle Squad were indicted for extortion and receiving bribes in connection with the moneymaking scheme. Woods suspended the officers immediately, but the courts reinstated them on the premise that they were innocent until proven guilty.

A separate investigation by Commissioner of Accounts Leonard Wallstein blamed the entire debacle on Woods's lax management style. Desk lieutenants failed to keep track of the summonses issued in their precincts. Woods issued new orders that fixed responsibility for reviewing all summonses on the desk lieutenants and directed that motorcycle patrolmen assigned to Brooklyn and Queens begin their tours at the Brooklyn headquarters on Poplar Street, while those from Manhattan, the Bronx, and Staten Island were to report to Traffic Station C on West Thirtieth Street in Manhattan instead of the stationhouse closest to their homes, as had been their practice.

Woods also revamped the missing person's procedures with the creation of the Bureau of Missing Persons. The unit was to be notified by telephone as soon as a person was reported missing to a policeman so that a general alarm could be transmitted to all precincts. Cases were tracked on special cards, called DB13s, that were duplicated and distributed throughout the department. The cards contained information that could be useful for identification if the missing person turned up unconscious at a hospital or, worse, dead at the city morgue.

As for Cocchi, he confessed to Italian authorities that he had murdered Ruth Cruger because she had resisted his advances. The Italian courts sentenced him to twenty-seven years in jail, bringing an end to one of the most embarrassing chapters in NYPD history.

Mitchel was tolerant of the department's occasional blunders because he and Woods shared a greater concern. The two men had spent 1916 developing contingency plans for New York City in the event that America was drawn into the war in Europe. Woods arranged for three thousand patrolmen to undergo special military training at Fort Wadsworth on Staten Island. He and Mitchel took part in the Citizen Soldiers Training Camp at the army base in

Plattsburg, New York. Woods encouraged uniformed personnel to join him and the mayor, but the cost was out of reach for most police officers because each participant was required to provide his own gear, pay for his own meals, and arrange for his own transportation. Since the vast majority of people who took part in the program were wealthy citizens, Mitchel's participation alienated many of his impoverished constituents. But when President Woodrow Wilson declared war against Germany on April 16, 1917, the NYPD was well prepared for any civil emergency, thanks to the foresight of Mitchel and Woods.

Although plans had been drawn up to evacuate New York in the event of a foreign invasion, Woods gave more practical consideration to the protection of its precious upstate water supply. The governor approved his request that several hundred special patrolmen be added to the Aqueduct Police Force to patrol the reservoirs.

To protect the vital East River crossings Woods established the Machine Gun Corps. Seventy-two patrolmen with prior military service attended a two-week training course where they practiced shooting .30 caliber machine guns capable of firing four hundred rounds per minute. After completing the course, the officers were detailed, in squads of six, to special duty on each of the East River bridges from Lower Manhattan all the way north to Spuyten Duyvil.

Special arrangements were also made by the police to safeguard utilities that provided gas, oil, and electricity to city residents. Woods even reestablished an old system of flag and searchlight signals called "wig-wagging" for officers to contact each other by Morse code from atop tall buildings in the event that telephone service, telegraph service, or the primitive police wireless radio used to communicate with ships at sea was disrupted.

Shortly after President Wilson's declaration of war, Woods activated the twenty-three-thousand-man Home Defense League (a forerunner to the modern-day Auxiliary Police), which he had first organized during 1915. The all-civilian force was funded by private donations and was meant to supplement the regular police force during emergencies. The volunteers were outfitted in forest green uniforms with bronze buttons, canvas leggings, black shoes, and campaign-style hats. For their protection they were provided nightsticks and whistles.

By utilizing the Home Defense League for routine patrol duties, Woods had more police officers available to patrol the vulnerable waterfront and to keep an eye on German sympathizers lurking in the city. But after little more than a month had passed, Woods's use of the Home Defense League was called into question. A large number of volunteers were on duty in Manhattan's predominantly black neighborhood of San Juan Hill while the regular patrolmen sat for the sergeant's test. An argument in a saloon between a bartender and a black patron over the price of a glass of soda ignited a full-scale race riot when a league member attempted to arrest the black man for disorderly conduct. The fight spilled out onto the street, where an estimated two thousand people of both races joined the fray.

Uniformed patrolmen who were called to the scene were confronted by flying bottles and knife-wielding rioters. Reservists armed with rifles were rushed in for reinforcement. It took several hours for the police to clear the streets, but a patrolman aiding a fellow officer who was being attacked with a knife ended up killing the black perpetrator. Critics claimed that if patrolmen had responded to the initial disturbance instead of Home Defense "guards," the entire melee might have been avoided.

While Mitchel and Woods were doing everything possible to keep New York free from foreign invaders, Tammany Hall's Charles Murphy was doing everything he could to get Mitchel and Woods out of office. He borrowed a page from his predecessor, Richard Croker, and tapped another little-known magistrate named John Francis Hylan to run for mayor.

Mitchel assumed that the people of New York would reward him with a second term for his honest and efficient administration and the steps he had taken to protect their well-being. But when he was challenged and defeated in the Republican primary by William Bennett, it became apparent that he had overestimated his popularity.

In October 1917 Mitchel announced his intention to run as an independent on the Fusion ticket. Although he was still considered the favorite, he and Woods were under constant attack for their handling of the Cruger affair, and Catholics still had not forgiven him for his comments after the priests' wiretapping trial. Mitchel also lost support from a large portion of the city's German population because of his anti-German rhetoric.

Just three weeks before the election the *New York Times* published an article by Mitchel. He wrote that if he lost, New York would be given back into the hands of men who for generations had unflinchingly betrayed their promises to the people and had prostituted the city for selfish and corrupt purposes. He reminded his constituents that his police had thwarted plots to destroy the water supply and obstruct communications. Meanwhile "Boss" Murphy kept a tight rein on his candidate by limiting his speaking engagements and refusing to let him debate Mitchel.

The mayor publicly challenged Hylan's fitness to run the city. "The marvelous incapacity of Judge Hylan for the office which he seeks is daily becoming a greater wonder. Two months ago there was no reason Judge Hylan should be mayor; there is now a multitude of reasons why he should be kept out of City Hall," he said.

Hylan countered that he had started out life in the ranks of the manual toilers and attended law school at night to better himself and the government. He reminded the patrolmen that when Mitchel had been trying to take away their right to appeal arbitrary dismissals by the police commissioner, he had supported their interests in fair play. This factor resonated with the force.

Although most newspapers endorsed Mitchel for reelection, by November the bookmakers saw it otherwise and put the odds two to one in Hylan's favor. When the final count was in, Hylan tallied 293,382 votes, while Mitchel, who had been elected mayor in 1913 with the largest majority of any mayoral candidate since the formation of the Greater City of New York, received only 148,060. Republican William Bennett received fewer votes than the third-place finisher, Socialist candidate Morris Hillquest, who nearly matched Mitchel's total. A Tammany Hall spokesman explained the mayor's demise: "Mitchel was too much Fifth Avenue and not enough First Avenue."

Two days after he won the election, Hylan informed reporters that he had no intention of keeping Woods on—not that it mattered. Woods was not interested in staying in office beyond December 31 without Mitchel by his side. "Few people seem to realize how essential to the success of a Police Commissioner is the whole-souled understanding and cooperation of the Mayor," he said. "Whatever success I may have had in conducting this department would have been impossible without the complete support which I have always had from Mayor Mitchel."

During his final days Woods named Inspector James Dillon to succeed Chief Inspector Max Schmittberger, who, after forty-three years with the department, had passed away from pneumonia. Although Hylan was consulted regarding Dillon's promotion, the new chief inspector would be forced into retirement before he had worked even one day for the new mayor.

Woods disbanded the wiretapping unit and gave the eavesdropping equipment the department had borrowed back to the telephone company. During his last week in office he visited several stationhouses to watch his men play Santa Claus and say his goodbyes. Woods left office having served longer than any of his predecessors. That longevity was due to Mitchel's full confidence in his abilities, despite several lapses. In turn, Mitchel's confidence in him allowed him to keep other politicians from influencing his decisions. He explained why it was so important to keep politics out of the NYPD. When a politician obtained a transfer or assignment for a policeman, that policeman owed favors to the politician, and those favors usually required that he break the law.

Despite having been considered the early frontrunner, Mitchel must have thought that there was a good chance he would lose the election because he submitted a request to the secretary of war for a commission in the U.S. Army on the same day the votes were being cast. But the secretary did not believe his brief experience playing soldier at the Plattsburg army camp warranted such consideration. While the decision upset Mitchel, whose father and uncles had distinguished themselves in battle during the Civil War, his burning desire to take part in the war led him to accept an offer to become a pilot in the Army Air Corps. The training would delay his going to fight in France, but at age thirty-nine he had few options.

After he completed the first phase of his flight training, which totaled just nine hours in the cockpit with an instructor and a solo flight, Mitchel was sent to Gerstner Field in Louisiana. On the morning of July 6, 1918, as he was practicing glides and banks, his plane began to nosedive. Witnesses reported that Mitchel was catapulted out of the plane as it flipped over. He died instantly upon impact. The investigators determined that he had failed to fasten his safety belt. Mitchel Field on Long Island was named after him.

Mitchel's first police commissioner, Douglas McKay, certainly fared better in retirement. He lived to the age of eighty-three and even returned to the police department for a time as a special deputy commissioner. During World War I he served as a colonel in the army and was placed in charge of overseeing the production of ammunitions for artillery. For many years he was president of the New York Title Insurance Company and state commander of the American Legion. He passed away at his home in San Jose, California, in 1962.

After leaving office, Woods joined the Committee on Public Information of Foreign Propaganda. He left to follow Mitchel into the Army Air Corps as a lieutenant colonel. Although Mitchel died before he saw action, Woods served overseas during the last two months of active fighting. He went on to become an assistant secretary of war, author of three books about policing, chairman of the board for Rockefeller Center, and the chairman for President Hoover's Committee for Employment during the Great Depression. He died in 1942 and was buried in Arlington Cemetery.

Few mayors and police commissioners worked better as a team than Mitchel and Woods. They shared a unique vision for what a police department in modern society should be through their early use of community-based policing. Although the nomenclature has changed, many of their innovations remain in effect to this day. As noted, the concept of the Home Defense League, an organization of trained volunteers to supplement the regular police, exists to this day in its current incarnation, the Auxiliary Police. The Junior Police are also now part of the Law Enforcement Explorer Program. Officers are still sent for special weapons training at military bases. Today the Emergency Service Unit still uses nearby military camps for that purpose. The Bureau of Missing Persons that Woods created in response to the Ruth Cruger murder is still in existence. Unfortunately in the end, being ahead of their time cost Mitchel and Woods many more votes than it got them.

1. NYPD patrolmen's shields, 1898–1902 and 1902–present. Dies struck from German silver. Courtesy of the authors.

2. NYPD chief of police and Tammany Hall favorite William "Big Bill" Devery, circa 1899. © 1900–1938 by the New York City Police Department. All rights reserved. Used with permission of the New York City Police Department.

3. NYPD lieutenant Joseph Petrosino in his uniform, circa 1908. Note the original lieutenant's shield had identification numbers on it. When Lieutenant Richard Enright became police commissioner in 1918, he did away with the numbers.

4. (*top*) NYPD medal ceremony. Mayor George McClellan, Police Commissioner Theodore Bingham, and Second Deputy Frederick Bugher presenting, circa 1908. Courtesy of the authors.

5. (*opposite*) The scene moments after Mayor William Gaynor was shot on board the ss *Kaiser Wilhelm der Grosse*, August 9, 1910. © 1900–1938 by the New York City Police Department. All rights reserved. Used with permission of the New York City Police Department.

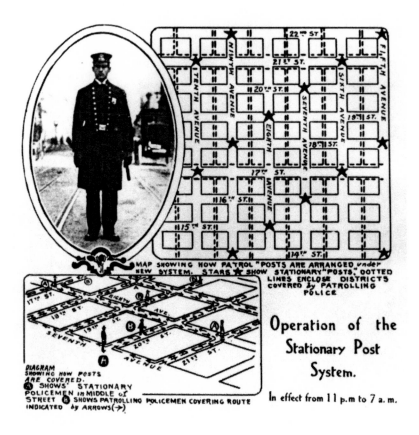

MAP SHOWING HOW PATROL "POSTS ARE ARRANGED *under*
NEW SYSTEM. STARS ★ SHOW STATIONARY "POSTS." DOTTED
LINES ENCLOSE DISTRICTS
COVERED *by* PATROLLING
POLICE

DIAGRAM
SHOWING HOW POSTS
ARE COVERED.
Ⓐ SHOWS STATIONARY
POLICEMEN *in* MIDDLE *of*
STREET Ⓑ SHOWS PATROLLING POLICEMEN COVERING ROUTE
INDICATED *by* ARROWS(→)

Operation of the
Stationary Post
System.

In effect from 11 p.m to 7 a.m.

6. (*top*) Diagram of Police Commissioner Rhinelander Waldo's Stationary Post System, June 1911. Patrolmen were required to remain in the middle of an intersection until relieved. © 1900–1938 by the New York City Police Department. All rights reserved. Used with permission of the New York City Police Department.

7. (*opposite top*) NYPD Police Headquarters at 240 Centre Street in Manhattan, circa 1912. © 1900–1938 by the New York City Police Department. All rights reserved. Used with permission of the New York City Police Department.

8. (*opposite bottom*) NYPD lieutenant Charles Becker and his devoted wife, Helen, during his trial for the murder of gangster Herman Rosenthal in October 1912. Becker was found guilty and sentenced to death in the electric chair. Courtesy of the authors.

9. (*opposite top*) NYPD patrolmen playing Santa Claus while distributing Christmas presents to needy children, circa 1915. © 1900–1938 by the New York City Police Department. All rights reserved. Used with permission of the New York City Police Department.

10. (*opposite bottom*) NYPD green light signal box in operation, circa 1915. The boxes were nicknamed the "Blinking Irishmen." © 1900–1938 by the New York City Police Department. All rights reserved. Used with permission of the New York City Police Department.

11. (*top*) NYPD patrolmen assigned to Police Commissioner Arthur Woods's Machine Gun Squad posted at the base of the Williamsburg Bridge during World War I in 1916. © 1900–1938 by the New York City Police Department. All rights reserved. Used with permission of the New York City Police Department.

12. (*top*) NYPD substation in a rural area of the Bronx known as the Melrose Section, circa 1917. © 1900–1938 by the New York City Police Department. All rights reserved. Used with permission of the New York City Police Department.

13. (*opposite top*) Police Commissioner Richard Enright at his desk at Police Headquarters in 1920. Courtesy of the authors.

14. (*opposite bottom*) The main lodge at the Police Recreation Camp in the Catskill Mountains, where policemen and their families could relax and enjoy a vacation, circa 1924. © 1900–1938 by the New York City Police Department. All rights reserved. Used with permission of the New York City Police Department.

INDIAN HEAD LODGE, MAIN BUILDING OF THE POLICE RECREATION CENTER

MISSING SINCE AUGUST 6, 1930

HONORABLE JOSEPH FORCE CRATER,
JUSTICE OF THE SUPREME COURT, STATE OF NEW YORK

DESCRIPTION—Born in the United States—Age, 41 years; height, 6 feet; weight, 185 pounds; mixed grey hair, originally dark brown, thin at top, parted in middle "slicked" down; complexion, medium dark, considerably tanned; brown eyes; false teeth, upper and lower jaw, good physical and mental condition at time of disappearance. Tip of right index finger somewhat mutilated, due to having been recently crushed.

Wore brown sack coat and trousers, narrow green stripe, no vest; either a Panama or soft brown hat worn at rakish angle, size 6⅞, unusual size for his height and weight. Clothes made by Vroom. Affected colored shirts, size 14 collar, probably bow tie. Wore tortoise-shell glasses for reading. Yellow gold Masonic ring, somewhat worn; may be wearing a yellow gold, square-shaped wrist watch with leather strap.

COMMUNICATE with CHIEF INSPECTOR, POLICE DEPARTMENT, 18th Division, (Missing Persons Bureau), New York City. Telephone Spring 3100.

15. (*opposite top*) Mayor Jimmy Walker swears in new police commissioner Grover Whalen in December 1928. Courtesy of the authors.

16. (*opposite bottom*) The Police College was housed on the top four floors of 400 Broome Street (across from Police Headquarters) between 1929 and 1930 before the institute was renamed the Police Academy. © 1900–1938 by the New York City Police Department. All rights reserved. Used with permission of the New York City Police Department.

17. (*top*) An NYPD missing persons poster seeking information regarding the whereabouts of Judge Joseph Force Crater, who vanished on August 6, 1930, without a trace and was never found despite a massive police investigation. Courtesy of the authors.

18. (*top*) NYPD Police Radio Dispatch Room at Police Headquarters, where one-way radio messages were transmitted to police cars in the field, circa 1935. © 1900–1938 by the New York City Police Department. All rights reserved. Used with permission of the New York City Police Department.

19. (*bottom*) NYPD 1939 Plymouth displaying the new tricolor green, black, and white paint scheme. © 1900–1938 by the New York City Police Department. All rights reserved. Used with permission of the New York City Police Department.

20. The cover to a comic book depicting the exploits of famed NYPD police detective Mary Sullivan. *True Comics*, no. 67 (December 1947). Courtesy of the authors.

21. The scene at the New York World's Fair in the aftermath of the explosion that killed two NYPD Bomb Squad detectives, Joseph Lynch and Frederick Socha, July 4, 1940. Courtesy of the authors.

6

HANDING THE FORCE
OVER TO A LIEUTENANT

Sometimes it is not what a man says but what he does not say that makes all the difference. Such was the case for Judge John Francis Hylan after Tammany Hall put him on the ballot in 1917 to run for mayor of New York against the heavily favored incumbent, John Purroy Mitchel.

Hylan was born in 1868 on a farm in Hunter, New York, a small town nestled in the Catskill Mountains. As the oldest son, he spent more time laboring in the fields than attending school. Although the hard work transformed him into a strapping youth, Hylan wanted more out of life than the family farm offered.

He began working part time on the mountain railroad at age fourteen. At nineteen he paid $2.00 to take a ferry down the Hudson River to New York City. He arrived in Brooklyn with $1.50 in his pocket, a satchel of worn clothes, and parting words of wisdom from his mother. She told him, "Be honest, be truthful, be upright, and do by others as you would have them do to you."

But her advice could not put food on his table or a roof over his head. Fortunately he was able to parlay his previous railroad experience into a job laying track on New York's elevated line. Hylan was content working for the railroad until the sudden death of his younger brother, a promising law student. He decided to pursue a legal career in his sibling's place and enrolled in New York Law School. Although he claimed not to be much of a student, Hylan passed the bar exam on his first try in 1897. He started a practice in Brooklyn specializing in civil litigation. By most accounts he was very good at it. In 1906, while reviewing the revised City Charter, he noticed a provision that required the mayor to appoint ten magistrates in his home borough of Brooklyn. There were only eight. When he brought the discrepancy to the mayor's attention, the incumbent, George McClellan, appointed him to one of the vacancies.

Hylan toiled in anonymity until 1914, when he ran for county court justice. His decisive victory caught the attention of the Tammany Hall sachem, Charles Murphy. Three years later, with Murphy's blessing, future police commissioner Grover Whalen, then chairman of the Businessmen's League, placed Hylan's name in the hat for mayor on the Democratic ticket. With strong backing from newspaper magnet William Randolph Hearst and Brooklyn Democratic Party leader John McCooey, Hylan secured the nomination.

Other than the Hearst newspapers, most of New York's dailies portrayed the forty-nine-year-old Hylan as just another Tammany Hall stooge. His campaign was further hindered by the fact that although he was a lawyer, he was not a particularly gifted public speaker. Whenever he fumbled for words, his detractors mocked his intellect. As a result Murphy took control of his public appearances. During the mayoral race Mitchel did most of the talking while Hylan spoke only when absolutely necessary. Normally such a tactic would have been a recipe for disaster, but many New Yorkers were tired of Mitchel's constant boasts about how honest and efficient he and Police Commissioner Woods were. Murphy's unorthodox strategy proved to be correct. Hylan was elected by the largest plurality up to that time. When asked about his silence during the campaign, Hylan said that he never aspired to be an orator and preferred actions over words.

In exchange for Tammany Hall's support, Hylan, like McClellan before him, agreed to let Murphy have a hand in most of the patronage appointments with the exception of his personal secretary and the head of the police department. The job of secretary went to the man who had nominated him, Grover Whalen, but finding someone to replace Woods turned out to be much harder than he had thought. His first choice, shipbuilder Lewis Nixon, said that constructing battlewagons for the navy was far more important to the country in a time of war than the post of police commissioner. It was also much more lucrative.

U.S. Marshal Thomas McCarthy also cited patriotic duties related to the war effort as his reason to decline the job. Chief Inspector James Dillon was thought to be in the running, but when Hylan passed over him, Dillon filed for retirement instead. For a short while it appeared that former commissioner James Cropsey's one-time second deputy, William J. Flynn, was a potential candidate, but his strong Republican ties ultimately eliminated him from contention.

It seemed that Hylan had boxed himself into a corner, but just before the New Year he announced that former first deputy Frederick Bugher had agreed to take the post. Bugher's appointment came as a surprise because his name had never come up, even though he had previously served as a deputy for two police commissioners.

Unlike Hylan, who was born into poverty, Bugher was born in 1876 in Cincinnati, Ohio, with a silver spoon in his mouth. As a young man he distinguished himself commanding a volunteer naval unit during the Spanish-American War. The experience had such a profound effect on him that he continued to adhere to the traditions of the military while in public service.

Although nearly two months had passed since the election, Mayor Mitchel was still feeling the sting of his loss. During the swearing-in ceremony Mitchel told Hylan, "The people of New York have selected you to serve as their Chief Executive for four years. I now formally deliver to you the office of Mayor."

Woods and Bugher were much more cordial to each other during their brief meeting afterward at Police Headquarters. As Woods handed him the commissioner's shield, Bugher promised to continue the admirable job that Woods had done in keeping the lid on crime. Bugher made it a point to inform reporters that Hylan's offer to him to become police commissioner was entirely unsolicited on his part and that before he accepted, he received personal assurances from the mayor that he would have a free hand in running the department. In addition, by selecting him, Hylan had someone who absolutely knew the department "from cellar to roof." Later that afternoon Bugher brought the department's inspectors into Headquarters and warned them to shun all politics. Regrettably he would not be able to do the same and still keep his job.

Despite Hylan's pledge not to interfere with the police department, two weeks into his term the *New York Times* was already reporting that the mayor was dissatisfied with Bugher because he was not moving fast enough to rid the city of the gambling parlors and disorderly houses. Hylan was also upset that Bugher had not appointed a woman as one of his deputies, as Hylan had suggested. It was said that Bugher felt the police department was no place for a lady, so he purposely disregarded the mayor's directive. A week later Hylan's brother-in-law, Patrolman Irving O'Hara, went to speak to Bugher about appointing a longtime family friend to the post of police property clerk. Bugher became so incensed by the very thought that he threw O'Hara out of his office.

After only three short weeks in office Bugher had grown so tired of Hylan's "guidance" that he wrote him a letter reminding him of the terms to which he had agreed to become police commissioner. The letter infuriated Hylan. The next morning he ordered Bugher to City Hall. Grover Whalen, who was present for the meeting, recalled that Bugher had made the mistake of presuming that the two would have a gentlemanly discussion about their differences. The mayor, however, was not of the same mindset. As soon as Bugher arrived, Hylan demanded his resignation. Bugher took several moments to regain his composure. Finally he said, "You may have it." Then he clicked his heels, did an about-face, and marched out of the office.

After Hylan calmed down, he told Whalen to get hold of Lieutenant Richard Enright and have him come to City Hall. Enright was manning the desk at the Stagg Street Stationhouse in Greenpoint, Brooklyn, when he received the telephone call from Whalen. Enright thought it was a hoax until Whalen said, "The mayor is waiting for you and the gift you are about to receive will startle the world." Lieutenant Enright could never have imagined when he reported for duty that morning that the mayor would offer him the police commissionership that afternoon. Hylan's only condition was that he accept his "guidance" without question. Enright agreed without hesitation.

It was the first time since consolidation that a mayor had selected a uniformed man to head the NYPD. In doing so, Hylan had passed over one hundred higher-ranking officers, including Inspector Daniel "Honest Dan" Costigan, whom Enright blamed, along with Police Commissioner Woods, for his having been passed over for promotion. With Woods gone, Costigan would soon find himself completely at Enright's mercy.

When asked why he forced Bugher out after such a short time, Hylan cited Bugher's refusal to suspend the officers involved in the bungled Ruth Cruger murder investigation after a presentment was returned by the grand jury in which probable cause for a crime was established, but not individual responsibility. For his part Bugher said that he had informed the mayor beforehand that he wanted time to study the complete record before he took action since the officers were bound to appeal any disciplinary action that he initiated. The mayor termed Bugher's attitude "negatively honest" and claimed that he had concocted legitimate excuses for sitting on his hands. Hylan said that he preferred a man of action and not someone who wanted to reinvestigate every little matter in the name of efficiency.

As for how he came to pick Enright as his replacement, Hylan explained, "If you want to buy a pair of shoes for yourself, do you go to a blacksmith? Policing is a profession that requires special knowledge. I would like every man walking a beat to feel that it is possible for him to head the department."

Richard Enright was born in Campbell, New York, a hamlet in the Finger Lakes region, in August 1871. His father had emigrated from Ireland. He worked as a telegraph operator in Elmira before joining the NYPD in 1896. He was one of 1,600 recruits appointed that year by Theodore Roosevelt under a revised civil service system in which patrolmen were hired for their physical and mental qualifications instead of their political connections.

By most accounts Enright was intelligent and well liked by the officers with whom he worked in the old Fourth Precinct on Oak Street in Manhattan. He was promoted to roundsman in December 1902 and for a short time served as president of the Roundsmen's Benevolent Association. He was elevated to lieutenant along with sergeants and detective sergeants as a result of the Bingham Bill and soon took charge of the newly formed Lieutenants Benevolent Association. In that capacity he championed better working conditions and higher wages for his colleagues. But his outspokenness caused him to become the subject of several internal investigations, including one by Inspector Costigan that caused him to be passed over for promotion to captain by Commissioner Woods, despite his having achieved the highest score on the written exam.

In all likelihood Enright would have retired a lieutenant if the mayor had not plucked him from obscurity. Enright showed his gratitude by giving Hylan his undying loyalty. Whenever the newspapers pressed him for comment on a controversial topic that Hylan had already weighed in on, he invariably said that he was in complete agreement with the mayor. That is not to say that Enright was the mayor's puppet. By acquiescing, he slowly gained the mayor's trust. Once he had that, Hylan gave him greater latitude to implement his own initiatives. But until that happened, Enright did exactly what he was told. His first official act was to suspend the officers against whom Bugher had refused to take action. Then he issued orders directing that all summonses be filled out in ink so that the facts could not be altered at a later date.

Enright allowed Hylan to pick all of his deputies, including the first female commissioner, a widow from Brooklyn named Ellen O'Grady. Hylan had made her acquaintance in his courtroom, where she had appeared in her capacity as a probation officer. As fifth deputy commissioner, Mrs. O'Grady was put in charge of a new branch called the Special Duty Division. It would investigate the white slavery trade and tend to the welfare of minors.

When Enright ended routine wiretapping at Hylan's behest, he put safeguards in place to prevent the abuse that had occurred under Woods. In the future police would have to seek the consent of the district attorney or a judge prior to tapping a suspect's phone line. He also did away with the merit system that Woods had created to monitor performance after Hylan told him that he thought the system caused police officers to make far too many unnecessary arrests solely to advance their careers. Enright agreed with the mayor and said, "A man who cannot show something of greater value than routine duty in gathering prisoners cannot expect to go on holding his job." Then he issued instructions to the force that arrests for minor offenses should not be made if a simple warning would suffice.

Since Enright came from the ranks, he knew the one thing that annoyed policemen the most: Inspector Costigan's shoofly squad. He not only abolished it, but he also transferred its members to distant precincts because, like former chief of police McCullagh, he did not think that patrolmen should be kept in line by a network of plainclothes spies.

Costigan subsequently asked for a leave of absence from the department to become the head of security for the nation's ports. Although it was a vital post, Enright denied his request, claiming that he could not afford to lose his "best man" in a time of war. He let Costigan stew for a few months before demoting him to captain and shipping him off to a precinct at the Westchester border.

The Republican leaning Citizens' Union rushed to Costigan's defense and asserted that such vengeful retaliatory actions by Enright would cause a drop in morale and a rise in crime. In response to the skeptics who claimed that his deeds would cause a return to the days of Chief Devery, Enright said, "For sixteen years we have had to submit to the dictation of outsiders, men who were not one of us. . . . [The police force] has suffered and endured the rule of strangers. . . . My own record is at stake. Do you think I am going to permit anything to tarnish the record of the department under my regime?"

When the emergencies that Woods had envisioned for the Home Defense League failed to materialize, many of the volunteers stopped participating in drills. Enright decided a complete overhaul of the unit was necessary. He called his new corps the Police Reserve, and in keeping with its new identity, he arranged for its five thousand members to be outfitted with blue uniforms and badges that more closely resembled those of the NYPD than the green military-style uniforms they had worn as members of the Home Defense League. In addition, he consolidated individual precinct companies into larger borough regiments to assist the police during what he described as the "disturbed times that confront us."

Although Hylan had arranged Deputy Commissioner O'Grady's appointment, it was up to Enright to put together her staff. But there were no civil service provisions for the department to hire female investigators. To circumvent the civil service requirement, Enright exploited a little-known section of state law that permitted him to appoint temporary patrolmen to the force during emergencies. He said that the law could also be applied to hire women temporarily. The emergency was to determine firsthand if women could protect young girls better than men could. The success of the program led to the creation of a new civil service title called "patrolwoman." A year later the title of matron was abolished. The former matrons were designated policewomen to distinguish them from patrolwomen. In reality, however, most of their duties were interchangeable, with one exception. Only policewomen had the authority to make arrests. Enright wanted to consolidate the two ranks, but it was not until 1937 that all females on the force became policewomen.

When Enright had joined the department, the two-platoon system was in operation. After a change in the law in 1904, the three-platoon system went into effect. While it was better than the two-platoon duty schedule, patrolmen still had to work the equivalent of twelve tours every nine days before they received a day off. Enright believed that working so many hours without sufficient time to recover made meaningful patrol physically impossible.

To help alleviate some of the stress patrolmen were under, Enright added an extra squad to the work schedule in October 1918. The new ten-squad duty system provided patrolmen with one day off a week for the first time, although they still worked the equivalent of eight tours over six days. In addition, Enright granted each officer a half-hour meal period during each tour. Critics noted that the new duty chart resulted in a 10 percent reduction in overall patrol coverage, but Enright countered that the additional time off would result in police officers being able to provide better service to the public on the days that they were working.

In November 1918 Enright married his landlady, a thirty-nine-year-old widow named Jean Smith. While the couple honeymooned in Cuba, ranking officers collected $1,200 to give them as a wedding present. When questioned about the propriety of such a large gift, First Deputy John Leach maintained that it was only natural for the superior officers to express their appreciation in return for all of the great deals Enright had given the force.

One of those "great deals" was the imposition of fixed probationary periods instead of monetary fines for patrolmen found guilty of minor infractions at the department Trial Room. If a patrolman stayed out of trouble during his entire probationary period, Enright waived the fine. This was a significant departure from the former policy, where harsh financial penalties were viewed by most as the best way to keep the force in line.

For several months the president of the Patrolmen's Benevolent Association, Joseph Moran, had been seeking a $200 per year wage increase for his members. Although Enright had taken a similar position when he was head of the Lieutenants Benevolent Association, the mayor considered Moran to be a troublemaker and ordered that he be transferred to teach him a lesson. Enright did as he was told, but Hylan had a change of heart after a strike by the Boston police force brought chaos to that city. The situation for the police officers of Boston was much worse than for those in New York. They had not received a raise in sixty years and went on strike only because their mayor refused to consider even a modest wage hike. As soon as the 1,100 officers walked out, the police commissioner of Boston, Edwin Curtis, fired them. Without police, looters ransacked the city. Governor Calvin Coolidge called in the state militia to restore order. Coolidge rose to national prominence for taking the position that "there is no right to strike against the public safety by anybody, anywhere, anytime."

Afterward Hylan told Moran that patrolmen would receive a raise but only in accordance with the city's financial ability to pay for it. He also made it very clear that under no circumstances would he tolerate a job action. Although there was no strike by police in New York, the low starting salary in particular proved problematic. There were seven hundred openings but few suitable applicants. The secretary of the New York City Civil Service Commission lamented, "Police jobs seem to go a-begging."

In September 1919 a series of high-profile robberies prompted Hylan to yet again offer "guidance" to Enright on how to deal with brazen criminals fleeing in getaway cars. He conveyed his advice through a letter that appeared in the *New York Times*: "May I not suggest to you [Enright] the advisability of having a special automobile squad detailed at points which you may select, so that immediate attention may be given to any car that looks as though it contains gangsters who are out for unlawful purposes?"

The next evening Enright flooded the streets with detectives to keep the mayor happy. But he was not convinced that the number of crimes committed under his watch had risen. Instead he blamed reporters for sensationalizing what little criminal activity there was in order to sell their newspapers. "Crime waves have been conjured up, directly and indirectly," he complained. "The citizenry of this city has been churned up and agitated by the most atrocious falsehoods and misstatements it was possible for the gifted scribes, as they call themselves, to conceive, in their effervescing and over-stimulated craniums."

It bothered Enright to no end that the press continued to lavish more praise on former police commissioner Woods's programs than on his own. "The only wonder," he said regarding Woods, "is that the Police Department, under the direction of an unpracticed civilian, was able to perform as high a quality of service as it did."

But the rash of getaway car robberies forced the department to purchase enough Ford Model T Runabouts (at a cost of $330 per automobile) to deploy at least one experimental motor patrol car in each precinct. There was a general reluctance on the part of patrolmen to volunteer for an assignment on motor patrol. It appeared to have had something to do with the rules governing the job. Unless the weather was particularly foul, the two-man crew was required to keep the automobile's canvas top down. But even in the up position, the roof offered little protection against the elements because there were no windows or heaters in the vehicles. In contrast, foot patrolmen always knew how to stay warm and dry in inclement weather.

The Eighteenth Amendment, prohibiting the sale of alcohol, was passed on January 16, 1919, and under the Volstead Act, states and local governments were given a year to begin enforcing it. When the national law took effect in 1920, police in New York City began the daunting task of shutting down every single business that was involved in the manufacture, sale, or transport of intoxicating liquor, which was defined as having an alcohol content in excess of 0.5 percent.

In theory prohibition was supposed to eliminate the public's access to alcohol. Ironically the department's arrests involving drunk and disorderly persons rose dramatically. But mass arrests for public intoxication had little effect on the consumption of illegal alcohol because most cases were dismissed by the courts. Despite the high number of arrests, teetotalers did not stop criticizing the department's efforts.

After several patrolmen were seriously injured during violent demonstrations by anti-government groups during 1920, Enright transferred the Machine Gun Squads that Police Commissioner Woods had formed during World War I to protect New York's bridges into a new unit called the Police Riot Regiment. The machine guns were mounted on armor-plated motorcycles that Enright nicknamed the "Flying Armor." As he envisioned it, these specially trained officers could respond to major disorders anywhere in the city with their motorcycles and provide a deterrent against "marauders and aggressors" that he said were seeking to create mayhem.

Unfortunately the Police Riot Regiment could not prevent anarchists from detonating a bomb on Wall Street, in the heart of New York's financial district, on September 16, 1920. The blast caused $2 million in damage, killed 39 people, and maimed at least 200. It resulted in the largest loss of life in the United States from a terrorist incident until Timothy McVeigh set off a bomb in Oklahoma City that killed 168 people in 1995.

Within an hour 1,700 patrolmen were rushed to the scene. Witnesses told detectives that they had observed a nondescript horse-drawn wagon pull up in front of the Morgan Bank shortly before noon. The driver had climbed down and disappeared into the crowd. Minutes later a powerful blast from within the wagon shattered windows and rained shards of glass down on the street. The impact of the metal shrapnel against the bank's marble facade left deep pockmarks that are still visible today.

It took several hours for the police, working in conjunction with the Justice Bureau of Investigation (a forerunner to the Federal Bureau of Investigation), to determine that the explosion had not been an accident. But the Wall Street bankers were more interested in clearing the street of debris so that they could open for business the next morning than solving the mystery of who had planted the incendiary device. As a result fragments of evidence that might have helped police figure out who was responsible for the bomb were inadvertently destroyed.

Authorities initially believed that the Morgan Bank had been targeted by Italian anarchists affiliated with the radical Luigi Galleani. Later they decided that another radical, Mario Buda, had caused the explosion in retaliation for the indictments leveled against a pair of fellow anarchists, Nicola Sacco and Bartolemeo Vanzetti, for the murder of two payroll guards in Braintree, Massachusetts.

It was no secret that patrolmen did not have much of an opportunity to spend quality time with their loved ones. There was little time off, and if they wanted to take their families on a vacation, the costs of travel, lodging, and food were too expensive for most of them to afford. Enright thought something should be done about such a situation. In November 1920 he convinced the trustees of the Police Relief Fund to purchase 332 acres in the Catskill Mountains for the exclusive use of police officers and their relatives.

The buildings and grounds were officially known as the Police Recreation Center, but to most cops the center was simply the "Police Camp." The facilities served double duty as a sanitarium for sick and injured officers to recuperate. Enright gave the job of overseeing improvements to the camp—including the clearing of land, installation of a sewage system, construction of bungalows, and remodeling of the main lodge—to his nephew. Free labor was provided by members of the Police Riot Regiment, who were dispatched to the campgrounds ostensibly for the purpose of disorder control training.

On December 14, 1920, Fifth Deputy Commissioner O'Grady resigned after quotes attributed to her appeared in the newspapers. She complained that Enright constantly interfered with her work and that the mayor did not back her up when she brought it to his attention. Enright denied any wrongdoing on his part. He claimed that O'Grady had barged into his office acting hysterically and had thrown her shield down on his desk while screaming, "I'm through with this department." He admitted that he did not try to change her mind.

With O'Grady out of the picture Enright took the opportunity to disband her command, the Special Duty Division. In its place he created the Women's Bureau and housed it in the old Twenty-Second Precinct stationhouse in Hell's Kitchen. Enright named Policewoman Mary Hamilton as its director and enlisted the services of Mrs. Julia Loft, whose husband owned the Loft Candy Company, as an honorary deputy commissioner to advise her.

In addition to Mrs. Loft, Enright gave a number of prominent businessmen the title of honorary deputy commissioner, a step that provided him an opportunity to mingle with New York's most rich and famous. Among the wealthy civic-minded citizens who joined the department were members of the Guggenheim and DuPont families. Each "Honorary," as they were called, was given a police shield, special parking privileges, and an office at Police Headquarters. While they received no salary, many of them provided expert advice on matters such as traffic enforcement, public safety, pension investment, and narcotics interdiction.

Honorary Deputy Commissioner John Harriss, for instance, was instrumental in the development of New York's first rudimentary electronic traffic control device, installed at the intersection of Fifth Avenue and Forty-Second Street. Patrolmen assigned to duty in the original traffic tower had to climb up to a booth sixteen feet above the roadway to operate a bank of five-hundred-watt floodlights fitted with red, amber, and green lenses. Red stopped traffic in all four directions. Green stopped north- and southbound traffic and permitted crosstown traffic. Amber stopped crosstown traffic and permitted north- and southbound traffic. Eventually there were fifty traffic towers in use throughout the city (many of them funded by the private sector). But they were very expensive to operate and required a great deal of manpower. When Grover Whalen was promoted by Hylan to be commissioner of plant and structures, he began to test a variety of cheaper automated traffic lights and semaphore systems. The experiments were so successful that within a short time all of the traffic towers were dismantled and replaced with traffic lights, and one hundred patrolmen were shifted to more important duties.

As the 1921 mayoral election approached, a number of Republicans vied for the chance to take on Hylan. In the end the race came down to two men, the president of the Board of Aldermen, Fiorello LaGuardia, and a former alderman named Henry Curran, who in 1913 had served as chairman of the Curran Committee, which had exposed widespread police corruption during Waldo's tenure. Curran won the primary by a wide margin and won the opportunity to challenge Mayor Hylan.

It was also the first election in New York since the Nineteenth Amendment, which gave women the right to vote, went into effect. For some reason, city Republicans presumed that a majority of the four hundred thousand first-time women voters would cast their ballots for Curran, but they seriously miscalculated his appeal.

By early October the oddsmakers already had Hylan favored three to one over Curran. In desperation Curran and the Republicans switched their campaign strategy from attacking the mayor to attacking the personal integrity of his police commissioner. Enright was under investigation because his bank account showed deposits of over $100,000 since he had become police commissioner when his salary over that same time period amounted to only $28,125. But somehow Enright's convoluted explanation about how the extra money had made its way into and out of his account proved satisfactory to the inquisitors, making the issue moot.

Once the discrepancy was resolved, the bookmakers raised the odds of a Hylan victory to ten to one. On Election Day Hylan swept all five boroughs, and to make matters worse for the Republican Party, every other important office in city government went to the Democrats as well.

Hylan's relationship with Tammany Hall had changed during his four years in office, however. After his first election win Hylan showed his gratitude to "Boss" Murphy by letting him hand out most patronage posts to Tammany Hall's favorite sons. This time around Hylan's margin of victory was so overwhelming that he was convinced that he was no longer beholden to the organization. Hylan asked his entire cabinet, including Enright, who was being wooed by a private detective agency, to remain by his side for another four years. His stance prevented Murphy from helping other loyal Tammany Hall partisans from advancing their political careers.

In January 1922 Enright began his own reorganization of the department and promoted six captains to a new rank, that of deputy inspector. He said that their primary function would be to maintain proper discipline and improve overall supervision within the districts. But since there was no money in the budget, Enright closed four precincts and used the savings to pay for their higher salaries.

The Board of Aldermen passed an ordinance in 1922 that required every driver in New York City to be in possession of a police-issued "Traffic Warning Card" when operating a motor vehicle and to produce the card whenever stopped for a traffic infraction. Each card had space for police officers to note up to five separate traffic infractions. After a driver had received five warnings, as indicated on the card, he was no longer eligible to receive a warning and was supposed to be arrested. Nothing in the law, however, prevented an officer from arresting a driver after the first offense if the violation was serious. In either case the intent was to identify and keep bad drivers off the road.

The Citizens' Union, however, proved that the Traffic Warning Cards had little impact on bad drivers because the police rarely complied with the ordinance. Its review of the department's own statistics showed that of the 306,000 Traffic Warning Cards issued to New Yorker drivers during the first year the law was in effect, police recorded only 2,147 warnings on the cards.

When the uniform for the consolidated police force was first introduced in 1898, awards for meritorious police service were represented by four-point gold, silver, or bronze metal stars sewn onto the cuffs of an officer's dress coat. In August 1922 Enright ordered a switch to military-style breast bars. Tricolored green, white, and blue one-and-a-half-inch enamel bars with gold, silver, or bronze stars representing awards for meritorious police service were from that time forward worn one inch above an officer's police shield.

Enright also thought that a promotion should be celebrated as a special occasion rather than having an officer simply report to Headquarters to be issued the shield of his new rank. With that in mind Enright called sixty-one patrolmen into his office for the department's first promotion ceremony. It was the largest single group of patrolmen promoted to sergeants at one time in department history. One of the new promotees, Arthur Wallander, would go on to become police commissioner.

The *New York World* printed a front-page story in November 1922 that caught Hylan's attention. According to the newspaper, the Ku Klux Klan had made arrangements with a Baptist minister in Brooklyn to allow the organization to recruit from within his congregation.

Hylan fired off a letter to Enright instructing him to "Ferret out those despicable, disloyal persons who are attempting to organize a society, the aims and purposes of which are of such a character that were they to prevail, the foundation of our country would be destroyed. Go after the Ku Klux Klan and do not let them get a foothold in New York City."

Enright put a team of detectives on the case right away. Three weeks later he turned over the names of eight hundred suspected Klansman to the Brooklyn district attorney. Included in the list, much to the embarrassment of the department, were thirty police officers. But nothing happened to the police or anyone else because none of the people identified had broken any law. Nevertheless, the threat of a crackdown drove Klansmen in New York underground for a while.

Since becoming police commissioner, Enright had dreamt that one day the long arm of the law would be able to reach out anywhere in the world to gather in lawbreakers. In September 1922 he invited representatives from seven hundred departments from across the globe to discuss his ideas at the First Annual International Police Conference.

The year before Enright had hosted a more informal gathering limited to department heads throughout the United States. During the meeting he had Third Deputy Commissioner Joseph Faurot (the former head of the Detective Bureau) demonstrate why fingerprints were superior to the Bertillon Method as a means of identifying criminals. Faurot placed a metal safe out of sight and told the group of police chiefs (whose fingerprints he had on file) to select, without telling him (Faurot), one of the chiefs to open the safe with the combination he supplied. Afterward Faurot dusted the surface of the safe, and after comparing the fingerprints he had recovered to those of the chiefs, he positively identified the culprit. The demonstration was repeated at the International Police Conference and led to the adoption of fingerprints over the Bertillon Method as the primary means of identifying criminals worldwide.

But policemen who worked with Faurot during his early days on the force knew that despite his advocation of fingerprints, he never completely relied on them to solve his cases. He was a well-known practitioner of the "third degree," a method of torture employed to gain a confession from a reluctant suspect. It was only after Faurot retired from the department that he admitted, "There is only one language that the criminal understands and that is the language of fear."

The usefulness of the department's original radio transmitter at Police Headquarters was limited to communication with ships at sea. To alert policemen of crimes in progress, the department relied on WNYC, the city-owned and -operated radio station launched by Grover Whalen after he became commissioner of plants and structures. Each stationhouse was provided with its own radio, locked in on the WNYC frequency. A light activated on the receiver whenever a police alarm was being broadcast over the air. The desk officer then relayed the information to the patrolman on post via the green signal box system. Unfortunately the transmissions of crimes in progress could also be heard by any citizen listening to the radio at home.

Enright felt that the department needed to have its own private radio frequency. He obtained a license for a special frequency from Secretary of Commerce Herbert Hoover, for sole use of the police department, with the call letters WLAW.

Next Enright entered into a contract with the Western Electric Company to install a more powerful transmitter atop Police Headquarters and individual radio receivers in each precinct tuned in exclusively to the police band. Reports of crimes in progress were transmitted to the stationhouses. Upon receipt of an alarm that a crime was taking place in his precinct, the sergeant monitoring the radio receiver would relay the information to the patrolman by means of the signal box on his post.

Despite its great promise, the technology of the day was not yet up to the task. Six years later Enright's successor auctioned off all of the radio equipment to the highest bidder, proving once again the old adage that the innovations of one police administration become the relics of the next.

A little noticed but important piece of legislation was passed by the New York State Senate on its final day before the summer recess of 1923. Two years earlier Chief Inspector William Lahey had been indicted for accepting an unlawful gratuity while he was acting as second deputy commissioner. An insurance underwriter had sent a check for $50 to Detective George Andrews of the Automobile Squad as a reward for recovering a car that had been reported stolen. It was a regular practice by insurance companies, even in instances where the NYPD had little or nothing to do with retrieving the vehicle. The check was logged in and turned over to then Second Deputy Lahey, who in the course of normal business forwarded it to the detective and mailed a receipt to the insurance company. Lahey's troubles started when Detective Andrews cashed the check at a tavern across the street from Police Headquarters.

Under the City Charter monetary rewards of this nature could be accepted only by the police commissioner. Twenty-five percent of the amount listed on the check had to be donated to the Pension Fund or Widows and Orphans Fund before the balance was given to the officer. According to the district attorney, since Lahey was not the police commissioner, he had accepted an unlawful gratuity when he had signed for the check himself.

Lahey denied the accusation, but there were no provisions in place for the department to cover his defense after the indictment, so he paid for his own attorney out of pocket. After his acquittal the bill in the Senate reimbursed him for the legal expenses. The episode soured Lahey so much that he asked Hylan to allow him to return to his former position as chief inspector. The mayor granted his request without consulting with Enright. As a result the relationship between Enright and Lahey deteriorated to the point that the two men communicated only through written memoranda.

Earlier in the year several articles had appeared in the press in which Assemblyman Louis Culliver claimed that at least 10 percent of the police force was profiting from prohibition and Enright was ignoring the problem. Culliver found an ally in Judge Joseph Corrigan, who stated that Culliver's estimate was much too low. As far as he was concerned, at least half of the police force was comprised of bootleggers, and it was Enright's fault.

Culliver and Corrigan ignored the fact that the department had made thirty thousand arrests and shuttered ten thousand speakeasies. Enright knew that he would never be given credit for the enforcement efforts he had made as long as statements by Culliver and Corrigan went unchallenged. He decided the best way to keep them quiet was to sue them for libel.

The case went before Brooklyn magistrate Thomas Crain in July 1923. After listening to testimony from seventy-one witnesses, Crain ordered Culliver and Corrigan to issue a public apology to Enright. However, he did believe that there was a considerable number of grafters on the force taking advantage of prohibition to line their own pockets. The judge suggested that a pay increase might lessen their temptation to take bribes.

Although Enright said that he did not agree with Crain's assessment of the force, he realized that prohibition had provided more opportunities than ever before for a small number of dishonest officers to make money illegally. Shortly after the trial Enright issued General Order No. 6, which relieved patrolmen of the responsibility of suppressing vice-related crimes on their posts and shifted the duty to members of a new unit called the Special Services Division.

As per the revised rules, patrolmen were required only to observe vice conditions on their posts. Instead of taking action, they were to notify their commanding officers whenever they spotted a breach of the law. Precinct commanders in turn were required to forward the information to the Special Services Division, which would address the situation. Enright predicted that the new arrangement would go a long way toward restoring the public's confidence in the force.

As a hobby Enright dabbled in creative writing. A short story that he wrote for a police magazine, called "Into the Net," was adapted into a silent motion picture starring Constance Bennett as a missing society girl who is rescued by the police. Enright served as the film's technical adviser. In the movie detectives traced automobile license plates, picked out suspects from the rogues' gallery, chased after suspects with patrol boats, and used signal boxes to alert patrolmen on their beats to apprehend the sinister Oriental perpetrator. The motion picture, one of the first to glorify the work of the New York police, opened to positive reviews in 1924. Enright parlayed that success into two subsequent police procedurals, *Vultures of the Dark* and *The Borrowed Shield*.

During the 1925 budget hearing Enright requested an additional 2,000 patrolmen. The Board of Estimate agreed only to give him an extra 450 patrolmen. Enright turned to Mayor Hylan, who convinced the Board to meet Enright halfway. The department's authorized strength was raised by 1,000 patrolmen.

The head of the Sergeants Benevolent Association was in attendance at the hearing and asked the mayor to give his members a raise since they earned only fifty-six cents more per day than their subordinates. Hylan scoffed at the notion that sergeants deserved extra money because Enright had initiated a pilot program that allowed them to drive automobiles instead of riding bicycles to keep a close eye on the patrolmen. Hylan insinuated that by using automobiles to supervise the force, sergeants were actually doing less work and therefore not deserving of any extra money.

But the sergeant countered, "We keep an eye on Bushwick too." Laughter erupted in the chamber because everyone knew that was where the mayor resided. Hylan was not known for his sense of humor, so everyone in the chamber was surprised when he suddenly chuckled and agreed to consider the matter. But his change of heart had more to do with his desire to win a third term in office than to raise sergeants' pay. Although the election was a year away, Hylan was already hearing whispers that Tammany Hall would not support his bid because he had frozen the organization out of his administration. He confided to Enright that if the rumors were true, the support of the police force would be more important than ever. The dilemma for Enright then became how to convince his men to vote for

Hylan while keeping his critics from using such an effort against them. Fortunately he had an idea.

In January 1925 Enright implemented a plan that he had been mulling over for several months, one that would allow him to substantially increase the number of officers detailed to perform investigative duties, at little cost to the city. He added another tier to the detective ranks. The newly designated third-grade detectives worked alongside seasoned detectives but received no extra compensation unless they advanced to a higher grade. Meanwhile, to keep the incumbent detectives happy, Enright arranged for the salaries of second-grade detectives to go up $200 and the salaries of first-grade detectives to go up $800, in order to put their pay on a par with sergeants and lieutenants.

In April 1925 Enright announced his intent to establish a world-class training facility to rival that of Scotland Yard and become for the NYPD what West Point was for the army, thus attracting a higher caliber of applicants seeking appointment to the force. The new Police Academy replaced the School of Instruction. The academy was located at Lexington Avenue and Twenty-Third Street in a school building that belonged to the College of the City of New York. He placed a deputy inspector, designated as the "commandant," in charge of all training, while the full-time staff taught classes specifically tailored for recruits, detectives, superior officers, policewomen, auto mechanics, and civilian clerks.

In August 1925 Hylan received official notice from Tammany Hall that the organization would not support his run for a third term. That meant that if he wanted to be the Democratic candidate, he would have to win a primary (the first ever held by the Democrats in New York City) against the Tammany-backed nominee, Jimmy Walker, a popular state senator who represented Manhattan's Twelfth District.

Retired chief inspector James Dillon was still bitter at being passed over for police commissioner eight years earlier by Hylan. He threw his support to Walker and urged his former colleagues to do the same. In response Enright issued a department-wide circular on official letterhead in which he reminded members of the force that Dillon had served as chief inspector for a shorter period than any other chief since the title was established and that he had left the department under a cloud. In a final volley Enright said that Dillon was supporting Walker only to get a second crack at the commissionership by reentering the department through the cellar.

Any speculation that Dillon would return to the department under a new mayor ended when he was found dead behind the wheel of his motorcar. The cause of death was attributed to a heart attack.

It turned out that Walker did not need Dillon's help. He defeated Hylan by ninety-five thousand votes. With the primary behind him Hylan took a brief respite in the Catskills. When he returned, he was asked to run for mayor as an independent for the Progressive Party. When Hylan declined, the party approached Fiorello LaGuardia. He too spurned the offer but admitted that he would have supported Hylan had he chosen to run against Walker.

Once Walker won the primary, the mayoral election became a mere formality. He routed his Republican opponent, Frank Waterman (of Waterman Fountain Pen fame), by four hundred thousand votes.

During the waning days of his administration Enright disbanded some of the less successful specialty units that he had created. The twenty-man Gun Squad, whose job it was to detect and apprehend armed felons before they committed crimes, was abolished because the unit did not make one single arrest relative to its function during the entire time it was in existence. He did away with the twelve-man Lounge Lizard Squad, which for the past year had trolled high-end Midtown saloons wearing formal evening attire while searching for clues regarding the murder of two young women. In one of his final chores as police commissioner, Enright presided over the December graduation ceremony for 483 rookie patrolmen from the new Police Academy. It was the largest class of recruits up to that time. Enright offered the graduates some personal advice: "No one can help or hinder you but yourselves."

On Christmas Eve 1925 Hylan sent a letter to Enright in which he praised his efforts to cleanse the department from within. He told him that he was "splendidly equipped to head the department" and that nobody in or out of the department had ever put one over on him.

Enright wrote back that the Hylan administration had set a "new standard of efficiency and honesty in the conduct of public office" and thanked the mayor for his unflagging support, which had made it possible for him to resuscitate a decaying police force despite false, malicious, and destructive criticism that had been leveled against him. Of the newspapers, whose stories he claimed put obstacles in his way when he tried to create harmony, Enright said, "They should be regarded as much an enemy of society as the convicted criminal." Last and perhaps most telling, Enright acknowledged that his administration of the NYPD was inseparable from the mayor's administration of the city.

Within weeks of leaving office, Hylan became partner in a law firm owned by his friend William Randolph Hearst. He remained bitter, however, at Tammany Hall for abandoning him. When a group of independents, calling themselves the Better Government Party, approached him to run for mayor again in 1929, he initially agreed, believing the city Republicans would join with them to form a Fusion Party. But when the Republicans chose Fiorello LaGuardia instead, he withdrew from the race and threw his support to Walker in exchange for a judgeship.

The Better Government Party morphed into the Square Deal Party and nominated Enright in Hylan's place. Unfortunately neither Enright nor the party had enough money to mount a real challenge. He received only 6,000 votes out of 1,465,000 total votes cast. He was also not aware of the deal that Hylan had made with Walker. After the election Walker was asked why he made Hylan a magistrate to the Children's Court. He quipped, "Now they can be tried by one of their peers."

Hylan remained on the bench until he suffered a fatal heart attack on January 12, 1936. He was sixty-eight years old. It was reported that his entire estate was worth less than $5,000 at the time of his death. Today the former mayor is remembered with a street in Staten Island named after him, Hylan Boulevard.

Hylan's first police commissioner, Frederick Bugher, who had served for a scant twenty-three days, passed away from typhoid fever in his Virginia home in November 1924. He was only forty-nine years old. His son would go on to found the world renowned Frederick H. Bugher Foundation in honor of his late father, providing money for groundbreaking cardiac research.

Enright eventually forgave Hylan for not supporting his mayoral bid. Other than his embarrassing foray into politics, Enright enjoyed a long and successful life in retirement from the police department. He published a police magazine, obtained a commission in the Army Reserves, sold real estate in Florida, worked for the National Recovery Administration, and opened his own private detective agency. Enright died in September 1953 after taking a bad fall. He was eighty-one years old.

While Enright was often ostracized for his close relationship with Hylan, in reality the association benefited the citizens of New York and the members of the police department. Whenever the mayor asked him to address a matter of import to the public, Enright took immediate action. His can-do attitude kept him in office longer than any police commissioner before him, and as time went on, a genuine friendship developed between the two men. Whatever his faults, there was no denying that Enright had more knowledge about policing in New York than anyone before him. Once he had the mayor's full confidence, Enright was able to institute changes that continue to benefit the force to this day.

Unfortunately after Enright left office, his legacy was tarnished by allegations that monetary donations made to several police funds under his control had disappeared. Most of the money was located, and what remained missing was attributed more to shoddy bookkeeping than any criminal act on Enright's part. When all the things he accomplished as police commissioner are put in proper perspective, it turns out that Enright had a pretty good career for a lieutenant who had been passed over for promotion to captain three times before he got a chance to shine.

7

POLICE COMMISSIONERS COME AND GO

Of all New York mayors perhaps none was more popular than the flamboyant former songwriter James J. Walker, and none spent less time actively involved in running the city than he did. When Fiorello LaGuardia tried to make a campaign issue out of Walker's giving himself a hefty raise, Walker wisecracked, "Think what it would cost if I worked full time." The city's constituents enjoyed Walker's wit at first, but in the end his laissez-faire attitude cost him his job.

Jimmy Walker's father, William Walker, had fled Ireland in 1857 to escape the potato blight. Like most immigrants, he arrived in America with little money and large aspirations. He was a carpenter by trade, and with help from his wife's politically connected father, he established a successful lumber business in Greenwich Village; in the process he made acquaintance with future Tammany Hall sachems Richard Croker and John Voorhis. His association with them helped him win four consecutive terms as a city alderman.

His son James was born in May 1881. The boy expressed little interest in following in his father's footsteps by either learning a trade or trying his hand at politics. He had another passion: composing music. It was so strong that after he graduated from New York Law School, he postponed taking the bar exam to concentrate on a career in music. His decision paid off in 1908, when he wrote the hit song "Will You Love Me in December as You Did in May."

The song gained Walker entrée into the fast-paced world of the Broadway theater crowd. Walker enjoyed the life of a well-heeled gadabout town, but when he was not able to parlay his success into a second hit, an uncle introduced him to "Boss" Murphy, who had taken over Tammany Hall from

Richard Croker. Murphy thought Walker's friends in the entertainment field would be an asset to the organization and put him on the Democratic ticket in 1910.

Walker easily won a seat in the State Assembly and became a protégé of Al Smith, the most prominent Tammany Democrat and the future governor of New York. Smith would have a great impact on the rise of Walker's political career. Another contemporary, Judge Samuel Seabury, known as the "Scourge of Tammany Hall," would bring about his fall two decades later.

In 1914 Walker moved up to the State Senate and soon afterward married a pretty showgirl named Janet Allen. He also got around to taking the bar exam so he could make some extra money practicing law. An elected office, despite its many perks, did not pay enough to fund his extravagant lifestyle. By 1921 Walker had become minority leader of the State Senate and championed such causes as legalized boxing, the five-cent subway fare, and the playing of baseball and showing of motion pictures on Sundays.

When "Boss" Murphy passed away in 1924, Judge George Olvany took over Tammany Hall. Soon afterward Olvany decided that Tammany Hall would not endorse Mayor Hylan for a third term. This caused a major rift in the party because the Democrats from Brooklyn, Queens, and Staten Island were in favor of keeping Hylan. Olvany appealed to Governor Smith. Olvany proposed that Walker challenge Hylan in the city's first-ever Democratic primary for mayor. But the governor was concerned that Walker's habitual late-night carousing would make him a bad candidate for such an important office.

When Walker learned of his mentor's objection, he abandoned the night-life long enough to convince the governor that he had genuine interest in becoming mayor. Hylan, however, was not as easily fooled. He warned the citizens that if Walker became mayor, prostitutes and thieves would run rampant in the city. But most voters did not care. Hylan lost big in every borough, including Brooklyn, where he resided. William Randolph Hearst, Hylan's longtime friend and financial backer was in California during the primary. When he called the managing editor of his New York newspaper to ask about the results, the editor informed him, "The people have spoken, but they needn't have been so loud."

Walker's win in the primary made the mayoral election a foregone conclusion. He easily defeated Republican Frank Waterman, with the rest of the Tammany slate riding on his coattails. It was the first time since the

Van Wyck administration that the entire city government was under the Democrats' control. Although the citizens of New York did not know it, the future would not bode well for them as a result of their decisions at the polls.

Ironically during the campaign the very same people who had lambasted Police Commissioner Enright every chance they got for the way he ran the department were suddenly concerned that his successor would do worse if Walker handed the post to a Tammany man. Walker heard the noise and decided that for him it would be best if an outsider were brought in, someone independent of politics and unaffiliated with the uniformed force. But finding the right man for the job once again turned out to be a long-drawn-out process.

With time running out the political reporter from the *New York Sun*, George Van Slyke, suggested on a lark that Walker might consider the New York State banking superintendent, George V. McLaughlin, for the post. Although his name had not come up before, McLaughlin fit the bill. He was an outsider, a Democrat, and well thought of by Governor Smith. "Banzai!" Walker was said to have exclaimed. "That's it. You named him!"

An editorial in the *New York Times* lauded Walker's selection. "Mr. McLaughlin appears to be a man of firm character and proved executive capacity." In comparing his potential against the record established by Enright, the article concluded, "Commissioner McLaughlin certainly has a great opportunity to heighten the prestige as well as the efficiency of the police force, which admittedly has been working under serious handicaps."

The new police commissioner was a sturdy six-footer with roots in Brooklyn. He was born in 1887 to a ferryboat captain and his wife. After graduation from Eastern District High School in Williamsburg, McLaughlin was hired by the North Side Bank and worked his way up the corporate ladder while pursuing simultaneous degrees at the New York University School of Commerce and Brooklyn Law School. In 1910 he passed a state civil service exam for bank examiner. His attention to small details caught the eye of Governor Smith, who promoted him to superintendent of banks in 1920.

After McLaughlin's swearing-in at City Hall he went to Police Headquarters. Enright introduced him to the inspectors and chiefs before leaving for good. He was overheard in the corridor sighing to a friend, "Well that's all."

Enright's departure also meant the end for a number of his initiatives. McLaughlin wasted no time in transforming the force into what he called "a real police department" by using every member of the force to combat serious crime.

McLaughlin was an accountant by trade. He viewed the department the same way a bookkeeper looked at the bottom line in a ledger book. Since he considered uniformed patrolmen to be the backbone of the force, almost all of his early moves to put more officers on the street were accomplished by disbanding specialty squads. One of the first to go was the Special Services Division. Enright had given the unit sole responsibility to enforce vice laws related to prostitution, gambling, and violations of the Volstead Act. McLaughlin felt the public would be better served by having all of the department's 12,657 patrolmen take part in vice enforcement rather than just a cadre of 391 plainclothes specialists.

The immediate results, however, were not very impressive. On the first night the order went into effect the precinct-level plainclothesmen who took over the job made only thirty-six arrests throughout the city, as compared to the same night a week earlier, when the Special Services Division rounded up over four hundred suspects. "This move is like everything else," McLaughlin said the next morning. "It will not be perfect in the beginning."

Another one of Enright's highly touted specialty squads that McLaughlin decided the department could do without was the Bureau of Criminal Science. He said that the examination of evidence through the use of science had not contributed to the solving of a single homicide in the three months that the bureau had been in existence. McLaughlin transferred its members back to the Detective Division and shifted their work back to the medical examiner.

The Police Academy was between classes. The instructors had planned to use the down time to update the curriculum for the next group of recruits. McLaughlin thought their time could be better spent on patrol. He transferred out the entire staff with the exception of the commanding officer.

McLaughlin abolished the annual police parade up Broadway because he thought that excusing so many patrolmen from work "amounted to an annual invitation to the thieves and stick-up men to visit the city and pursue their criminal practice." (The senior member of the force, seventy-eight-year-old patrolman William Wells, sided with the commissioner, not because he was concerned about a possible increase in crime but because he thought that the parade caused an unnecessary hardship for the officers who had to travel by ferry from Staten Island to Manhattan to take part in the march. Wells retired later that year after completing nearly fifty-two years of service. Although he predicted that he would live to be one hundred, he died four years later.)

During Enright's tenure sixty-one separate funds were in existence to raise money for a hodgepodge of police causes. The amount in the funds purportedly totaled $3 million. Since most of the funds were under the direct control of the police commissioner, McLaughlin arranged for an audit to be conducted. When he was informed that there were discrepancies in many of the accounts, he launched an immediate investigation.

It turned out that the money had not been stolen but rather that Enright had spent it however he saw fit, even if the money in a particular fund had been raised for another purpose altogether. For example, in 1920 a committee of concerned citizens had approached Enright about building a police hospital. He thought it a worthy project and permitted his name to be attached to it. When the committee failed to raise enough capital to build the hospital, the project was shelved, but the money remained in the hospital account. Several years later Enright took $5,000 from the dormant hospital fund to help pay for repairs to the main lodge at the Police Recreation Center after it had been destroyed by a fire. Enright had also used the funds to pay for a number of dubious police-related expenses, such as dinners for the attendees of the international police conferences, badges for the honorary commissioners, and the refurbishing of the Teddy Roosevelt room at the old Police Headquarters on Mulberry Street.

McLaughlin wanted Enright to pay back the money. When Enright refused, McLaughlin threatened to charge him with larceny, but since there were no specific guidelines for the distribution of the money in the funds, there was nothing more McLaughlin could do. Fortunately Enright had never touched the two largest and most important funds: the Police Pension Fund and the Police Relief Fund.

When McLaughlin took over, it was assumed that he would replace all of Enright's deputies, but he retained the top three, including sixty-year-old

First Deputy Commissioner John Leach. In total Leach would serve a record seventeen years as a deputy commissioner for five different mayors and eight different police commissioners before his retirement in 1935.

Mary Hamilton, Enright's director of the Women's Bureau, would not last nearly as long. While she was in office, Hamilton wrote a book about her experiences, *Her Services and Ideals*, in which she established principles to guide future generations of policewomen. She believed that for policewomen to be effective in the community, they could not by reasons of their gender be expected to do the same type of work that policemen did.

Hamilton's departure after five years proved fortuitous for her colleague Mary Sullivan. Sullivan had joined the department as a matron in 1911, but her outstanding work as an undercover resulted in her being promoted to detective. Instead of naming her director, McLaughlin made Sullivan a lieutenant—a first for a female in the NYPD—and designated her the commanding officer of the Women's Bureau. But since "lieutenant" was a civil service rank, he did not have the authority to grant her that title. She was later designated detective first grade, which paid the same money as lieutenant. It would be another thirty-five years before policewomen won the right to take the same civil service tests for promotion as male members of the force.

Sullivan shared her predecessor's views and said when she accepted the post that "women should not be assigned to perform duties that could be better performed by men." She went on to become one of the founders of the Policewomen's Endowment Association and to advocate for their special interests.

Police Commissioner Enright had had a long-standing beef against the "Honest Cop," Lieutenant Lewis Valentine, who had earned his nickname while working for his mentor, Inspector Daniel "Honest Dan" Costigan. Enright passed him over for promotion three times, a situation that under civil service rules put Valentine at the end of the captain's list, where it would never be reached. McLaughlin restored Valentine to his rightful position on the list and then promoted him. He not only resuscitated Valentine's career, but also put him on a trajectory that would one day result in Valentine becoming police commissioner.

In May 1926 McLaughlin promoted the first black, Patrolman Samuel Battle, to sergeant. Fifteen years earlier Police Commissioner Cropsey had passed over Battle when his number was reached on the hiring list. It was only the personal intervention of Cropsey's successor, Rhinelander Waldo that righted the wrong. Battle would go on to become the department's first black lieutenant before he retired to take a post with the Parole Board.

It did not take very long for the ramifications of McLaughlin's decision to disband Enright's Special Services Division to come back to haunt him. Returning the responsibility for vice enforcement to precinct plainclothesmen had not yielded the results for which McLaughlin had hoped, but he also had no desire to revive the Special Services Division, so he tried a new approach to deal with vice crimes. He formed the Confidential Squad, which reported directly to him. Then he elevated the "Honest Cop," Captain Valentine, to deputy inspector and put him in charge of the unit. Valentine's handpicked team spied on the force and infiltrated gambling establishments, gathering evidence against lax precinct commanders and district inspectors. While the strategy proved effective at keeping officers in line, it also caused a serious rift in McLaughlin's relationship with Walker.

In July 1926 McLaughlin's efforts to put more patrolmen on the street at any cost backfired badly when he ordered the six-week recruit training class cut short so that he could utilize probationary officers to supplement the beleaguered patrol force, which was overburdened by a violent railroad strike. The recruits, however, had no equipment because their instructors had told them not to purchase uniforms or revolvers until they were sure they that would graduate from the Police Academy.

One of the unarmed recruits, probationary patrolman James Broderick, was detailed to safeguard the payroll of the Loft Candy Company. Unbeknown to him or anyone else in the NYPD, the notorious Philip Oberst gang, a.k.a. the "Crybaby Bandits," intended to steal it. Broderick caught Oberst and his associates trying to sneak into the factory and confronted them with only a nightstick. It was no match for their guns. He was struck by three bullets, but the gang fled without taking a penny from the payroll. The next day McLaughlin admitted that he had made a mistake putting an unarmed rookie in harm's way. Although he pledged that it would never happen again, several recruits resigned that afternoon.

It took two weeks for the police to apprehend the perpetrators. During the Oberst gang's crime spree, the bandits murdered two people, wounded two more, and made off with $16,532 in cash.

When Broderick returned to full duty, McLaughlin promoted him to second-grade detective and awarded him the Medal of Honor. Unfortunately Broderick's career took an unexpected downturn when a sixteen-year-old girl accused him of accosting her in his car. Although Broderick denied the charge, he was stripped of his gold detective's shield and never got it back. He retired from the police department in 1943 on a disability pension related to the wounds that he had suffered during the payroll robbery.

When Hylan was mayor, he was so uncomfortable appearing in public with dignitaries and celebrities that he delegated those duties to his secretary, Grover Whalen. After he returned to the private sector (as manager of Wanamaker's department store), Whalen continued to perform that function as chairman of the Mayor's Reception Committee. The first events Whalen oversaw were the ticker-tape parades and City Hall ceremonies for the victorious American Expeditionary Forces returning home from the war in Europe. Several more high-profile receptions followed as the city honored a president, a general, a king and queen, a prime minister, and a host of gold medal Olympians.

Although Whalen became the public face of these extravaganzas, he freely admitted that it was only because of the cooperation of the police department that he was able to fete the honorees in such grand style. Enright had always been happy to provide Whalen with whatever police resources he needed, but McLaughlin was not nearly as accommodating.

Whalen told McLaughlin that he expected that the crowds lining Broadway and welcoming hometown heroine and Olympic gold medalist swimmer Gertrude Ederle would be the largest that the city had ever seen and that he would therefore need more police than ever before. But instead of taking Whalen's advice, McLaughlin cut the number of patrolmen assigned to the detail.

An estimated ten thousand people waited that day for Ederle's motorcade to arrive at City Hall, where Walker was to present her with a medal for her athletic achievements. The fervent crowd easily broke through the severely undermanned police line and swarmed around Ederle as she tried to get out of the car. Somehow Whalen managed to get her through the mob and into City Hall for the award ceremony. Meanwhile, the anxious spectators lingered on the grounds, waiting for her to come back outside. When she stepped out onto the steps to have her picture taken with Walker, the horde overwhelmed the police for a second time. A quick-thinking patrolman hefted Ederle over his shoulder and grabbed the mayor by the arm. They followed another patrolman, who cleared a path for them. Once they were back inside City Hall, Walker admonished the inspector in command of the detail and called in the reserves. It took three hundred patrolmen to finally restore order.

Although Walker did not blame McLaughlin for understaffing the event, after that incident the police department gave Whalen whatever manpower he thought was necessary for keeping the crowd under control.

There had always been plenty of patrolmen found unfit for duty due to intoxicants, but not one policewoman had ever been charged with the offense until Belinda Milatz reported for duty at the Bedford Stuyvesant stationhouse in an inebriated condition. She was suspended for thirty days without pay.

It was the beginning of her downward spiral. Prior to becoming a policewoman, Milatz had worked as an investigator in the New York State Department of Narcotics Control. During an interview by a newspaper reporter on the day she was hired, Milatz told the reporter that kindness should be used as a weapon against crime when dealing with juveniles. But the department was ill equipped to help her with her drinking problem. There were no counseling programs. She was relieved of her investigative duties and reassigned to watch over female prisoners.

Things got worse when her husband abandoned their family. Milatz struggled to keep her job and raise two children. Her predicament finally overwhelmed her. In June 1931 the same policewoman who had once advocated using kindness as a weapon was arrested for committing a brutal assault on her young son.

Milatz denied the charge, but the boy was put into temporary protective custody. At the Children's Court hearing, her son, despite being covered with welts, recanted his story and said that his mother had hit him only because he had disobeyed her. Since excessive corporal punishment was not considered a crime, the judge dismissed the charge, but neither mother nor son was better off for his ruling. Milatz died the following spring from complications related to her drinking. She was only forty-five years old. Her son was sent to an orphanage on Staten Island while a distant relative reared her daughter.

Walker had kept his word and given McLaughlin a free rein to run the police department as he saw fit, but in reality his frequent extended absences from the city meant that he was not around to question McLaughlin's operational decisions. In fact the mayor was out of town so much that even Governor Smith complained that he had a hard time scheduling an appointment with him.

Walker's arrangement with McLaughlin worked until the Confidential Squad raided the Democratic Party clubhouse in Greenpoint, Brooklyn, that was operated by Alderman Peter McGuinness. According to the *New York Times*, McGuinness was alleged to have cried out the now infamous phrase, "Cheese it! Here come the cops," when Valentine's men came crashing through the door. McGuinness, however, claimed that when the police barged onto the premises, he merely instructed his fellow club members to sit down. He further asserted that if there was illegal gambling going on somewhere inside the clubhouse, it was certainly without his personal knowledge.

A judge dismissed the charges against McGuinness, despite the fact that Valentine's men recovered $114,000 in horse race receipts locked in a safe that had the alderman's name on it. Meanwhile, other Tammany Hall district leaders approached Walker and told him that the "friendly games of cards" that the members of their clubhouses played were being misconstrued by the police as illegal. They expected him to intercede before the situation with the police got further out of hand. Walker was forced to broker a deal between the parties in which McLaughlin agreed that there would be no more raids as long as no "commercialized" gambling took place inside the clubhouses.

A week later McLaughlin informed Walker that he was resigning to take a job in the private sector as executive vice president of the MacKay Companies, a conglomerate that provided telegraph cable services in Europe and North America. He denied that his sudden announcement had anything to do with the controversy caused by the police raids. He insisted that his decision had been made strictly in terms of "dollars and sense." His new position paid $65,000 more per year than the job of police commissioner.

Although reported crime under McLaughlin had dropped to its lowest level since 1922, few from Tammany Hall were sad to see him go, especially Alderman McGuinness, who said, "I always win," when he heard the news.

Judge Olvany pledged that Tammany Hall would have no hand in deciding the next police commissioner, but rumors that it would be Walker's close personal friend and Tammany Hall associate Joseph Warren turned out to be true. Walker believed that Warren had an expert knowledge of the law, integrity of character, and the zeal of a crusader, all of the important traits that he wanted in his next police commissioner. Warren's friends described him as "honest beyond a doubt."

Joseph Warren was born in Jersey City in 1882. He and Walker first met at a Jesuit high school in Manhattan. Both men attended New York Law School and later served together for one term in the New York State Assembly. When Warren lost his bid for reelection, he became a lawyer for the State Health Department. In 1921 he left the public sector and started a private practice in Lower Manhattan. Walker rented a suite in Warren's office from which to run his practice. Walker said that Warren had the best legal mind he had ever known. Unfortunately he was also somewhat frail. Once he became police commissioner, the stress of office took a great toll on his health. He began to suffer psychotic episodes that impaired his ability to run the department. But none of that could have been predicted when Walker offered him the job.

McLaughlin met Warren at Police Headquarters on April 26, 1926, and handed him his police commissioner's shield. When asked by reporters what his plans were for the department, Warren said that the mayor had promised him exactly the same thing he had promised McLaughlin: a free hand to run the department. He pledged to continue to follow the course set by McLaughlin. He conceded, however, that there would be some minor changes, no doubt suggested by Walker to keep his associates happy.

One of the first ranking officers Warren met with was Inspector Lewis Valentine of the Confidential Squad. Valentine assumed that he would be stripped of his command, but to his surprise Warren told him, "Your duties are unchanged. I like your work." A few days later he promoted Valentine to deputy chief. Warren allowed the raids to continue on the poolrooms and betting parlors, but the only political clubs targeted were those in which Valentine's men uncovered overwhelming evidence that organized gambling was taking place.

Warren's first crisis began on his second day in office. The department had received word that a ruthless gang had kidnapped a wealthy realtor named Abraham Scharlin and was demanding $400,000 in ransom for his safe return. Deputy Chief Inspector John Coughlin, commanding officer of the Detective Bureau, put his best man on the case, Detective John Cordes.

Over the next few days the kidnappers made several calls to the victim's residence. Cordes instructed the family to string the kidnappers along by negotiating over the ransom amount and to demand proof that the abductors were actually holding Scharlin. The kidnappers mailed the family one half of Scharlin's Elks Club card, along with special instructions that it be placed in a bag with the ransom money, which had been lowered to $20,000.

The police caught a break when a stool pigeon identified Bernard Marcus, a.k.a. "Jack Thompson," as one of the abductors. Cordes was familiar with Thompson from past encounters. He and his partner tailed him into Central Park. There Thompson met with another hood whom Cordes knew to be David "the Jew" Berman. Cordes noticed a handgun tucked into Berman's belt. The concealed weapon was enough reason to bring him and Thompson in for questioning, but with so many innocent bystanders in the area, Cordes thought it best to have his partner call for backup rather than risk a shootout.

The suspects apparently sensed that they were being watched and got up to leave. As luck would have it, Cordes caught the attention of a nearby motorcycle cop, Patrolman Richard O'Connor. Since O'Connor was in uniform, Cordes told him to keep an eye on the suspects from a distance while he discreetly moved closer. But he got too close. Berman suddenly whirled around and pointed a gun at him. Cordes knocked it out of his hand. Thompson drew his own revolver, but before he could pull the trigger, Patrolman O'Connor shot and killed him. Cordes recovered the missing half of the Elks Club card in Thompson's pocket, thereby confirming his involvement in Scharlin's kidnapping.

Berman fled the scene but was apprehended a short time later hiding in the brambles. He remained tight-lipped about his role in the kidnapping, despite being subjected to an intense interrogation at Police Headquarters. His accomplices read about what had happened in the newspapers the next morning and got spooked. They freed Scharlin a few hours later from a Brooklyn warehouse where he was being held. The kidnappers also released a second victim, identified as James Taylor. The police were not aware that he was missing because his wife was afraid that her husband would be killed if she told the authorities.

Berman was not charged with kidnapping because neither Scharlin nor Taylor could identify him. He did, however, receive twelve years for his part in the attempted murder of Detective Cordes. Four of Berman's cohorts, thought to be part of the Dougherty Brothers gang out of Chicago, were eventually arrested after police discovered that both victims originally hailed from the Windy City.

Warren offered Patrolman O'Connor a promotion to detective for his heroic actions, but O'Connor refused because he liked motorcycle work better. Cordes, meanwhile, became the first member of the NYPD to be awarded a second Medal of Honor.

In May 1927 Charles Lindbergh became the first person to fly across the Atlantic Ocean. It was a feat of such heroic proportions that after he landed in France, he was feted for several days by the mayor of Paris. Walker had no intention of being outdone by his European counterpart. He announced that New York City would host Lindbergh for four days starting on Monday, June 13, 1927, with a massive ticker-tape parade up Broadway. He left the arrangements in the capable hands of Whalen and Warren.

Whalen was a pro at coordinating such events, but when the mayor declared June 13 a municipal holiday so that a million schoolchildren could take part in the celebration, even he wondered if there were enough patrolmen on the entire police force to control the crowds. Warren wanted to call in the state militia but was talked out of it by high-ranking officers who had no interest in having outsiders provide assistance. The final plan called for five thousand officers to be detailed along the parade route, starting in Battery Park and ending in Central Park. In order to maintain sufficient manpower along the entire procession, patrolmen were instructed to take the subway to posts further ahead on the parade route once Lindbergh had passed through their sectors.

Another major concern for Warren was that with so many people at the parade and so few patrolmen on duty in the precincts, vacant homes would become easy targets for burglars. So before the parade he had the department distribute flyers to homeowners advising them to lock their doors and keep their shades drawn during the celebration.

Lindbergh arrived on the morning of June 13 by seaplane and landed in New York Harbor, where an enormous flotilla was assembled in his honor. He was greeted by Whalen and conveyed to shore by the city's official yacht, the ss *Macom* (a name derived from the words "mayor" and "committee"), under police escort.

Over eighty thousand spectators were crammed into Battery Park hoping to catch a glimpse of Lindbergh as he disembarked. The police escorted Lindbergh and Whalen to the city's official car. As the motorcade started to roll, Lindbergh climbed on top of the back seat to make it easier for the multitude lining Broadway to see him, although he was barely visible in the deluge of white ticker tape floating down from the sky.

The motorcade's first stop was City Hall, which had been cordoned off by the police. There Walker presented Lindbergh with a Medal of Valor on behalf of New York City. After the ceremony Lindbergh headed to Central Park, where he met Governor Smith. Later that night Lindbergh and his mother attended a dinner in his honor on Long Island. Since the Nassau County Police Department did not have enough patrolmen to provide for his security, Warren detailed a hundred motorcycle cops to escort Lindbergh there and back. The evening festivities, much like the parade, went off without a hitch, although Lindbergh disappointed guests when he left the affair earlier than expected.

Not one serious mishap was reported during the entire four-day event. Warren had assigned Sergeant Arthur W. Wallander, the head drill instructor at the Police Academy, as Lindbergh's personal bodyguard. Before he left for St. Louis, Lindbergh conveyed his personal thanks to Warren for the fine protection afforded him by the police and singled out Wallander in particular. A week later Wallander was promoted to lieutenant. As a reward Warren granted every member of the force an additional day of vacation. Of the gala celebration the *Evening World Journal* wrote, "Hats off to these boys in blue! New York has reason to be proud of the men who guard her peace."

While the Lindbergh visit took place in New York, other events far beyond the city border kept NYPD busy during the summer of 1927. Seven years before a bomb had exploded on Wall Street two days after a pair of anarchists, Nicola Sacco and Bartolemeo Vanzetti, had been arrested in Braintree, Massachusetts, for the murder of two payroll guards. Supporters sympathetic to their case believed the evidence was circumstantial and that neither man was actually being tried for the murders, but rather because they advocated an overthrow of the American government. Sacco and Vanzetti were found guilty and sentenced to death, but before their execution was carried out, a fund was established to pay for their appeal. Over $300,000 was raised, much of it from prominent American citizens who believed that the men had a constitutional right to speak out against the government.

It took seven years for the appeals process to be exhausted. On August 3, 1927, the governor of Massachusetts set August 10 as the date for their execution. Two days later in New York City, anarchists detonated a bomb in the Twenty-Eighth Street subway station. No one was killed, but twelve people were injured.

Warren mobilized the entire force and posted patrolmen around the clock to watch over subway stations, power plants, and public buildings. Ironically police also had to guard several buildings housing anarchist organizations because of the threats of retaliation they received for the subway explosion.

Supporters of Sacco and Vanzetti—an eclectic group of anarchists, Fascists, Communists, Socialists, civil libertarians, trade union workers, and disfranchised immigrants—scheduled a two-hour rally at Union Square Park the day before the scheduled execution to demand clemency. Thirty-five thousand were expected to take part in the protest. But the police were more than ready for them. Chief Inspector Lahey told reporters beforehand that the department had made the most elaborate arrangements in the history of the city to keep the demonstration under control. That afternoon 1,000 uniformed officers, including patrolmen on horseback and motorcycles, encircled the park, while a reserve force of 2,400 patrolmen hid in a nearby subway station and on rooftops.

As a result of the large police presence, the rally concluded without incident. But the huge protest, along with dozens of others across the nation, convinced the Massachusetts governor to issue a temporary stay of execution so that the State Supreme Court could review the case. After the high court affirmed the jury's verdict, additional demonstrations followed in New York City.

The night before the execution Congressman Fiorello LaGuardia spoke on Sacco and Vanzetti's behalf at a church assembly in Manhattan. His pleas for clemency had no effect. Both men were electrocuted shortly after midnight August 23, 1927, but to this day, the fairness of their trial has remained a subject of controversy.

After several incidents had occurred where policemen accidentally shot and killed innocent bystanders during shootouts with armed adversaries, Warren decided to increase the number of days patrolmen spent on target practice from two to three days per year. More important, he also raised the passing grade from a 30 percent hit rate to 50 percent.

As a method of gun control Warren proposed to cut in half the number of pistol permits the department issued each year. But in a letter to the editor of the *New York Times*, the writer, T. R. Mullen, pointed out that the percentage of people who committed murder with licensed firearms was extremely low because thugs were not concerned with obtaining pistol permits. Mullen had no problem, however, with pistol owners being able to demonstrate an ability to shoot accurately. He also noted sarcastically that if New York's police officers were required to meet the same standard expected of ordinary citizens, a very small percentage of the force would qualify for a pistol permit.

Although Warren escaped his first year in office without a major scandal, crime was on the rise and police morale was said to be plummeting. Walker was hearing rumors that his police commissioner was becoming increasingly unstable, but for the sake of their friendship he chose to let him remain in office even as Warren's public proclamations became more convoluted. For example, following a rash of motor vehicle accidents in which a number of pedestrians had been run over and killed, Warren erroneously claimed he could do nothing about it. But that was not true. The police department regulated vehicular and pedestrian traffic. When informed of his misstatement, Warren said that the primary task of the police department was to prevent crime, and he had no intention of sacrificing that function simply to reduce the number of vehicle accidents even if it saved lives. Then he belittled the fine work that policewomen had done with juveniles and said that as far as he was concerned, they were only good as matrons.

Another indication that all was not right occurred when Warren announced that a drastic shakeup would take place after detectives had failed to apprehend the killer of a known narcotics peddler. In the end a handful of detectives were demoted, but none of the ranking officers who were involved were affected.

Arnold Rothstein was New York's most notorious gangster. He made a fortune running gambling houses and poolrooms and was alleged to have been the brains behind the infamous Black Sox scandal of 1919. His own lawyer described him as "a gray rat waiting for his cheese." The advent of prohibition provided ample opportunities for Rothstein to diversify. He used his ill-gotten gains to ingratiate himself to the politicians of Tammany Hall, many of whom enjoyed spending their evenings in his gaming establishments.

For years Rothstein had lived the highlife, seemingly impervious to the law, until he unwittingly took part in a marathon poker game in which he lost $320,000 over the course of three days. Word of his predicament got out. If he did not satisfy his obligation, he would be rubbed out. Two months later, on Sunday evening, November 4, 1928, Rothstein joined in on a floating card game in room 349 of the Park Central Hotel at Seventh Avenue and Fifty-Fifth Street. Although no reliable account was ever told of what happened that night, hearsay had it that one of the players called Rothstein a "welch" for not paying his debts.

Normally such an insult would have sent Rothstein into a rage, but in this instance he told the man to come back and repeat it when he sobered up. The player, upset by the slight, pulled a pistol from his pocket and shot Rothstein in the lower abdomen. Rothstein reportedly muttered, "Is that all?" as he staggered out of the room clutching his stomach. But the wound was serious. Rothstein managed to hobble down the stairs to the street, where he told a passerby, "Get me to an ambulance. I've been shot."

Walker received the news of Rothstein's shooting while dancing with his mistress, actress Betty Compton (the woman for whom he would eventually leave his wife), at a nightclub in the North Bronx. It was one of his favorite places to unwind. A lot of gangsters liked the joint too, and as usual they were also there that night.

According to the bandleader, there was a sudden stir in the club around midnight. He observed a man whisper into the mayor's ear. Seconds later Walker grabbed Compton's hand and said, "We're leaving." As Walker got up, the bandmaster pointed at the gangsters in the back of the room and said, "Something's happened. . . . The boys are acting kind of funny." Walker nodded. "Rothstein's just been shot. . . . That means trouble from here in."

Meanwhile, back in Manhattan, Rothstein was transported by ambulance to Polyclinic Hospital on West Fiftieth Street. Although he was conscious when detectives arrived, he refused to identify his assailant to them. Even as his condition deteriorated, he still would not talk. His passing two days later inflicted a mortal wound on Warren's police career.

The homicide fell under the jurisdiction of Deputy Chief Inspector John Coughlin, commanding officer of the Detective Division, but since gamblers were involved, Deputy Chief Lewis Valentine was summoned to assist. The poker players were long gone by the time Valentine arrived on the scene, but he reported that the hotel room still reeked with tobacco smoke. Coughlin's men recovered an overcoat with the name of a well-known underworld figure sewn into the lining. The coat belonged to George "Hump" McManus, and although he became the prime suspect, the police had no idea at first where he or the other players were hiding out.

To make matters worse, Warren inexplicably allowed Coughlin to take a sudden extended vacation, a move that brought the investigation to a complete halt. Walker was said to be furious, but for public consumption he said that he was satisfied that Warren was doing the best he could to solve the case. In reality, however, he was secretly wooing Warren's replacement.

The Christmas season was the busiest time of year for Grover Whalen at Wanamaker's department store. Although he and Walker had become good friends through his work with the Mayor's Reception Committee, the last thing he wanted was the distraction of a visit from the mayor.

According to Whalen, Walker strode into his office and said, "Grover, I've got to make a change of police commissioners. This Rothstein murder has raised hell. I'm afraid Joe Warren must go. . . . I'm here to ask you to be the 'top cop.'" Then he went on to explain that Warren's once steady judgment had been faltering in recent months and that he thought it was time for a businessman to try his hand at running the department.

Whalen thanked Walker for the consideration but said that he was not interested. He believed that was the end of it, but several days later he was called to the corporate headquarters in Philadelphia to meet with William Nevin, Wanamaker's chairman of the board. "I met your Mr. Walker the other day," Nevin told Whalen. "We talked mostly about you and how he hoped he could secure your services as police commissioner. The mayor seemed terribly concerned about this unsolved murder case—the gambler."

Whalen confessed that he had been flattered by the offer but said that he could not afford to take the job. He made $100,000 a year as the store manager, whereas the position of police commissioner paid only $10,000. It would be unfair to his family for him to take such a drastic pay cut. Nevin seemed to understand, so Whalen once again considered the matter closed, especially after New York's most wanted gangster, George McManus, arranged to turn himself in to Detective John Cordes. Although there was very little tangible evidence against McManus, a grand jury indicted him for first-degree murder anyway.

To some the arrest appeared to have saved Warren's job, but Walker was determined to bring Whalen on board. The mayor used his consider-able persuasive powers to convince Nevin to put the difference between Whalen's annual salary as head of Wanamaker's and that of the salary of the police commissioner in escrow so that taking the police job would not harm him financially.

Whalen was genuinely surprised at the lengths Walker was willing to go to secure his services. He agreed to serve as police commissioner for one year, during which time he would reorganize the police department as he saw fit. Walker could not make any request of him for promotion, transfer, or appointment. The minute that happened, Whalen said that he would resign. Walker accepted all of his conditions, and although he did not admit it, he was glad that Whalen wanted to serve only one year as police commissioner because that was long enough for him to get reelected.

Walker decided his best campaign strategy would be to defer all law enforcement decisions to Whalen. Then assuming Walker won the election, Whalen could bow out without having his feathers ruffled the way Warren's had been after he was told that he was being replaced. When Warren left police headquarters for the last time, he muttered to reporters that he had wasted three years toiling for the city.

Whalen was born on the Lower East Side in 1886, and it happened to be the same day that President Grover Cleveland was getting married. While Whalen's father, a proud Tammany Hall Democrat, thought it appropriate that his son be named after the Democratic president of the United States, his wife was upset because there were no Saint Grovers in the Catholic Church. As a compromise, they agreed that Michael would be Grover's middle name, along with Aloysius and Augustine.

As a boy, Whalen made his first money performing chores on the Sabbath for the Orthodox Jews in his neighborhood. Within a short time he was pocketing fifty cents a week tending to the special needs of his customers. He claimed that it was this early experience that taught him how to be a good salesman.

After Whalen graduated from De Witt Clinton High School, his father enrolled him into an accounting class. He did so well in the course that he was offered a teaching position, but his father nixed the idea. He wanted his son to become a lawyer. It was at New York Law School that Whalen took his first lesson in public speaking and discovered that he had a talent for it.

After his father died, Whalen gave up the legal profession to take over the family business but sold it after just three years to take a job at Wanamaker's department store. It was at Wanamaker's that Whalen joined the Businessmen's League.

In 1917 Tammany Hall was seeking a candidate who could beat incumbent mayor John Purroy Mitchel. Whalen used his connections in the Businessmen's League to put Judge John Hylan's name into the hat. When Hylan won the election, he asked Whalen to become his personal secretary. There Whalen got a firsthand look into New York City politics.

Whalen felt that his two most important tasks as police commissioner were to restore the public's confidence in the police department and to raise the department's standards of efficiency. In his first sit-down with reporters, Whalen said that he intended to reorganize the department along the lines of the Ford Motor Company, wherein each man had certain responsibilities, and if he did not fulfill them, management knew exactly whom to blame.

Sweeping changes began just twenty-four hours after he took charge and continued on an almost daily basis for the next eighteen months. The first ranking officers jettisoned were Chief Inspector William Lahey and the commanding officer of the Detective Division, Deputy Chief Inspector John Coughlin. Lahey had been good friends with Whalen's father, so he was surprised that his son wanted to force him out of the department. Coughlin did not bother questioning Whalen's reasoning. He knew that he had been lax in overseeing the Rothstein case—some thought on purpose in order to protect the politicians who owed money to the gambler and benefited by his demise. With Rothstein's death the chits were forgotten.

Whalen elevated Deputy Chief Inspector John O'Brien and Inspector Edward Mulrooney to take Lahey's and Coughlin's places. He ordered them to review the Detective Division's investigation of the Rothstein homicide and determine which officers had neglected to perform their duty.

Then Whalen rescinded the demotion of acting lieutenant Patrick Fitzgibbons, head of the Glee Club. Warren had demoted Fitzgibbons to sergeant on his last day in office after Deputy Chief Valentine had determined that $18,000 was missing from the Glee Club's bank account, which Fitzgibbons oversaw. Whalen said that he reinstated Fitzgibbons to his former rank because he had no faith in the man who had prepared the complaint—namely, Lewis Valentine—and tossed the charges into the wastebasket explaining that "there were more important matters at hand."

Whalen's decision spelled bad news for the Confidential Squad, whose methods he described as tyrannical. He put the squad out of business. As long as he was police commissioner, he said that patrolmen no longer would have to worry about plainclothesmen peeking around the corner to spy on them.

The public learned of the "Honest Cop's" fate when the news was flashed across the electronic news streamer in Times Square: "Valentine, Crown Prince of the Police Department, demoted to Captain." Whalen transferred him to a precinct in Long Island City. Valentine turned down an offer from the town of Hempstead on Long Island to become its chief of police. While addressing his first roll call at his new precinct, Valentine told the men, "A good cop goes where he's told and does what he's told. I expect you to do that for me."

The axe fell next on the head of the Homicide Bureau. Deputy Inspector Arthur Carey had been its commanding officer since it was established in 1908 by Police Commissioner Bingham. Police Commissioner Baker abolished it in 1910, but Police Commissioner Woods brought it back in 1914.

Since then Carey had taken only seventeen vacation days. When given the option to retire with dignity or be forced out, he chose the latter.

It was not just Carey's bungling of the Rothstein investigation that convinced Whalen he had to go. There were 228 murders in 1928, and homicide detectives had solved only two of them. Carey explained that by the time his men arrived on the scene of a murder, the precinct detectives were reluctant to turn their information over to his men out of fear that the Homicide Bureau would get credit for solving the murder. Whalen realized there was merit in what Carey said, although it did not save his job. Instead of having a centralized Homicide Bureau working out of Headquarters, Whalen established individual homicide squads in each borough so that the specialists could reach the scene as fast as the precinct detectives.

The botched Rothstein murder investigation had played a big part in Warren's downfall. Whalen wanted to make sure that did not happen to him under his watch, but homicide squads helped solve murders; they did not prevent them. During the first three months of 1928 under Warren, there were seventy-one homicides in the city. In comparison, during the first three months of 1929 under Whalen, the number of homicides rose to eighty. William Bullock, a high-ranking Republican, made note of the increase to embarrass Mayor Walker as he was preparing to mount his bid for reelection. Whalen called the statistics "political propaganda" because 67 percent of the city's murders were committed indoors, where the police could not see them. Bullock's assertion, however, made it clear that crime would be a major issue in the upcoming mayoral election.

In a concerted effort to drive what he called the "loafers, criminals, gangsters and disorderly characters" out of the city, Whalen formed a plainclothes Gunmen's Squad and gave it instructions to "treat 'em rough."

It most instances it was easy for a police commissioner to exert control over the ranking officers because their careers were under his direction. It was quite another thing to convince the lowly patrolmen to pledge their absolute loyalty to him. Abolishing the Confidential Squad was a good first step by Whalen, but he won the patrolmen over with General Order No. 36, issued on New Year's Eve 1928. He dismissed all but the most egregious disciplinary complaints lodged against members of the force. As a result, nearly every single officer started off the new calendar year with a clean slate.

It took a month for Chief Inspector O'Brien to complete his investigation into the Rothstein assassination. Ironically his report implicated the department's most decorated detective, John Cordes, even though he was the man who had arrested George McManus. Whalen suspended Cordes immediately and scheduled a department hearing to take place just two days later over which he would preside.

The hearing lasted only seven minutes—just long enough for Cordes to enter a "not guilty" plea and request that his trial be delayed for a week so that he could prepare his defense. If Whalen had denied his motion, Cordes would have called former police commissioner Warren and the former head of detectives, Deputy Chief Inspector Coughlin, to testify on his behalf since both were present in the trial room, as was Manhattan district attorney Joab Banton.

Banton did not want Cordes questioned by the department for fear that his testimony might jeopardize the McManus murder trial. When Banton asked for an adjournment, Whalen agreed to postpone Cordes's disciplinary hearing until after the McManus trial. Then he rescinded Cordes's suspension and ordered that henceforth any policeman accused of wrongdoing would either get a speedy trial or be restored to duty, pending the resolution of the charges against him. No longer would policemen go months without pay waiting for their disciplinary cases to be heard. That is not to say that Cordes did not receive punishment in the interim. Whalen banished him to the distant Bronx for two years.

Whalen took a vacation to Florida with his family just six weeks into the job. When he returned, he learned that the American Civil Liberties Union (ACLU) was very upset with his "treat 'em rough" policies. The ACLU complained to the mayor about the large number of arrests that the police had made in the short time Whalen had been in office. According to the ACLU, even if the focus of the police raids was to curtail the criminal activity of gangsters, patrolmen were violating the civil rights of ordinary, law-abiding citizens caught up in the sweeps. The ACLU was particularly upset with Whalen's instructions to the force that when arrests were not enough, the end of a nightstick could take care of the problem. "If a Police Department exceeds the bounds of the law," the ACLU lawyers asserted, "it becomes in itself a menace to the rights of citizens."

Whalen shrugged off the ACLU's criticism but agreed to meet with its delegates to discuss their concerns. He thought that he could convince them that law-abiding citizens had nothing to fear from the police. During the meeting Whalen explained that he meant for his patrolmen to use their nightsticks only in self-defense and not to needlessly harm innocent bystanders. He then took the delegates upstairs to the Lineup Room to show them the condition of prisoners. Despite his best efforts to convince them the police were their friends, the delegates were not satisfied with his answers or actions. Eventually the ACLU attorneys would petition Walker to remove Whalen from office.

When Rhinelander Waldo was first deputy commissioner, he replaced the tall gray helmet that New York's patrolmen had been wearing for years with a navy blue hat that featured a round, flat crown and visor. Former chief of police William Devery derided the new cap for its European flair, but it turned out to be a better piece of equipment.

Whalen thought that it was time to replace the Waldo hat with an even more practical model, but few members of the force were interested in buying a new hat. So he tested out a flexible, eight-point cap called the "Windbreaker" on a small group of patrolmen first. They reported that its unique pliable shape made it stay on their heads better than the old-style Waldo cap. After the successful wear test, Whalen ordered each member of the force to purchase the new hat in time for the annual police parade, which he reinstated in May 1929. But when the policemen grumbled about having to buy new headgear when their old hats were still in good condition, Whalen arranged for his friends in the private sector to donate enough money for him to reimburse every single police officer two dollars for the cost of the cap.

Margaret Sanger was born in 1879. In 1914 she distributed the first pamphlet in America advocating birth control for women; it was called *Family Limitation*. Although Sanger was a nurse, she was charged with breaking the law because only physicians were permitted to dispense that type of information and then only to married women. Sanger was arrested, but the charges were dropped when her five-year-old daughter died unexpectedly during the trial.

Sanger went on to establish the country's first birth-control clinic in Brooklyn in 1916, and she was arrested again by the police. Her case garnered national attention. She was found guilty and sentenced to thirty days in jail. Over the next several years she opened more birth-control clinics across the country, including one in Manhattan that was staffed by female doctors.

As head of the Women's Bureau, Detective Mary Sullivan considered it her duty to keep tabs on Sanger. In April 1929 she sent an undercover policewoman into the Manhattan clinic to inquire about contraception. When the female doctor provided her with the information without first determining her marital status and condition, Sullivan secured a warrant from the chief magistrate, William McAdoo, and had the doctor and nurses arrested. This led to an immediate outcry by Sanger's supporters.

After looking into the matter, Whalen decided it best to remove Sullivan from her post and for the first time put the Women's Bureau (which he renamed the Bureau of Policewomen) under the control of a male, Captain James Brady. He said that the reason for his action was that Sullivan failed to consult with her immediate superiors knowing the potential trouble the arrests would cause. A month later the court dismissed the charges against Sanger's medical staff because the prosecution could not prove the defendants had acted in bad faith when they provided birth-control information to the undercover officer.

Although Sullivan's career suffered a setback as a result of the controversy caused by her raid on Sanger's clinic, she went on to write a best seller about her police experiences titled *My Double Life* and had a comic book published based on her exploits, *Lady Detective*. Before she passed away in 1950, Sullivan hosted a popular weekly crime-fighting radio serial and operated her own confidential investigation business.

As an experienced businessman, Whalen knew how important it was to provide clear, concise directions to subordinates, so he was surprised to discover that police department orders were convoluted, confusing, and often in conflict with previous directives still in effect. To make matters worse, copies of orders were extremely difficult to locate because each precinct was only allotted two copies per command. The situation was further exasperated by the fact that precinct commanders routinely promulgated their own orders without consulting superiors at Headquarters.

The last time an attempt had been made to make sense of the department's myriad regulations was in 1924, when Police Commissioner Enright had distributed a series of pamphlets to replace the rule book that Police Commissioner Woods had issued in 1914 called *Police Practice and Procedure*. All members of the force were required to keep the individual pamphlets in their possession and update them by hand as new orders were issued.

After studying the problem for several months, Whalen replaced the pamphlets with a book called *The Manual of Procedure*, in which rules and regulations were correlated by subject matter. Every uniformed member of the force was given his own copy. Whalen explained that the new reference manual would "eliminate indecision and doubt from the minds of members of the force and instill a feeling of confidence and tranquility in the conduct of official business."

In conjunction with the new rule book, Whalen set out to create the most modern and comprehensive police-training program in the country. Back in 1898 police recruits underwent training at the School of Instruction, which became the Training School of the New York Police Department in 1914, under Police Commissioner Woods. In 1925 Enright founded the Police Academy. Whalen replaced the Police Academy with the short-lived College of the Police Department of the City of New York, which lasted until December 1930, when his successor changed the name back to the Police Academy.

Nevertheless, the Police College, as it was called, was a giant step forward. The department converted an eight-story building, leased from the Lofts Candy Company, as an annex to Police Headquarters. In addition to relieving overcrowding at Headquarters, the former candy factory, at 400 Broome Street, provided enough classroom space for a modern training school that Whalen staffed with a corps of experts in all branches of police work because, as he said, "Police work is a profession that must be taught as such." In addition, for the first time recruits were provided with gray uniforms, paid for by the city at a cost of $4.75 each, which they wore until they graduated from the revamped sixty-day training course.

The results after Whalen's first six months in office were impressive. After an initial increase, homicides had dropped by 8 percent, and burglaries had fallen an impressive 19 percent as compared to the same six-month period in 1928 under Police Commissioner Warren.

Whalen's mid-year crime report was good news for Walker as he geared up for reelection, but his main opponent, Republican congressman Fiorello LaGuardia, disputed the figures. Apparently Whalen had cited a 19 percent reduction in the amount of money paid out by insurance companies for burglary claims rather than counting the actual number of break-ins reported to the police. LaGuardia said that the apprehension of criminals was a much better indicator of the effectiveness of a police force, and according to his statistics, the number of arrests in New York City had remained stagnant since Walker had become mayor despite Whalen's much ballyhooed crackdown on gangs. Although LaGuardia's rhetoric was intended to repudiate the administration's assertion that crime was on the ebb, it had little effect convincing the public that Walker and Whalen were not doing a good job.

Once LaGuardia realized that this strategy was not going to get him the votes he needed to defeat Walker, he changed his tactics and accused the mayor of impropriety in office. "I know one thing," he told supporters, alluding to Walker's expensive wardrobe. "You cannot get rich in public life honestly, and I am speaking from personal experience." Although LaGuardia's instincts about Walker's misconduct would ultimately prove true, at the time few voters seemed to care even after the stock market collapsed and started the country's downward spiral just weeks before the election.

Walker routed LaGuardia in November 1929 by nearly a half million votes. In his concession speech LaGuardia said prophetically, "I am licked . . . but I hope the election is all for the best."

A third candidate in the mayoral race proved to be a non-factor despite his crime-fighting reputation. Former police commissioner Richard Enright ran on the Square Deal Party ticket. In explaining his extremely poor showing, Enright paraphrased a quote attributed to Abraham Lincoln: "If this is the sort of thing the people want, it is the sort of thing they want." He added in Latin, "The voice of the people is the voice of God."

Walker took a parting shot at LaGuardia during his victory speech and said that his large margin of victory proved that a man could wear whatever clothes he wanted so long as the people of New York were satisfied with the past four years. Walker also declared Whalen the greatest police commissioner the city had ever known, but he was overheard later that night telling his Tammany Hall cohorts, "Now Grover can go."

Democrats were also victorious in races for controller, Manhattan district attorney, and president of the Board of Aldermen. In fact Joseph McKee, the second-term Aldermanic leader who became president of the Board of Aldermen, tallied even more votes than Walker. His popularity worried the sachems of Tammany Hall because McKee considered himself to be a reformer.

Another matter that was extremely important to the members of the police department was also resolved by the ballot. Efforts by the Patrolmen's Benevolent Association to secure a raise previously had been stymied by Warren, who deemed patrolmen's salary to be sufficient for attracting "intelligent and decent men to the force." He thought that the money could be better spent hiring more officers at the lowest wage possible. Whalen, however, called the patrolmen's salary "entirely inadequate for them to decently support themselves and their families and maintain their self-respect." He agreed with Alderman McKee, who prior to the election had proposed that the people of New York City and not state lawmakers should decide whether or not the patrolmen deserved a raise. Then Whalen set about selling the idea to the public, relying on his skills as a salesman. After he convinced the state legislature to put it up for a referendum, Whalen promised New Yorkers that patrolmen would render the best type of police service possible and make life and property safe from harm in the city if they were appropriately compensated.

Despite the crash of the stock market, the referendum passed. The starting salary of patrolmen jumped from $1,450 to $2,000, and top pay after five years went from $2,500 to $3,000. In the meantime the raises created a whole new set of problems that had to be resolved because senior patrolmen were suddenly being paid the same wages as second-grade detectives and higher-ranking police sergeants.

It took nearly a year for District Attorney Banton to bring McManus to trial for the Rothstein murder, and by that time he was a lame duck preparing to leave office and return to private practice. After the state rested, the defense made a motion to dismiss the charges against McManus claiming that the prosecution had not made its case. The presiding judge concurred. Fifteen minutes later McManus walked away a free man.

Banton blamed the loss on the shoddy police investigation. "Looking back on the case now," he said, "we can see many things might have been done differently at the start had we known what we know now." In his autobiography, *Mr. New York*, Whalen wrote that the failure to obtain a conviction was due entirely to the laxity of the police who had been assigned to the case originally.

Otherwise Whalen gave himself high marks for his first year in office. He attributed most crime to youth gangs and juvenile delinquents. He addressed the problem with the establishment of the Bureau of Crime Prevention on January 1, 1930. He told reporters, "If we can nip it at the source we have done a great deal to solve the problem."

Whalen's interest in aviation had been kindled by his former boss, the late Rodman Wanamaker, who early on understood the impact that regular air service across the Atlantic Ocean would have on business in America. In 1914 Wanamaker formed the American Trans-Oceanic Corporation to construct a long-range aircraft capable of making the journey, but the war in Europe forced him to shelve his plans.

After the armistice Frenchman Raymond Orteig offered $25,000 to the first person or team to complete a nonstop flight across the Atlantic. Many pilots took up the challenge, but none succeeded and six died trying. Wanamaker followed their attempts with great interest. When naval commander Richard Byrd and his copilot Floyd Bennett became the first men to fly over the North Pole in 1926, Wanamaker had Whalen contact the flyers with an offer to build an aircraft to their exact specifications if they would agree to pilot it across the Atlantic. When they said yes, Wanamaker put Whalen in charge of the arrangements. The first thing Whalen did was to sign a contract with Roosevelt Field on Long Island to extend the airfield's dirt runway from one mile to two miles to accommodate Byrd's large, single-wing tri-motor Fokker aircraft.

Although other aviators continued to make preparations for their own attempts, the combination of experience and financing made the Byrd/Bennett team the favorite for the prize until their plane crashed on one of its final test flights. The delay the accident caused opened the door for a plucky twenty-five-year-old Army Air Corps reservist named Charles Lindbergh to enter the contest.

In early May 1927 Lindbergh landed on Long Island in an airplane that was essentially a single-winged, 450-gallon flying fuel tank called the *Spirit of St. Louis.* The press dubbed him the "Flying Fool." Lindbergh asked Whalen for permission to use the extended runway for his takeoff. Whalen was skeptical of Lindbergh's chances but agreed, provided the lanky aviator give him advance notice of his departure date so that he could be there to witness the historic moment for himself.

The forecast for Friday, May 20, called for clear skies. Lindbergh telephoned Whalen the night before and told him that he was taking off in the morning. Whalen arrived at the airfield well before dawn only to find a throng of newspapermen waiting in the hangar. He later learned that a hotel switchboard operator had been bribed by reporters to listen in on his private conversations with Lindbergh.

As the *Spirit of St. Louis* rumbled down the muddy landing strip, Whalen sped alongside it in a motorcar accompanied by mechanics toting fire extinguishers in the event the plane crashed. The airplane barely cleared the electrical wires at the end of the runway and then headed for Europe. The entire nation waited anxiously for the next thirty-three and a half hours until word reached home that the "Lone Eagle" had landed safely in Paris. At that exact moment Lindbergh became a celebrity the likes of which the world had never known before.

It was Whalen's association with Lindbergh that led to the formation of the NYPD's first aviation unit in 1929. Police pilots were recruited from within the ranks and sent to flight-training school at Roosevelt Field. But when they were ready, there were no planes to fly because the Board of Estimate refused to appropriate money to purchase them. Whalen turned to Rodman Wanamaker's nephew and fellow aviation enthusiast for help. The junior Wanamaker used his family connections to acquire two aircraft for the department: an amphibious, bi-wing Keystone-Loening K-84 "Commuter" and a smaller, Italian-designed Savoia Marchetti flying boat. The planes were christened PD-1 and PD-2 respectively. Three months later, in March 1930, two more Savoia Marchetti flying boats were obtained, bringing the department's total compliment of airplanes to four, all of which were stationed at the North Beach Marine Air Terminal in northern Queens, the future home of LaGuardia Airport.

In return for Wannamaker's help, Whalen appointed him deputy commissioner to oversee the department's new flying squadron. Wannamaker was assisted by Whalen's personal secretary and noted aviation expert

Arthur Chamberlain. The uniformed head of the Air Services Division was acting captain and future police commissioner Arthur Wallander.

In February 1930 Whalen founded a magazine for the force called *Spring 3100*, after the old telephone number to Police Headquarters. The cover of the inaugural issue depicted a department airplane soaring over the dome of Police Headquarters.

Whalen borrowed an idea from Police Commissioner Enright to attract budding police writers for the periodical and offered them twenty-five dollars for their best original short stories. In addition, the magazine featured articles by police department experts on topics such as traffic regulations and fingerprint identification. Within each issue were illustrations, promotional exam study questions, and news of interest to the force regarding promotions, retirements, weddings, births, and, sadly, deaths. The back pages of the magazine had a panel of cartoons called "Kop Komics," which humorously depicted a policeman's lot. Although Whalen wrote an article about the new Police College for the first issue, he would not be a longtime contributor to the magazine.

The collapse of the stock market and the mass unemployment that followed had expanded the base of the American Communist Party. Nowhere in the country were Communists more active than in New York City, and they had little use for the police. The local branch of the Communist Party regularly called Whalen the "Capitalist Police Commissioner" and referred to members of the force as "Cossacks."

Whalen believed the Communists were getting out of hand. In order to keep an eye on their activities, lawful and otherwise, he restructured the Police Intelligence Squad and recruited fifty rookies to infiltrate the organization, much the same way Police Commissioner Woods had used undercover officers to spy on anarchists fifteen years before. Whalen's covert operatives informed him that the Communists planned to hold a massive rally at Union Square Park on March 6, 1930, and that it was expected to get violent.

After discussing the situation with the mayor, Whalen had the local Communist Party leader, William Foster, and four of his associates brought to Police Headquarters for a sit-down. Whalen informed them that they needed a permit to hold a demonstration of that size and that he had no intention of giving them one. Foster countered that since he did not respect the laws of the United States, he had no intention of applying for a permit. Whalen would later say that he doubted that any police commissioner had ever been more openly defied than he was at that meeting.

On the day of the rally Whalen and his top aides established a temporary headquarters inside the park grounds. When the number of demonstrators swelled to sixty thousand, Whalen activated the department's contingency plans. First he closed the Union Square subway station to keep the crowd from getting any bigger. Then he had Foster brought over to the temporary headquarters and warned him not to incite a riot. Instead of cooperating, Foster climbed onto the podium and exhorted his comrades to bring their grievances directly to City Hall and suggested that while they were en route, they stop in front of Wanamaker's Department Store and break all of the windows.

Whalen immediately mobilized one thousand reservists, the Emergency Service Division, and three hundred mounted and one hundred motorcycle police to coral the demonstrators in the park. But Foster's speech had stirred his followers into a frenzy. The rally exploded into a pitched battle between police and protesters. Had the Communists advanced past the police blockade and made it to City Hall, they would have been met by a squad of armored motorcycles outfitted with machine guns. Fortunately the police prevented most of the demonstrators from advancing very far out of the park.

Lawyers from the ACLU denounced Whalen for what they described as the NYPD's "liberal use of nightsticks" and offered to represent for free anyone who claimed to be a victim of police brutality. Norman Thomas of the Socialist Party accused Whalen of stirring up "anti-red hysteria" and compared his actions to the infamous Spanish Inquisition.

During the ensuing weeks the ACLU pressured Walker to remove Whalen from office. Newspapers began to print stories that Whalen's resignation was imminent. Although both he and the mayor denied the reports, rumor had it that Walker had grown tired of seeing Whalen's name in the papers more often than his own. Whalen admitted in his autobiography that he felt that Walker was finding it more difficult to be accommodating to him as time went on. He tendered his resignation shortly after persuading the owners of Madison Square Garden not to rent the arena to the Communist Party for its upcoming May Day festivities. He had been in office for a year and a half.

In recounting his time as head of the police department, Whalen wrote to his men, "I shall always look back with pride on the privilege that was accorded to me to serve by your side and shoulder to shoulder with the most fearless and finest organization in the world, the police of the city of New York."

Sixty-four-year-old Chief Inspector John O'Brien was initially considered as a possible replacement for Whalen since Walker made it known that this time around he wanted to appoint someone from within the department, but his advanced age factored against him. In the end Walker selected Assistant Chief Inspector Edward Mulrooney to be his next police commissioner.

Mulrooney was so quiet and unassuming that the reporters covering the press conference at City Hall did not recognize him even though he was standing beside the mayor. Walker appreciated the fact that the low-key Mulrooney would not compete with him for publicity or popularity. Tammany Hall liked him because he was a staunch Democrat with family ties to the organization

Edward Pierce Mulrooney was born in July 1874. His grandfather had sold chickens on the site of Police Headquarters in Manhattan. His father, an Irish immigrant, made his living piloting boats along the Hudson River. Mulrooney dropped out of Cooper Union High School at age sixteen to join his father on the waterfront. After five years navigating the treacherous waters of New York Harbor, he answered Police Board president Theodore Roosevelt's call for able-bodied honest men to join the police department in 1896. His prior experience on the river served him well. All three of his departmental citations involved taking action in water, including the rescue operation during the *General Slocum* disaster.

There was a general consensus that Whalen had left the department in far better shape than he had found it. Mulrooney thought it best to follow the course set by him. Other than to say that he expected the men to show more restraint, he indicated that he would not make any drastic changes. For himself, however, he discontinued Whalen's practice of being accompanied everywhere he went by a police bodyguard. When reporters asked him why he was shedding his security officer, Mulrooney pointed to the revolver on his hip and said that it was all the protection he needed.

Mulrooney had hoped that his policy of police restraint would appease the ACLU, but soon after he took office, another violent confrontation between police and Communists occurred at Union Square. The ACLU once again alleged that the police had turned a peaceful demonstration into "a bloody massacre." Mulrooney ordered Deputy Chief Inspector James Bolan, who was in command of the detail, to review the conduct of his police officers during the rampage. But the ACLU called the inquiry a farce and advised the alleged victims not to cooperate with the investigation. Bolan had no choice but to produce a report based solely on his interviews with the police participants. Naturally it was one-sided. Without any evidence to the contrary, Mulrooney could only conclude that the police had not employed undue force in their attempts to control the demonstrators during the riot.

On the evening of August 6, 1930, Judge Joseph Force Crater said good night to two dinner companions on West Forty-Fifth Street. He told them that that he was off to catch a Broadway show, but he was never seen again, despite being the subject of the most intensive missing-person search in department history to that point. The mystery might have been solved if the judge's wife had not waited several weeks before informing the police that her husband was missing. Although Crater's public persona was that of a devoted husband, in reality he was a cad who regularly cheated on her—not that she seemed to mind. Mrs. Crater enjoyed the perks that went along with being married to a prominent public figure. The couple lived on Fifth Avenue and had a summer cabin in Maine, which was where she had last seen him. He told her that he was returning to New York to take care of a problem. She never thought to ask what the problem was.

Mrs. Crater began to make inquiries only after several days had passed, but both his chauffer and a private investigator she hired to find her husband assured her that he would return soon. Finally, after almost a month had gone by without her having heard from him, she notified the police. Crater's disappearance immediately became front-page news.

Within a week detectives had a pretty good idea of every place that the judge had been in the months leading up to the night he vanished, but after that the trail went cold. They learned that he had taken his mistress to Atlantic City for an overnight stay the day after he left his wife in Maine. They knew that he had visited his office the day before he disappeared and removed some files. Later that day he withdrew $5,150 from his bank account. There was also evidence that Crater had paid an unknown benefactor with ties to Tammany Hall $22,500 for the privilege of sitting on the bench.

News of the payoff was soon linked to a special investigation already under way by Samuel Seabury, at the request of Governor Franklin Roosevelt, to determine whether or not a judge named George Ewald had paid someone in Tammany Hall $10,000 to secure his appointment. Testimony at the Ewald hearings would force several municipal judges connected to Tammany Hall, including New York's first woman magistrate, Jean Norris, to resign in disgrace. Meanwhile, Crater's disappearance lent credence to the theory that he had gone into hiding to avoid suffering the same fate as his colleagues. Others insisted, however, that he had been murdered for fear that his testimony would bring down the careers of several prominent Tammany Hall politicians.

A special grand jury was convened by the newly elected Manhattan district attorney, Thomas Crain, to determine what had happened to Judge Crater. Over the next several months Crater's wife, friends, coworkers, political associates, and paramours were questioned under oath. Leaked testimony concerning the judge's scandalous affairs with showgirls and divorcees kept the public riveted at a time when it should have been much more interested in the country's worsening economic crisis. Although the police tracked thousands of leads over the years, it was all for naught. In 1939 the Surrogate's Court declared Judge Crater legally dead so that his wife, who had declared bankruptcy, could finally collect on his insurance policy.

Seabury's inquiry sparked separate investigations into the NYPD and the Walker administration. Corruption in the judiciary was just part of a much larger money-making scheme that involved the police department and the highest levels of city government.

Policemen assigned to vice enforcement quickly returned to their old ways once they no longer had to worry about Valentine and the Confidential Squad looking over their shoulders. Seabury's primary witness against the Vice Squad was a stool pigeon who went by the name of Chile Mapocha Acuna. The police had another name for him: the "Human Spittoona."

Acuna had worked closely with plainclothesmen to frame innocent women for profit, until the police double-crossed him. He decided to tell his story to Seabury, but he feared that he would not live long enough to testify once his identity was made public. Fortunately for him Mulrooney had no use for corrupt officers. He detailed six lieutenants to watch Acuna around the clock and told them that if anything bad happened to Acuna before his appearance, their own careers would be finished as well.

Acuna's tale was so lurid that Seabury ordered that all women be removed from the courtroom during his testimony. According to Acuna, he earned $150 a week framing innocent women as prostitutes. One of his ploys was to pose as a patient at a doctor's office. If the nurse was alone, he would discreetly slip a marked bill on the examination table and proceed to disrobe. The Vice Squad would then bust through the door and arrest the unsuspecting nurse for prostitution. At some point a plainclothesman would pull the nurse aside and pretend to be concerned for her reputation. Then he would offer to overlook her indiscretion in exchange for cash.

Acuna employed a similar ruse on female landlords. The police would give him marked money to rent a room in a boarding house. Then he would invite over a gullible young lady. As soon as the girl entered the boarding house, the police would barge in and arrest her for prostitution and charge the landlord with running a brothel. Of course the police would agree to look the other way for the right amount of money. Sometimes the women waited until they were before a judge to cut a deal. In those instances the police had to share their profits with the magistrate to get the women off.

It was a lucrative racket for all involved. Every cop assigned to vice enforcement had a "tin box" stashed somewhere with a wad of cash. Mulrooney was so disgusted by what he heard that he suspended every plainclothes officer Acuna identified as taking part in the scheme. Many of them wound up in jail; the rest he transferred back to uniformed patrol after their department trials. But this created a whole new problem for Mulrooney. Very few officers were willing to take their place, so Mulrooney drafted patrolmen who had passed the sergeants exam and were waiting for their list numbers to be reached. Since any blunder on their part could result in their being passed over for promotion, he felt that they would not succumb to the temptations that had ruined the careers of their colleagues. The draftees, however, were reluctant to make arrests for fear that a mistake would derail their careers.

As for Acuna, he died from a brain tumor two years after his appearance.

By November 1930 it was evident that the Depression would not end any-time soon, despite President Hoover's claim that prosperity was just around the corner. Walker directed that each city agency make provisions for the destitute. In the police department the assignment was given to a new unit called the Unemployment Relief Bureau. Its primary function was to acquire canned goods, vegetables, and apparel through private donations and then deliver the products to New York City's most impoverished families. In addition, all NYPD officers were required to contribute between fifty cents and five dollars per month, depending on their rank, to a special fund to help the poor who were strapped for cash. In his 1930 Christmas message to the force, Mulrooney said that despite the hard times, he was consoled by the fact that for many families in New York City blue-uniformed patrolmen had filled the role of red-suited Santa Clauses.

In June 1931 the Crime Prevention Bureau that Whalen had formed the year before as an experimental unit to combat juvenile delinquency was made permanent, along with provisions in the City Charter for a sixth dep-uty commissioner to administer it. Mulrooney appointed the department's second-ever female deputy commissioner, a native Georgian named Henrietta Addison, to the post. Addison was a renowned social worker, author, and authority on childhood delinquency. "Preventing these delinquencies is the job of both policewomen and patrolwomen as well as the policemen," she said.

Addison's staff was comprised of 182 members of the force, the highest-ranking being Inspector Louis Costuma, who would go on to one day become the first Jewish member of the department to reach the rank of chief inspector. Of her work Addison explained to the *New York Times*, "It is not highbrow, but just a simple attempt to help children." In reality the children she spoke of were teenage ruffians who ran with gangs. She hoped to modify their behavior with the help of a new organization called the Junior Police Athletic League, otherwise known as PAL. It was to provide wholesome recreational activities for the wayward youth of the city. The New York Yankee slugger Babe Ruth, who had had his own share of problems growing up, became spokesman for the league, while Mulrooney served as honorary chairman.

After he had exposed the dirty dealings of the NYPD Vice Squad, Sea-bury let it be known that he was setting his sights on Mayor Walker.

Governor Roosevelt made a halfhearted effort to stop Seabury, whom he had appointed, but he was more concerned about his presidential prospects and how it would look if he tried to shield Walker. He decided to let Seabury continue his inquiry.

Seabury called the "Honest Cop," Lewis Valentine, to the stand in September 1931. Captain Valentine insinuated that Walker had forced Warren out of office because Warren had refused to stop the raids on the political clubs. Valentine said that Walker considered the gambling taking place inside the political clubs to be petty, but in many instances the raids the Confidential Squad conducted netted professional gamblers. One man who was paying particular attention to Valentine's testimony was Fiorello LaGuardia. Valentine's disclosure would prove useful for his campaign when he ran for mayor in 1933.

Valentine's appearance was followed by that of former police commissioner Grover Whalen. Seabury did his best to coax him into admitting that he had demoted Valentine and disbanded the Confidential Squad at Walker's behest to prevent any further raids on the political clubs. Whalen insisted that was not the case. He said that he had done what he had done because the Confidential Squad under Valentine had become so powerful that its authority superseded that of the chief inspector. Since he had been appointed to bring a corporate, businesslike acumen to the police department, Whalen thought it bad policy for an underling to wield so much influence. For the moment it appeared that Whalen had saved the mayor, but there were other witnesses that Seabury wanted to hear from.

Twenty-month-old Charles Lindbergh Jr. was kidnapped from his nursery on the second floor of the family residence in Hopewell, New Jersey, on the night of March 1, 1932. A ransom note demanding $50,000, splotches of red clay caked on the nursery floor, and parts from a crude wooden ladder located some distance from the house were the only clues left by the kidnappers.

Although the crime had been committed seventy-five miles away from New York City, Mulrooney put every available cop on the case. He instructed his men to search tenements and tunnels, canvass hospitals and hotels, and look anywhere and everywhere that the kidnappers might hide out. He told them to be alert, keep on their toes, and investigate every clue.

Over the next several days Lindbergh received two more ransom notes from the kidnappers. Since both letters were postmarked in Brooklyn, Mulrooney sought Lindbergh's permission to set up a surveillance of all mailboxes in the borough. In the event a suspect was discovered, Mulrooney wanted to have his detectives follow the suspect and raid whatever premises the suspect entered. Lindbergh adamantly opposed the plan for fear that his son could be killed during the raid. He threatened to personally ruin Mulrooney's career if he carried through with the plan. Mulrooney realized Lindbergh had enough clout to do it, so he backed off the idea.

In the meantime a person outside of law enforcement named John Condon convinced Lindbergh he had a better way to get the baby back. Condon took out several newspaper ads using the alias "Jafsie" in an attempt to communicate with the kidnappers. His plan worked, but Lindbergh did not notify the police that Condon had been contacted by his son's abductor. Instead Lindbergh let Condon arrange for a midnight rendezvous with the kidnapper in St. Raymond's Cemetery in the Bronx. Lindbergh and Condon arrived at the graveyard with a box containing $50,000 in gold certificates. The arrangement called for Condon to hand the money over in exchange for information from the kidnapper concerning the whereabouts of Lindbergh's young son.

Lindbergh kept to the shadows and watched as Condon passed the ransom money to a man who identified himself only as "John." From where he was standing Lindbergh never actually saw the man's face, nor did he or Condon attempt to follow him when he left the cemetery with the money. It was only several hours later, when Lindbergh discovered that he had been duped, that he finally called the police and informed them about what had transpired in the cemetery. For all of the mistakes he had made, Lindbergh fortunately had kept a record of the serial number for each bill in the ransom packet. This information would become crucial to police two years later, when one of the marked bills turned up at a bank in the Bronx.

Sadly the toddler's badly decomposed corpse was found a month later by a truck driver named William Allen, who had happened to stop by the side of the road near the Lindbergh residence to relieve himself.

Despite testimony from Whalen that seemed to contradict that of Valentine, Seabury had amassed enough evidence against Walker through other witnesses to bring charges against him. In particular he wanted Walker to answer questions about $26,000 worth of bonds that he had accepted from J. A. Sisto, a major investor in the taxicab industry. Sisto's profits were being eroded by the large number of privately owned cabs prowling the streets for fares. In exchange for the bonds, the mayor sponsored legislation to limit the number of taxicabs operating in the city, a limitation that in turn increased the dividends for Sisto and his fellow shareholders.

After consulting with his own legal experts and determining that he had no choice in the matter, Walker quipped to reporters that there were three things that a man must do alone: "be born, die, and testify." He was scheduled to appear on May 25, 1932. Walker was cagey, witty, charming, and congenial in the courtroom. After his first day on the stand he felt so confident that he had won the day that he punned, "Life is just a bowl of Seaburys." But the mayor was wrong. His next hearing did not go nearly as well when he could not explain how $700,000 ended up in his bank account. It did not help matters that the accountant who handled his personal finances had fled to Mexico.

Seabury submitted his findings to Governor Roosevelt in a letter on June 8, 1932. Roosevelt waited until he had secured the Democratic Party nomination for president before calling Walker to Albany to discuss the best way to resolve the case against him. Walker waited until the end of the summer to submit his letter of resignation, along with a statement defending his administration. Although Walker had secretly struck a deal in which the charges would be set aside in exchange for his resignation, he proclaimed that Seabury had proved nothing. Ten days later Walker sailed for Europe, after making a promise to return and seek reelection. But he apparently had a change of heart while overseas. Walker stayed away for three years, during which time he divorced his wife and married his longtime paramour, actress Betty Compton. The president of the Board of Aldermen, Joseph McKee, assumed the office of mayor on September 2, 1932, as per the City Charter.

McKee was born in Newark, New Jersey, in 1889. His father was an engraver by trade who hailed from Glasgow. When McKee was a youngster, his family moved to the Bronx, where he attended public school and Fordham University. After graduation McKee stayed on at the university, teaching Greek and Latin while pursuing a law degree.

In 1918 McKee won election as a state assemblyman representing the Seventh Assembly District in the Bronx and became friendly with his colleague

Jimmy Walker. Governor Smith appointed him to a judgeship in 1924, but after just one year on the bench McKee left to run for president of the Board of Aldermen. Although he was a staunch Democrat, he was often at odds with his own party, so when he took over as mayor pro tem, Tammany Hall demanded that an interim election be held to determine who should rightfully finish out the remainder of Walker's term. McKee and his supporters thought the charter was clear on the order of succession but agreed that they would let the courts make the final decision.

In the meantime McKee let it be known that he intended to keep Mulrooney on, while he did what he could to rein in the city's budget. Walker's failure to enact any real cost-cutting measures had left the city $80 million in the red. Before he resigned, Walker had given police officers the option to accept a voluntary pay cut equal to one month's wages or face layoffs. The policemen voted to accept Walker's proposal to reduce their salaries, but his legal troubles prevented the plan from being implemented. Rather than reopening the matter for discussion, McKee told the police that he would institute immediate pay cuts across the board to help make up for the deficit. Although the deputy controller disagreed with him about the amount of savings the pay cuts would actually produce for the city, individual officers saw their top salaries and intermediate pay steps go down between $110 and $140 per year, depending on their rank. Even Mulrooney was forced to take a 10 percent pay cut.

Once the Court of Appeals ruled in Tammany Hall's favor that an interim election was necessary, McKee announced that he would not run for mayor. That left Tammany Hall free to nominate whomever it wanted. The organization selected Surrogate Court justice John P. O'Brien, a longtime party man who had once served as the city's corporation counsel. O'Brien's platform was simple: hold the line on taxes and provide more home relief to the destitute.

In the November 1932 election O'Brien tallied more than a million votes on the coattails of Franklin Roosevelt, who easily defeated Herbert Hoover for president. O'Brien hailed his victory and those of his fellow New York Democrats, Senator Robert Wagner and Governor Herbert Lehman, as a landslide for democracy. Although O'Brien won by the largest plurality of any mayoral candidate in city history, McKee, whose name did not appear anywhere on the ballot, received an unprecedented 234,000 write-in votes. He would remain acting mayor until January 1 and then return to his duties as president of the Board of Aldermen.

On December 14, 1932, at one o'clock in the morning, Patrolman George Gerhard, assigned to the Twentieth Precinct was killed in the line of duty. He had inadvertently interrupted the holdup of a cordial shop on Amsterdam Avenue. According to police sources, Gerhard had gone into the store after a driver whom he had observed running a red light, while his partner, Patrolman James Galligan, remained outside with the vehicle. Neither officer realized until it was too late that an armed robbery was under way. Gerhard was shot seven times.

Galligan captured one of the two perpetrators fleeing the shop. The second gunman commandeered a taxicab with two female passengers in the back seat. (The women were later identified as the mother and sister of comedian Milton Berle.) During the pursuit the police officers and the holdup man exchanged multiple rounds until the taxi crashed and came to a halt. Although the sedan was riddled with bullet holes, not a single shot had struck either woman. The robber, however, took a round to the chest. He was identified as William Vogel, a twenty-four-year-old ex-convict.

Vogel's accomplice, Ralph Florence, was a seventeen-year-old with a long record of juvenile offenses. Florence pinned Gerhard's shooting on Vogel, who was unable to give his side of the story due to his condition. The next day a grand jury indicted both men for murder. The officers involved in the apprehension received medals for their efforts, and Gerhard's name was forever enshrined on a bronze tablet at Police Headquarters.

Gerhard was the twenty-first officer killed in the line of duty in the two and a half years that Mulrooney had been police commissioner, and although Mulrooney had preached restraint, he decided the time had come to issue new orders to the force for dealing with armed criminals. The orders went far beyond Whalen's "treat 'em rough" policies. Mulrooney told his men, "The bandits and youthful criminals of today are ruthless killers. You must shoot first."

At the trial Vogel claimed that he was drunk the night of the robbery and had no recollection of the shooting. His testimony did not sway the jury. Six months later he was executed at Sing Sing Prison. Vogel's young cohort was declared insane after faking fits while in detention. Florence spent the next thirty years in a state mental hospital before being released in 1963, without ever having had to answer for his part in Gerhard's death.

Mayor O'Brien was born in 1873 in Worcester, Massachusetts. His father was a building superintendent. After high school he attended Holy Cross College and Georgetown University Law School. Then he moved to New York City in 1897 and entered private practice. In 1901 he was appointed an assistant corporation counsel until 1920, when Mayor Hylan put him in charge as corporation counsel. In 1922 he won election as a Surrogate Court judge and remained in that post until his nomination for mayor. As a judge he steadfastly opposed subway and utility increases, a stance that was very popular with the public. He married Helen Madigan in 1908 and had four sons and a daughter. In addition to his longtime affiliation with Tammany Hall, O'Brien was involved with many Catholic organizations, especially the Knights of Columbus.

During his inaugural address he pledged, "Every phase of City government will be examined," but he offered no specific plan or timetable for change. He also gave Mulrooney time to find another post rather than have him suffer the embarrassment of being let go after such a long and dignified career with the NYPD. Three months later Mulrooney left to become head of the newly formed State Alcoholic Beverage Control Board. He said that he expected that his new job would keep him very busy because the long drought was about to end and thousands of former speakeasies were already seeking to become legitimate places of business.

When reporters asked O'Brien whether Mulrooney's successor would be a member of the force or an outsider, the mayor said, "I have no word on that yet," an indication that the decision was not entirely his own. Behind the scenes various factions within the Democratic Party were pushing their own candidates for the post. Finally the new Tammany Hall boss, John Curry, made the decision for them and told O'Brien that Deputy Chief Inspector James Bolan, the cop who had put down the Communist riot at Union Square Park, would be the new police commissioner.

Bolan was of Scottish descent. Like Mayor O'Brien he was born in 1873 in Worchester, Massachusetts. Prior to joining the police department in 1896 he had worked at a hotel in Ossining, New York. Bolan moved up the ladder fast. By 1915 he was already an inspector, but his career stalled for several years after Police Commissioner Enright charged him with a failure to enforce the prohibition statutes. Congressman Fiorello LaGuardia, who was disgusted by the hypocrisy of prohibition, offered to defend him at the department trial for free against the charges, but Bolan accepted a fifteen-day fine instead.

When McLaughlin became police commissioner, he elevated Bolan to deputy chief inspector and placed him in command of the Third Inspection District in Manhattan. The area included the notorious Tenderloin and Union Square Park, the site of the violent "Red" demonstrations where his tactics had come under fire. It was said that Bolan's life revolved around police work, and as such he never had time for a wife.

As Mayor O'Brien pinned on Bolan's new shield at a low-key ceremony at City Hall, he stated, "In all of your endeavors, you will have my complete support." "I wish to assure you," Bolan responded, "that no act of mine will ever cause you to regret the confidence you have placed in me." In other words Bolan had no intention of letting another embarrassing police scandal ruin O'Brien's chances for reelection to a full four-year term in the fall. Bolan was expected to keep the lid on crime and the police department off the front page.

In order to do that Bolan decided that the department needed to shape up. He was a martinet who detested laxity among ranking officers. He hated the half-hearted salutes policemen gave to superiors. He despised scuffed shoes and wrinkled uniforms. He loathed poor posture and a slovenly appearance. To correct all such problems he ordered his sergeants to attend a special three-day training course on how to properly supervise subordinates and act like superior officers. He wanted smart salutes, polished shoes, and uniforms with sharp creases. He also thought that police officers should be able to communicate in proper English. "Police problems call for courteous public service, involving accurate information spoken in clear-cut grammatical language," he explained after he contracted the City College of New York to teach English to policemen during their off-duty hours.

After the embarrassing revelations that had come out of the Seabury Committee hearings, Mulrooney had reorganized the Vice Squad by limiting the number of plainclothesmen to a small cadre of draftees. Bolan considered the arrangement untenable because the staffing level was too small to effectively deal with the problems. He did not believe that vice crimes could be reduced in the city by having fewer police officers take less action, even if it resulted in fewer police officers getting in trouble. So he returned to the old system whereby district inspectors picked their own plainclothesmen in numbers they thought sufficient to address vice complaints. He also changed the unit's name to the Public Morals Squads and for the first time paid officers in the detail an extra $240 per year as an incentive to stay honest. The men in uniform immediately cried foul and sought additional compensation for themselves. Bolan called their complaint "rubbish."

The 1933 mayoral election was fast approaching. O'Brien was being challenged by two men who had previously served as presidents of the Board of Aldermen. The Fusion Party candidate was former congressman Fiorello LaGuardia. He had lost his congressional seat the year before during the Roosevelt sweep and had lost the mayor's race in 1929 to Jimmy Walker while running as a Republican. Joseph McKee, bolstered by his strong showing as a write-in candidate for mayor the year before, was actively running this time as an independent on the Recovery Party ticket. Of the three main candidates he was considered the most polished orator, but he was tainted by his previous affiliation with Tammany Hall even after his fallout.

During the campaign O'Brien pushed his agenda, while LaGuardia and McKee traded insults. LaGuardia called McKee a Tammany hack and a bigot. McKee fired back, calling LaGuardia a Communist who wanted to destroy the capitalist system. Shortly before the election Tammany Hall issued a statement that if what the two candidates were saying about each other was true, then the only logical choice for mayor was the Tammany man, John O'Brien.

Bolan put the entire force on a thirty-two-hour shift to prevent any voting irregularities during the election. Over 2 million ballots were cast. LaGuardia won with a plurality of 800,000 votes. McKee placed second, while O'Brien came in third, but between the two of them they received more votes than LaGuardia.

Samuel Seabury, who had championed LaGuardia during the campaign, was thrilled that Tammany Hall had been defeated. He declared that with LaGuardia's victory the cause of good municipal government would be won in New York City and promoted in every city in the United States. Ironically years later Seabury and LaGuardia would have a falling out after LaGuardia, as a favor to his friend President Roosevelt, appointed Jimmy Walker as an impartial arbitrator to hear disputes in the women's garment industry. Seabury accused LaGuardia of stepping down from his leadership role among those striving for decent municipal government.

Bolan had done a good job, but he knew that LaGuardia had already decided to replace him even before the election. Bolan could have returned to the uniformed ranks but chose to bow out gracefully instead. He sent LaGuardia a telegram congratulating him on his victory and informing him that he planned to leave office at the end of O'Brien's term. His last official duty was to oversee the giant end of a prohibition celebration at Times Square on New Year's Eve. For the first time in thirteen years liquor was being freely consumed by the public. The police made a handful of arrests during the night to show that even if drinking was legal, drunken behavior still was an offense.

With O'Brien's loss to LaGuardia went Tammany Hall's fortunes. The Democrats were forced to take a back seat to the Fusionists for the next twelve years. O'Brien returned to his private law practice and resumed his association with Catholic charities. He died in 1951 after a long illness at the age of seventy-eight. His close personal friend, Cardinal Francis Spellman, presided over his funeral mass at St. Patrick's Cathedral.

Joseph McKee never again sought public office after he lost his bid for mayor. He did, however, accept a post as commissioner of commerce under Mayor William O'Dwyer for one dollar per year. During his four months in office as acting mayor McKee gave O'Dwyer a big career boost when he appointed him as a judge. McKee passed away in 1956 after suffering a fatal heart attack. He was sixty-six years old. Although he was mayor for only a short time, he made tough choices when cutting the policemen's salaries and trimmed the budget to start the city on the road toward fiscal stability.

As for Jimmy Walker, the *Daily News* wrote upon his departure from office, "He has been the most charming and attractive public official possibly that we ever had. But he has been deplorably lacking, we believe, in a sense of dignity of his office."

Walker did not let such comments bother him. "I have long known that if one goes into politics, he must be prepared to take it on the chin. I have taken it on the chin many times," he mused. Even after receiving word that the charges against him had all been dropped, Walker did not hasten to return home. For three years he and his bride roamed the continent. When Walker finally came back to New York in 1935, he received a hero's welcome. Everywhere he went crowds swarmed around him, just as they had when he was mayor. Although he had many offers for employment, he turned them all down. When asked why, he explained, tongue in cheek, that taking gratuities from friends was what got him into trouble in the first place.

In 1937 Walker accepted a position on the State Transit Commission. The following year, as noted, LaGuardia appointed him as a labor arbitrator at President Roosevelt's behest. Seabury claimed the mayor had betrayed him, but LaGuardia believed that Seabury was more upset with Roosevelt's liberal agenda than with his giving Walker a job.

After Walker's second wife died in 1944, he moved in with his sister. He continued to make public appearances, but over the next two years his health began to show signs of decline. Walker was speaking at a testimonial dinner honoring the owner of the New York Giants football team in the autumn of 1946 when his loose dentures slipped right out of his mouth. Although he made a joke of it, he was humiliated. When he got home that night, he told his sister, "It's all over."

From that point on his health deteriorated rapidly. He passed away several weeks later on November 18, 1946. He was sixty-five years old. Judging by the enormous number of mourners who attended his funeral at St. Patrick's Cathedral, the citizens of New York had forgiven him for his many faults. Despite Seabury's efforts to convince the public otherwise, the people really did love Jimmy Walker in December as they had in May.

Walker's first police commissioner, George McLaughlin, fared very well after he left the department. After a short stint as the vice president of a telegraph conglomerate, he returned to banking as president of the Brooklyn Trust Company and oversaw the finances of the Brooklyn Dodgers. While he had a real talent for banking, he said that the job he enjoyed most of all was that of police commissioner. On occasion, usually after imbibing a bit, he would tell anyone willing to listen that he was the best police commissioner the city had ever had. There is no doubt that he had reshaped the department during his brief tenure and restored a modicum of accountability. In his later years he served as vice chairman of the Triborough Bridge and Tunnel Authority and later as director of the 1964–65 World's Fair Corporation. He died of a heart attack in December 1967. He was eighty years old.

Police Commissioner Joseph Warren died in August 1929 after suffering a paralytic stroke while under psychiatric care at the Blythewood Sanitarium in Greenwich, Connecticut. His friends attributed his premature death at the age of forty-seven to the strain of being police commissioner.

If Warren's successor ever felt the stress of the office, it certainly did not show. After he resigned, Grover Whalen continued to put his salesman skills to good use on behalf of the city that he loved. After he was named president of the 1939 World's Fair, which was to take place at Flushing Meadows Park in Queens, he traveled around the world trying to convince heads of state to have their countries take part in what he described as the greatest exposition ever created.

Whalen said that his most memorable encounter was with Benito Mussolini. The dictator spoke English quite well for an Italian, as Whalen recalled. But before he could tell him about the fair, Mussolini said, "I understand you served as police commissioner of New York." Whalen said that he had.

"How did my people behave?"

Whalen shrugged, "Some good, some bad."

"The bad ones," Mussolini shrugged, "from Sicily."

Then the two men discussed fascism, which Mussolini claimed was the same as President Roosevelt's "New Deal." By the end of the meeting Whalen had won him over. Mussolini committed $5 million for the construction of an Italian pavilion at the fair.

While the two-year World's Fair exhibition was not the financial success its sponsors had hoped for, it kept Whalen in the spotlight. He continued to host ticker-tape parades until Mayor Robert Wagner replaced him in 1953.

In 1955 G. P. Putnam's Sons published Whalen's autobiography, appropriately titled *Mr. New York*, wherein he recounted his many exciting life experiences, including his days with the police department.

When Whalen died at age seventy-five in April 1962, the police magazine he founded, *Spring 3100*, praised his seventeen months at the helm of the department. The editors touted his successful efforts to improve morale and train recruits. Among his long-standing accomplishments was putting an end to the long dreaded reserve duty and establishing the modern Emergency Service Division and Aviation Division (known today as the Emergency Service Unit and Aviation Unit). He put the men in more comfortable uniforms and created the Bureau of Crime Prevention to deal with juvenile problems. It eventually gave way to the Youth Division and is presently called the Youth Services Section.

Police Commissioner Edward Mulrooney was not nearly as flashy as his predecessor, precisely why Walker selected him in the first place. He came through the ranks and served as police commissioner for three years, longer than any of the other men Walker appointed, and was in office during the administration's most turbulent times.

As chairman of the State Alcoholic Beverage Control Board, Mulrooney deftly managed the transition from illegal to legal drinking in the state. He then went on to serve as commissioner of the state prison system and later served as an impartial arbitrator mediating labor matters involving workers in the hotel industry. Mulroney passed away at his Manhattan residence in 1960 at the age of eighty-five after a long and debilitating illness.

Although John Bolan was police commissioner for only a brief time, he reaffirmed the notion that a police department must enforce the law even at its own peril. Bolan went on to found his own private detective agency and later formed the Bolan Academy, a correspondence school for students interested in the study of criminology. He died of heart disease in May 1952 at his home in the Bronx, where he resided with his sister. He was seventy-nine years old.

The five men who had served as police commissioners during the administrations of Walker, McKee, and O'Brien had each been hindered to some extent by each mayor's association or disassociation with Tammany Hall, yet great strides were made by the police department through the introduction of new technologies such as radio motor patrol cars, automatic traffic lights, improved communications, and modern aircraft. In addition, the size of the patrol force grew by several thousand men. Unfortunately budget realities brought about by the Depression forced the department to put most of those advancements on the back burner until the end of World War II.

8

AN "HONEST COP"
LEADS BY EXAMPLE

The collapse of the stock market in October 1929 proved to New Yorkers just how fragile their lives really were during the "Roaring Twenties." In the panic following the crash citizens turned to their elected officials only to discover that the very men they had entrusted to be their saviors in times of crisis were little more than thieves and con artists themselves. It became all too evident that no amount of political rhetoric could save anyone once the slide began. When people finally realized what had been happening and that the questionable and often criminal activities had been at their own expense, the outcry shook the very foundations of party politics in New York City.

During times of prosperity New Yorkers tended to shrug off such questionable occurrences with benign indifference. Corrupt public officials were certainly nothing new. They had become an accepted reality of life in the city. But after the crash honesty and integrity became important again. Men who could not be bought were the ones to whom the public turned. The reemergence of the Fusion Party brought together a new breed of leaders who owed their alliance to no single political party, only to the people who had elected them. The hero of the Depression era was a nominal Republican who ran as the Fusion candidate for mayor of New York and defeated the most powerful political machine of his generation, dealing Tammany Hall such a crippling blow that it never fully recovered its former prominence.

Fiorello LaGuardia, affectionately known as the "Little Flower," was the son of a Jewish mother and an immigrant Italian musician who had come to America in the late 1800s and settled in New York. Although the future mayor was born in Greenwich Village in 1882, he was reared on the western frontier, where his father, an army bandmaster, was stationed. His boyhood experiences in and around Fort Whipple, Arizona, served him well later in life.

After reading Jacob Riis's famous expose, *How the Other Half Lives*, describing the brutal conditions in the city slums, LaGuardia became determined to make a difference in people's lives. But to achieve his goal he needed an education. He took evening classes at New York University Law School and earned a living as an interpreter for the Immigration Service. During his final year of study LaGuardia was assigned to Night Court to determine if any of the immigrants the police had arrested for vice crimes could be deported. The experience proved to be an eye-opener. Within a short time LaGuardia became familiar with the system of payoffs at the heart of the city's commercial vice racket. He saw police officers usher in prostitutes with whom they appeared to have a congenial association. He watched lawyers negotiate deals off to the side with judges who willingly doled out light sentences in exchange for money.

LaGuardia was not the only witness to this form of organized corruption, but he was one of the few extremely repulsed by it. It was all too evident to him that such arrangements were in place to fatten the bank accounts of the politicians who sanctioned them. Memories of his early courtroom experiences stayed with LaGuardia for the rest of his life.

Although his grades suffered from his busy schedule, LaGuardia said that he did not go to law school to become a legal scholar; he went to become a politician. To that end he joined the local Republican club. In 1914 LaGuardia ran for Congress. The Fourteenth Congressional District was regarded as solidly Democratic and controlled by Tammany Hall. LaGuardia was given no chance to defeat the incumbent. Undaunted by the odds, he campaigned fervently, and even though he lost, he polled enough votes for the Republican Party leadership to help him secure a patronage appointment in the attorney general's office.

LaGuardia ran for Congress again in 1916. This time he upset the same Tammany Democrat who had beaten him two years before. But he wanted to be more than a Capitol Hill lawmaker. He wanted to make his mark on society. He decided to join the war effort overseas, not with words but with actions. In July 1917 LaGuardia enlisted in the U.S. Army's Aviation Section as a pilot and was stationed in Foggia, Italy. His passion to serve captured the country's attention. Almost overnight the "soldier statesman," as he was called, became the nation's most famous legislator. But a war hero in far off Italy left his constituents without a voice in Washington, and Tammany Hall was anxious to regain the lost seat. The Democrats forwarded a petition with three thousand signatures to the Speaker of the House, demanding that LaGuardia's seat be declared vacant and that a special election be held to fill it. When LaGuardia heard the news, he said that if any of his constituents wished to take his place in a Caproni bomber, he would be more than happy to return to his "upholstered seat in the House."

The Speaker refused to act on the petition, noting that Congressman LaGuardia's military service entitled him to the loyal support of his constituents. LaGuardia returned from Italy just one week before the election and immediately hit the campaign trail, still wearing his uniform. He won reelection with nearly 70 percent of the vote.

When World War I ended, LaGuardia resigned his commission and returned to Congress. He could have basked in his wartime glory and reaped the fruits of his nationwide fame, but he wanted to be mayor of New York. In 1919 he relinquished his seat in the House and ran for president of the Board of Aldermen, New York City's second most prominent political office and a potential stepping-stone to mayor.

LaGuardia won handily, but he soon discovered that prominence was not to be confused with importance. For the most part LaGuardia found the Board of Aldermen to be an inept legislative body. Its weekly meetings were devoted to naming streets, changing numbers on buildings, regulating theaters, authorizing parades, and designating play streets. It seemed to him that the job for which the board had been created—that is, to oversee the city's massive fiscal budget—had been long forgotten. Half-billion dollar budgets were approved after little more than a cursory examination. LaGuardia used his power as Aldermanic president to try and harness the city's ever-expanding budget, and while he was incorruptible, he operated on the assumption that most other politicians were not. As he increased his knowledge of municipal operations, he uncovered rampant profiteering in nearly every branch of city government. When he thought that he had learned enough, LaGuardia resigned from office in 1921 to run against Mayor Hylan, but he overestimated his popularity and failed to muster enough support within the Republican Party to even get on the ballot.

The following year LaGuardia set his sights on Congress again in the newly created Twentieth District in East Harlem. He defeated the Tammany candidate in another close race. In 1929 he was nominated by the Republicans to run against the flamboyant incumbent mayor, James Walker. Despite reports of Walker's political ineptitude and allegations of personal immorality, the mayor was extremely popular. LaGuardia got trounced, but his instincts proved correct. Walker resigned from office during his second term.

Joseph McKee, president of the Board of Aldermen, succeeded Walker as acting mayor until a special election could be held to decide who should finish out Walker's term. That contest was won by Tammany Hall loyalist John O'Brien, riding the coattails of Franklin Roosevelt's landslide victory over Herbert Hoover. The same landslide swept many Republicans out of Congress, including LaGuardia. Although he was anxious for another shot at the mayoralty, he knew that the Republicans by themselves did not possess the strength to defeat even a mediocre Tammany candidate in the 1933 mayoral election. It would be necessary for a political reform movement to attract the support of many disenchanted factions. LaGuardia called for a "sincere Fusion movement," a merging of parties to reclaim city politics from the Tammany machine.

The Fusion Party's choice came down to two candidates who were complete opposites. Fiorello LaGuardia was a liberal Republican with Socialist leanings. General John F. O'Ryan was a staunch conservative, a distinguished lawyer, and the vice chairman of the state Republican Party. His views were tempered by his military experiences in the famed Seventh Regiment, where he began as an enlisted man and rose all the way to major general during World War I.

Each man had a solid core of boosters, but the Fusion Party could support only one candidate. On August 4, 1933, with the election just three and a half months away, O'Ryan withdrew from the race with the understanding that if LaGuardia became mayor, he would appoint O'Ryan as police commissioner.

During the campaign LaGuardia stressed integrity in government and promised to eliminate corruption. He claimed that Tammany Hall's ties to organized crime had allowed gangsters to clamp the city in a stranglehold.

Former acting mayor Joseph McKee's late entry into the race as an Independent Democrat turned the election into a three-way contest. All through

Election Day LaGuardia and O'Ryan kept watch on the polling sites to make sure Tammany's minions did not corrupt the balloting. Although LaGuardia tallied only 40 percent of the overall vote, he achieved a plurality. With O'Brien placing a distant third in the contest, it left little doubt in the minds of even the most ardent Democrats that LaGuardia had tamed the Tammany Hall tiger.

Shortly after midnight on January 1, 1934, LaGuardia was sworn in as New York City's ninety-ninth mayor overall but only the tenth since the consolidation of the five boroughs in 1898. LaGuardia selected the police department, the city's most visible arm of government, to demonstrate his commitment to an honest administration. If he could clean up the NYPD with its entrenched and inherent corruption, he believed that all other city agencies would fall in line. Later that morning LaGuardia made good on his promise and pinned the gold police commissioner's shield on O'Ryan's lapel. "I picked General O'Ryan (O'Ryan preferred being called "general" over "commissioner") because I have confidence in him," LaGuardia told the brass assembled at Headquarters to witness the ceremony. He continued:

He is your only commanding officer, remember that. There will be no interference in the regular performance of police duty, anywhere, anyplace, anytime, and I can't make that too clear. If there is interference, the men in the department must eliminate it. Promotions will be made on the basis of merit. There is opportunity for everyone. If you believe otherwise, now is the time to speak up or get out of the Department. I am hopeful for the future. I don't expect any trouble. We've got to live together for four years. The people of this city are entitled to adequate police protection without intimidation by racketeers or gangsters. I expect every district to be cleaned up.

Despite philosophical differences O'Ryan shared the mayor's passion for reform. During a radio broadcast that afternoon he said, "I have generally high regard for the New York City police. I am also sure that esteem does not blind them to the fact that there is room for substantial improvement in their efficiency and their dependability."

Morale was said to be at an all-time low because of widespread outside interference. Seabury had shown that crooked politicians used their influence on policemen to determine which crimes were solved and which crimes were ignored. This was an arrangement O'Ryan planned to eliminate right at the start. "For the ordinary citizen to be dishonest may constitute a crime," he said. "For a policeman to be dishonest in the performance of his duties is a defilement of the home, your civic home."

In a speech to subordinates that he called "The Policeman as a Soldier," O'Ryan said patrolmen were at war a full twenty-four hours each day, 365 days a year, and that the principles of organization that governed an army had an application to the command, discipline, and administration of a large police force. But he cautioned, "When the policeman becomes a shirker, a grafter, his conduct is not to be treated as if it were a prank or due to a lack of understanding displayed by a boy recruit in an army, but rather as a serious major offense of a matured man of tested intelligence, necessitating dismissal."

O'Ryan stressed the highest standards of behavior for members of the force every time he got a chance: "When a policeman acts dishonestly in the performance of his duty, he is no more than a thief. He becomes a traitor to the cause he has sworn to serve—a traitor as well to his organization and his comrades—a traitor to the public who honored him and trusted him, paid his salary and provided for his security, and finally a traitor to his family." He viewed his authority to dismiss the traitor, the grafter, and the shirker as his three most important weapons in righting the ship.

During an address to members of the Patrolmen's Benevolent Association, O'Ryan called patrolmen the backbone of the police department. "They are the infantry of our army of 18,000 men—the body of combat forces of the Department. I confess that, sentimentally, I am a New York Police Department patrolman."

But O'Ryan's rigid adherence to military protocols created conflict with the rank and file almost from the start. An early incident occurred when he countermanded former police commissioner Bolan's order that allowed patrolmen to remove their dark blue woolen blouses in the summer so long as they wore a long-sleeved uniform shirt and necktie. O'Ryan decreed that policemen would be required to wear their coats all year round, even during the hot summer months. "Every member of the department will have to stand up like he-men and take it and like it," he said. Fortunately for the members of the force, the thorny issue was resolved when LaGuardia, who had promised no interference, instructed the general to modify his order before the hot weather set in. O'Ryan reluctantly agreed to a compromise. Patrolmen could remove their blouses during the day and evening hours if the temperature reached eighty-five degrees or more, provided the coat was readily available in the event the temperature dropped. LaGuardia, however, let stand O'Ryan's order for officers to wear only black socks.

The last annual police parade occurred in 1931, when Grover Whalen was police commissioner. General O'Ryan announced his intent to revive the tradition, complete with prancing horses, brass bands, and marching formations of immaculately clad patrolmen. But LaGuardia overrode him and declared there would be no police parade until all the criminals were taken care of. His decision put an end to the annual march for good. While O'Ryan was not happy with LaGuardia's meddling, the issues were minor until a taxi strike brought the simmering underlying philosophical discord between them to a full boil. O'Ryan would soon discover that despite the deal he had made with LaGuardia, he served at the mayor's pleasure, not the other way around.

An illegal taxi excise tax had been enacted by the previous administration as a method to generate revenue for the city. When the courts overturned the tax, a dispute between the hacks and the fleet owners occurred regarding who was entitled to the money that would be refunded. When negotiations between the parties collapsed, the disgruntled cabdrivers went on a rampage. Police on the scene allowed the riot to continue unchecked for a full fifteen minutes before attempts were made to restore order. The delay was caused in part because LaGuardia had ordered the brass to allow picketing by the cabbies to take place around the fleet garages. He also forbade the officers assigned to the strike detail from carrying their batons, so they were not properly equipped to deal with the situation once it got out of hand.

In the past the liberal use of nightsticks had been the preferred method to control rowdy demonstrators. If it had been up to O'Ryan, he would have met the strikers with an immediate show of force, but he bowed to the mayor's authority and ended up maligned by the press for failing to take proper action.

A month later, in March 1934, the department was embarrassed a second time by striking cabbies who were roused to a frenzy by union organizers. The disturbance resulted in the destruction of 150 cabs and numerous injuries to scab drivers. Once again LaGuardia personally prevented the police from taking action at the onset until he received so many reports detailing the wanton recklessness of the strikers that he finally had no choice but to turn the police loose.

Although the sides ultimately agreed to settle the taxi strike through binding arbitration, a grand jury inquiry into the cause of both riots criticized the police for failing to act swiftly to control the drivers. The jury accused the mayor and the police commissioner of abetting the disorder. O'Ryan was deeply upset by the criticism leveled against him and told reporters that in the future either he would have the authority to handle tumultuous situations as he saw fit or he would resign.

LaGuardia made light of the grand jury findings and insisted that the reports of violence were "exaggerated." However, remarks by his police commissioner did not go unnoticed. He began to circumvent O'Ryan's authority by passing his orders directly to Chief Inspector Lewis Valentine, the former head of the defunct Confidential Squad. During his thirty-one years in the department Valentine's career had suffered a series of disappointments and political retaliations that would have driven a lesser man from the force. He had been praised by some police commissioners, passed over for promotion by others, and demoted by yet another simply because he was incorruptible.

Shortly after winning the November election, LaGuardia invited the "Honest Cop" to his flat on the Upper East Side to discuss his testimony at the Seabury hearings. It was supposed to be a short breakfast meeting, but it ended up lasting most of the day. Valentine thoroughly impressed LaGuardia with his knowledge of the inner workings of the department and his thoughts about what could be done to improve it. As a result of their discussion LaGuardia promoted Valentine from captain all the way to chief inspector.

As head of the uniform forces, Valentine found himself caught in the middle of an escalating ideological battle between the mayor and the police commissioner. He wanted to remain faithful to his new boss, but LaGuardia was the one who had revived his career. Although the acrimony between the two men became more apparent every day, Valentine did what he could to keep each of them happy and to free the city from the stranglehold of organized crime.

O'Ryan had the foresight to realize that social and criminal problems would grow exponentially if narcotics enforcement was not made one of the department's top priorities in the 1930s. To attack the problem he expanded the Narcotics Bureau and arranged for treatment for any addict who came forward voluntarily.

While narcotics trafficking was lucrative, it was just one of many illegal enterprises that were thriving in New York during the Depression. Dozens of notorious gangsters—Dutch Schultz, Meyer Lansky, Joe Adonis, Francesco Castiglia (a.k.a. Frank Costello), and Charles "Lucky" Luciano—were operating in plain sight throughout the five boroughs, and each controlled an element of the rackets that made the gangster rich and his clientele poorer. Luciano was so brazen that he complained to the newspapers when O'Ryan's men roused him from his suite at the Waldorf Astoria and dragged him down to Police Headquarters for a sit-down. He said the police did it to make the new administration look good. But LaGuardia wanted O'Ryan to convey a message to the gangsters that now that he was mayor, he wanted the "tinhorns" out of town once and for all.

Previous administrations had viewed slot machines with benign indifference. In 1934 there were approximately twenty-five thousand one-armed bandits in the city, most operating out of small mom-and-pop grocery stores. In total it was estimated that these slot machines grossed upward of half a million dollars per day, with profits going directly into the silk pockets of underworld kingpin Frank Costello.

Valentine formed a special squad to confiscate slot machines. Most ended up in the deep murky waters of Long Island Sound, but a few were used at a gambling fair set up by the administration at Radio City Musical Hall, where New Yorkers were invited to try their luck with the "mechanical pickpockets." LaGuardia's idea was to convince members of the public that the games were fixed so that they would not play them.

But the racketeers had no intention of surrendering $180 million a year without a fight. To get around the city's authority to confiscate his machines, Costello converted them into candy-vending machines and obtained a court order banning the police from seizing them. The city appealed the court decision. LaGuardia proclaimed that not even a federal judge could turn a slot machine into a vending machine and ordered the police department to continue impounding the machines. When the court order was overturned on appeal, Costello decided to seek greener pastures. He found sanctuary in Louisiana, where his new partner, Governor Huey Long, agreed to allow the one-armed bandits in his state so long as a percentage of the profits would be donated to charity. About sixty dollars found their way to the needy for every million dollars raked in. The rest was shared between the gangster and the governor.

O'Ryan was fascinated by the burgeoning field of forensic science and thought that the nation's largest police force should become a leader in that field despite past failures. He invited Swedish crime detection expert Dr. Harry Soderman to assist the department. By midyear 1934 the NYPD's fledgling Technical Research Laboratory was in full operation. Although primitive by today's standards, the lab was state of the art in its day, complete with a darkroom, a workshop, and a library. The scientific equipment consisted of a large microscope capable of magnifying objects eight hundred times, a binocular microscope, a tintometer, precise weight scales, magnifying glasses, micro-photographic apparatus, and a movie camera.

Perhaps O'Ryan's most enduring legacy was the creation of the Combat Cross, which became the department's most prestigious award after the Medal of Honor. The Combat Cross, patterned after the Maltese Cross, has been presented annually since 1934 to police officers who have performed "an act of extraordinary heroism while engaged in personal combat with an armed adversary at imminent personal hazard to life in the intelligent performance of duty." Adding to the historical significance of the award is that each medal is numbered sequentially, starting from the first in 1934, so that each recipient knows exactly how many officers have received the Combat Cross before him or her.

Ironically because of the lingering effect the taxi strike had on his relationship with LaGuardia, O'Ryan would not be in attendance when the first member of the department, Sergeant Harry Bilms, received Combat Cross No. 1 for shooting two stickup men attempting to rob a diner.

On the evening of September 20, 1934, O'Ryan declared that his department had solved the "crime of the century." Over the course of the past two and a half years the NYPD, working in conjunction with the Department of

Justice's Division of Investigation and the New Jersey State Police, had been slowly recovering some of the gold certificates from the ransom money that Charles Lindbergh had paid his son's kidnapper. Lieutenant James Finn had been tracking the locations where each bill was discovered on a large map that he kept in his office. Although bills were occasionally recovered as far away as Chicago, he noticed a pattern begin to develop in New York City. It appeared that an unidentified suspect was most frequently passing the bills in the Yorkville section of Manhattan and the Fordham section of the Bronx, so Finn began to concentrate his team's efforts on those two neighborhoods.

The real break in the case came when the U.S. secretary of the treasury announced that the federal government was switching from the gold standard to the silver standard and that any gold certificates that were not exchanged for the new currency would soon be worthless and illegal to possess.

On September 15, 1934, a male customer put ninety-eight cents' worth of gas in a Dodge sedan at a filling station in Upper Manhattan and paid for it with a ten-dollar gold certificate. The wary gas station attendant jotted the license plate number on the bill; in the event that the bank rejected it, he would still be able to find out who had given it to him through the Motor Vehicle Bureau. Unbeknown to the attendant, banks had their own list of serial numbers from the ransom money. When the ten-dollar gold certificate in question turned out to be one of the ransom money bills, bank officials immediately notified the police.

Lieutenant Finn questioned the station attendant who had deposited the gold certificate. The attendant explained the circumstances that had led him to write the license plate number on the bill. Finn then contacted the Motor Vehicle Bureau and asked a clerk to trace the plate. It came back to a thirty-four-year-old white male named Bruno Hauptmann who resided at 1279 East 222nd Street in the Bronx.

Hauptmann was arrested on Wednesday, September 19, 1934. Finn's men recovered another $13,750 in gold certificates from the ransom money in Hauptmann's garage. After a lengthy interrogation Hauptmann was remanded to the New Jersey authorities.

The press conference at which O'Ryan announced Hauptmann's capture was his finest hour. A few days later, after yet another disagreement with the mayor over the handling of pickets, O'Ryan resigned, ostensibly to resume his law practice. For the proud soldier the partnership with LaGuardia had left a bitter taste in his mouth. As he left office, O'Ryan blasted LaGuardia's coddling of strikers and called them "Communists and the vicious elements of the city."

It did not take LaGuardia long to name a successor for O'Ryan. The next morning, after some confusion as to who was bringing the police commissioner's shield to the ceremony (O'Ryan had no intention of delivering it to City Hall), Chief Inspector Valentine was sworn in at an annual salary of $12,500, $500 more than he made as chief inspector.

Lewis J. Valentine was born in 1882 and reared in a section of Williamsburg, Brooklyn, then known as "Irishtown." In 1902 he took civil service exams for both the fire department and the police department. He was hired by the police one year later at a starting salary of $800 a year and assigned to the then Forty-Ninth Precinct in Brooklyn.

In 1904 Valentine married a local girl, Elizabeth Donohue, and the two of them proceeded to build a family. Tragedy struck in 1910 when his wife died from tuberculosis, a sad fate that he shared with LaGuardia. Her death left Valentine a widower with four young children. Thankfully his sister-in-law stepped in to fill the void. The two became so close that they wed in 1914.

Valentine's appointment to police commissioner marked the first time that a member of the force had served in each rank. (Enright had been a lieutenant, and both Mulrooney and Bolan were chiefs but never chief inspectors.) As LaGuardia affixed the gold shield to Valentine's suit coat, he took a parting shot at O'Ryan and said, "It is not the badge that makes the office; it's the man."

Although O'Ryan had had some innovative ideas about policing, he was still learning the ropes. Valentine, on the other hand, had over thirty years of service behind him, a significant portion of which had been spent on investigating corruption within the department. He had no intention of letting the force carry on business as usual. After an uneventful week settling into his new position, Valentine selected the department's vaunted Detective Division for overhaul. Although he recognized the fine work for which NYPD detectives had become world-renowned, he was also aware that the division harbored more than its share of shirkers and malingerers.

Each morning felons were brought to Police Headquarters for viewing by detectives in a ritual called the "daily lineup." The procedure had become so routine that most detectives spent their time during the lineup drinking coffee (occasionally something stronger) and shooting the breeze. It was a practice that Valentine would not tolerate. During a surprise visit to the lineup he climbed on the stage and warned the detectives, "If you are not making good now, you are on your way out. No one will remain unless he produces. Merit alone is the only thing that is going to advance you. I have observed as many as ten [detectives] in a squad room at one time, listening to radios and in conversation. That's not the kind of detective I want. One or two detectives in a squad room at a time is enough. The rest should be out on the street working. Don't wait until crimes are reported. Go out and prevent crime."

Valentine's "be good or be gone" attitude had been shaped by his many years with the Confidential Squad. Now that he was in charge, he intended to mold the department into his idea of what a competent, duty bound, incorruptible police force should be, not someone else's. He told his patrolmen, "I'll stand up for you, but I'll crucify a thief. And I'll be quicker to punish a thief in a police uniform than an ordinary thief. The thief in uniform is ten times more dangerous."

The person most responsible for Valentine's attitude was his mentor, Inspector Daniel "Honest Dan" Costigan, who had convinced him that the street cop was the first and basic requirement for good law enforcement. Valentine believed that cops had to be alert, tough, and—above all—honest, but he was not unsympathetic to their plight.

Early on Valentine established "open-door Friday" and made himself available to members of the force seeking an audience with the police commissioner. Valentine would lock the disciplinary reports of patrolmen found unfit for duty due to intoxication in the "drunk drawer" of his desk. As long as an officer remained sober, he kept his job.

To deal with hardened criminals on the street, Valentine revived a special detail of plainclothesmen, the "Strong-Arm Squad." He made it clear that they were not to coddle the suspects they arrested. Valentine said that he wanted gangsters to tip their hats to cops when they walked by, and he offered promotions "for the men who kick those gorillas around." LaGuardia agreed with the strategy. "If gangsters speak well of the Police Department," he said, "it's a sign there is something wrong in the department."

Valentine was slowly earning respect from some members of the force, but the majority still could not forget the many years he had spent spying on them, no matter what he said or did. That all changed on the morning of November 7, 1934. Valentine had spent the night consoling the family of deceased patrolman John Monahan. Monahan had been fatally wounded a week before when he entered a dwelling in Brooklyn to investigate a crime in progress. He languished for seven days before finally succumbing to his injuries. To make matters worse, the gunman had escaped and was still on the loose.

Valentine left the hospital and headed straight for the Lineup Room. He had planned to scold his men for not solving the murder of one of their own. But as he walked into the room, he spotted a dapper hoodlum among the suspects waiting to be called onto the stage. This particular thug was wearing a Chesterfield overcoat with a velvet collar and a pearl gray fedora, cocked atop his head at a wise-guy angle. He was identified as Harry Straus, and although Straus had a rap sheet with seventeen prior arrests and was now charged with the murder of a garage attendant, Valentine noticed that he did not appear overly concerned with his predicament.

The sight incensed Valentine. He pointed at Straus and told his detectives in no uncertain terms, "When you meet such men, draw quickly and shoot accurately. Look at him. He's the best-dressed man in this room, yet he's never worked a day in his life. When you meet men like this, don't be afraid to muss 'em up. Men like him should be mussed up. Blood should be smeared all over that velvet collar. Instead, he looks as though he just came out of a barber shop." Then Valentine vowed, "You men will be supported by me no matter what you do, if what you do is justified. Make it disagreeable for men like these. Drive them out of this city. Teach them to fear arrest. Make them fear you."

Valentine was vilified in the national press for what he said, but he stood by his words. "I'm responsible for the protection of and safeguarding of the people of this city and of the men at my command, and it is my intention to support them in every undertaking regardless of criticism, when I'm satisfied that their action is justified." He added: "Habit to most of us is much like a malady—it is not easy to shake off. For a great many years many men in the Police Department of the City of New York have come to believe that racketeers, thugs, criminals, especially those whose nefarious activities gained them financial and political standing, must, of necessity, be treated with kid gloves. The habits of years cannot be erased in a day, and I am satisfied that more than one 'pep' talk similar to yesterday's will be required." But Valentine was shrewd enough to add a caveat: "If it develops that this stand must be modified, I will not hesitate to modify it as the occasion demands."

Arthur Flegenheimer, a.k.a. Dutch Schultz, was wanted on numerous felony charges. After months on the lam he came to the conclusion that it would be better to turn himself in in Albany instead of New York City. Schultz's unexpected surrender, coming on the heels of Valentine's "muss 'em up" comments, created the impression that crooks like he were running scared. But Valentine muttered that he would have been happier if Schultz had been brought in "in a box." The police commissioner got his wish several months later when Schultz was gunned down inside the bathroom of his favorite restaurant, the Palace Chop House Tavern in Newark, New Jersey.

During the Depression the city's fiscal crisis severely limited the number of experimental radio motor patrol cars the department was able to put out on the street. As the city's financial conditions began to improve, additional radio motor patrols were deployed to provide expanded coverage throughout the city. Department propaganda claimed that the system was so efficient that whenever a law-abiding citizen notified the police of a crime in progress, a modern, radio-equipped car would appear on the scene within minutes to arrest the perpetrator before he or she got away. The decrease in reported crime was hailed as statistical proof that radio motor patrol was on its way toward eradicating all criminal activity in the city.

In 1934 radio motor patrol was credited with effecting 4,500 arrests and recovering stolen property valued at more than $1.5 million, as compared to 1933, when there were only 1,150 arrests by radio car teams and less than $350,000 worth of stolen property was recovered.

The Telegraph Bureau, a forerunner to the present day Communications Division, was responsible for maintaining the communications link between Police Headquarters and radio motor patrol cars in the field. The bureau was commanded by the superintendent of the telegraph and operated out of the Operations Room, which was located on the top floor of the north end of Police Headquarters. Messages were broadcast over police radio station WPEG using a powerful five-hundred-watt transmitter, also at Police Headquarters. In the event that the main transmitter experienced operational difficulties, auxiliary four-hundred-watt transmitter stations were set up in Brooklyn's Seventy-First Precinct with the call letters WPEE and in the Bronx's Fortieth Precinct with the call letters WPEF.

On a typical day in the mid-1930s there were two hundred radio motor patrol cars on duty at any one time. The superintendent's staff kept track of each patrol car's whereabouts by utilizing a large, nine-by-twelve-foot map of the five boroughs fastened to a U-shaped desk called the "indicator table." One patrolman assigned to the table was designated as the "dispatcher." He worked in tandem with a second patrolman designated as the "announcer."

Radio-equipped cars were represented on the map by small, round brass disks, about the size of a standard checker. They were black on one side and white on the other, and they were distributed across the map according to their patrol territories. Other colored disks were used to indicate when the cars were out of service for routine maintenance, personal necessity, and so forth.

As soon as a call for service was received by the main switchboard, it was routed to the dispatcher. He scanned the table map to determine which radio motor patrol car should respond. Whenever a radio car was available for assignment, the disk displayed the vehicle's identification code number on the white side. Once the dispatcher made his decision, he passed the information over to the announcer, who transmitted the alarm to the radio motor patrol car designated by the dispatcher. Other radio cars in the vicinity were expected to respond as backup.

A typical radio-run transmission from the announcer would be as follows: "Car Number 292—Northeast corner Lenox Avenue and 125th Street, Manhattan—Signal 30. Authority Telegraph Bureau—Time 1:43 p.m." Then he would repeat the message.

Each radio car crew was responsible to listen for calls directed at its unit. Messages were presumed to have been received by the radio motor patrol car assigned since all communications were one way. The dispatcher flipped the disk over to its black side to indicate when a car was on an assignment. It stayed black until the radio car crew reported back by telephone with a final disposition.

For all their capabilities radio motor patrol cars were of little use when major riots erupted, such as the one in Harlem on March 19, 1935. The events of that day would have a profound effect on the neighborhood's relationship with the police for years to come.

A Puerto Rican teenager named Lino Rivera was caught stealing a ten-cent pocket knife from the E. H. Kress department store on West 125th Street. Rivera bit the hands of the store manager and a floor guard during a search of his pockets. The employees managed to restrain him and summoned Patrolman Raymond Donohue to the store. From that point on the situation escalated from a routine shoplifting arrest into a massive disturbance and huge political embarrassment for LaGuardia.

A rumor spread like wildfire across Harlem (fueled by Communist agitators) that Donohue had taken Rivera into the back room to beat him. Although the story was not true, the unconfirmed report drew a large crowd to the front of the store. Donohue attempted to assure the people that no harm had come to the boy, but he had made the mistake of releasing Rivera beforehand through the rear basement door instead of the front door, where the crowd would have been able see him.

The situation further deteriorated when an ambulance arrived on the scene to treat the injured employees. The attendants bandaged the bite wounds and left without transporting the employees to the hospital. A short time later a hearse parked in front of the store. Its arrival fueled speculation that Rivera had died while in police custody. (It was later explained that the driver had stopped by the department store to speak to his brother-in-law before returning the hearse to the funeral home.)

Donohue's failure to produce the boy combined with the appearance of a hearse resulted in Rivera's supposed "death" suddenly becoming a "fact." It was not long after that the uprising began. Roaming gangs smashed windows and looted stores along 125th Street. Black shop owners attempted to protect their property by placing large placards in their windows that read, "Run by COLORED people," while Caucasian merchants hastily posted signs of their own informing the protesters that they employed "Negro workers."

Heavily armed police reserves flooded the neighborhood. Patrolmen beat the rioters into submission with their batons and rifle butts. Emergency Service Division snipers took positions on rooftops and opened fire to disperse the crowd. By the time police brass had the sense to have a black lieutenant, Samuel Battle, escort Rivera back to the scene to prove that he was unharmed, the reason the melee had started in the first place was no longer relevant. When it was finally over, 3 rioters were dead (including a black teenager), 100 were injured, and 125 were under arrest. Despite the carnage Valentine praised his men for showing discipline, tact, and courage during the disorder.

LaGuardia, however, was appalled by the NYPD's actions. His administration stood for all the people, and in his mind that most certainly included blacks in Harlem. He immediately established a biracial commission, chaired by a prominent black dentist, Dr. Charles Roberts, to review the entire incident from start to finish. The panel interviewed over 160 witnesses and concluded that police hostility was "evident at every stage of the riot." It also ridiculed the department for circulating a picture of an uninjured Lino Rivera in the company of a black police lieutenant in the immediate aftermath as a way to justify its heavy-handed response. In fairness to the department, the commission noted that the explosion on March 19 would never have been set off by such a trifling incident had not existing economic and social forces created a state of emotional tension that sought relief upon the slightest provocation.

As a remedy the panel proposed sweeping changes to attack poverty, crime, and racism with an infusion of municipal funds. While LaGuardia was not ready to allocate enough money to correct all of Harlem's ills, he broke ground in July 1935 for the city's first public housing project. However, the question of how to best deal with racial disturbances was never resolved during LaGuardia's mayoralty.

A month after the Harlem riots Valentine invited dozens of news reporters and press photographers to the Brooklyn piers to witness the destruction of hundreds of craps tables, roulette wheels, and blackjack tables that had been seized by the department since he became police commissioner. This time instead of sinking them in Long Island Sound, as had been done with metal slot machines, he intended to burn the gambling paraphernalia in a huge bonfire.

Valentine presided over the event, which was to be filmed and shown in movie theaters throughout the city. Before the betting accouterments met their fiery doom, the script called for Valentine to give a lecture on the evils of gambling and then provide a demonstration. Clad in a dark Chesterfield coat and a snappy black fedora, he stood behind a roulette wheel and he placed a chip on the number seven. "Roulette is a sucker's game," he declared. "Watch me and see."

With the newsreel cameras rolling Valentine gave the wheel a firm spin. The tiny white ball skipped across the revolving numbers until it settled into the seven pocket. After a moment of stunned silence, the reporters began to howl with laughter. Valentine, despite his best intentions, had beaten the odds, but he found little amusement in the irony. He grabbed the roulette wheel and hurled it onto the ground. Once he regained his composure, he said that winning a bet under these circumstances was in fact unlucky for him.

Keeping the police force on the straight and narrow was a task that Valentine refused to leave to chance or in the hands of a small cadre of dedicated men, such as the Confidential Squad.

There were eighty-four precincts (patrol and traffic) in the city, and the ratio of sergeants to patrolmen (including detectives) was approximately one to seventeen. Much of the supervision relied on the honesty of the patrolmen in the field, who were required to contact the stationhouses at predetermined intervals from the green signal boxes located on their posts. For the most part so long as a patrolman made his "ring" and was logged in by the sergeant on the switchboard, he was free to do whatever he pleased.

Patrol sergeants and the plainclothes "shooflies" on the street were limited in their ability to deter corruption by the sheer number of officers on whom they had to keep tabs. Once a patrolman had been inspected by a supervisor on his post, he could be fairly confident that that was the last he would see of him on that tour.

In an attempt to improve supervision Valentine issued orders that directed precinct sergeants to utilize "a radio motor patrol car to monitor the response and performance of the men assigned to radio car sector duty and also regularly to inspect the patrolmen on their foot posts." The idea of a sergeant visiting them on their beats up to fifteen times per tour horrified patrolmen. However, the order ultimately set a new standard for supervision of policemen in the field.

While Valentine could issue orders to make improvements in supervision, the fundamental nature of police work continued to take its toll on the families of patrolmen. In June 1935 Mayor LaGuardia received an anonymous letter from the wife of a patrolman. It was signed "Heartbroken Mother." Apparently the young woman's husband was one of dozens of junior plainclothesmen drafted into the Vice Squad after Valentine had transferred out most of the senior officers for failing to vigorously enforce the law. The wife wrote that she was concerned about her husband carousing "with all kinds of bad women." She begged LaGuardia to have Valentine return the older, wiser, and more seasoned detectives back to the detail.

LaGuardia recalled only too well his early experiences in Night Court. He had often seen the same type of harlot that the policeman's wife feared would ruin her marriage. LaGuardia chose to address her concerns in the pages of *Spring 3100*. "If a man is good, decent, and clean, he will continue to be so, regardless of the work he may be assigned to," LaGuardia replied. "It is indeed a poor alibi for a husband and father to either attempt to ease his own conscience or justify his weakness and conduct by blaming unfortunate and depraved persons with whom he comes in contact by reason of his police duties." He concluded his letter with some homespun advice for the wife to keep her husband happy. "Avoid nagging and make allowance for little irritations."

The NYPD took another step forward in the scientific evolution of solving crimes when the Technical Research Lab began to blood-type samples recovered at the scene of homicides. Valentine predicted at the International Association of Chiefs of Police convention in Atlantic City that this science would become as invaluable to police in solving complicated murder cases as fingerprints had become to identify suspects.

While Valentine was impressed by the department's technological achievements, he never forgot that the most important rule in solving a crime was capturing the perpetrator. Only then did he feel that the scientific wizardry could be of real value. In this regard Valentine preferred a tried-and-true method that, in his opinion, had as much to do with solving a crime as anything the technical boys could dream up. The "Honest Cop" advocated the use of "stool pigeons," and he made money available for detectives to pay off reliable stoolies who had provided the department with "good information."

Valentine was also willing to turn a blind eye when his officers employed the "third degree" to obtain confessions from otherwise reluctant suspects once they were in custody. For most people involved in law enforcement, the third degree was either an accepted investigative technique or a tolerated form of police brutality that was necessary because the underworld had its own ironclad rule for dealing with law enforcement: "Don't talk."

To loosen their lips the police often resorted to beating information out of lock-jawed suspects. When the usual methods—such as kicks to the shins, sharp pokes in the ribs, or crushing out lit cigarettes on the skin—did not work, detectives switched to blackjacks and rubber hoses. Cop killers were subjected to the most barbaric forms of punishment. The officers were not concerned about the consequences because district attorneys accepted at face value the department's explanation that a suspect's suspicious injuries had occurred when he had fallen down a flight of stairs while trying to escape.

Although the third degree played a prominent role in police work, the more time he spent in office, the more Valentine realized that he did not want the public to think that the policemen charged with the people's protection were more brutal than the thugs who preyed upon them. He attempted to defuse complaints of police brutality by referring to it as the "myth of the third degree" and insisted that such beatings were figments of the criminals' imagination.

As important as it was to solve crimes, the police department was also in the business of preventing crimes. Its motorized fleet created a sense of omnipresence, but it seemed that there were never enough police officers on patrol. Valentine thought that too many cops were pushing pencils and brooms. Of the nearly eighteen thousand able-bodied men on the force, only three hundred were civilians. As a result it was necessary for thousands of uniformed patrolmen to act as dispatchers, switchboard operators, cell attendants, brooms, and stationhouse clerks.

As far back as when he had been president of the Board of Aldermen, LaGuardia felt such menial chores were inappropriate for patrolmen. During the depression NYPD staffing levels fell well below the authorized quota because of a hiring freeze that lasted until 1936, when 204 new patrolmen were added to the force for the first time in five years. But LaGuardia was not interested in just hiring more police officers. In planning his budget for fiscal year 1937, he made civilianization in the police department a real priority. He directed Valentine to identify jobs that could be performed by civilians at a lower rate of pay and gradually integrated them into the force. During LaGuardia's twelve years in office the number of civilians working in the police department grew from 300 to 1,291.

For all their good intentions LaGuardia and Valentine still served at the will of the people. Without LaGuardia as mayor Valentine could not be police commissioner. That was why the mayoral campaign of 1937 was so important to him. Up until then Valentine had made it a practice of remaining politically neutral, but now he found his career entirely dependent upon LaGuardia. He could no longer stand on the sidelines and let the course of political events unfold on their own.

Tammany Hall had managed to regain some of its influence when its candidates won midterm elections for comptroller, Board of Aldermen president, and Kings County (Brooklyn) district attorney. Each of these wins bolstered the machine's confidence that it could unseat LaGuardia, just as it had done in the past with Fusionist mayors Low and Mitchel.

Valentine was keenly aware that his men were not as enamored by LaGuardia's tough law-and-order stance as the mayor liked to believe. He also knew that many of them were upset by the intense supervision he employed and that they would welcome a return to the old system where merit had little to do with career advancement. To make matters worse, former police commissioner O'Ryan's personal animosity toward LaGuardia had grown greater than his distaste for Tammany Hall since his resignation. He declared his support for the Democratic Party nominee, Supreme Court Justice Jeremiah T. Mahoney, who had branded LaGuardia as a Communist sympathizer for his failure to act during the taxi strikes that had derailed his career.

Valentine spent several weeks preceding the election drawing up a plan to prevent Tammany Hall from "stealing" the election. He posted ten thousand patrolmen at three thousand polling sites throughout the city. Then he dispatched all of his his six deputy commissioners and the highest-ranking uniformed members of the department to personally monitor the polling places, while he remained at Police Headquarters to oversee the counting of the ballots. When the final results were tabulated, LaGuardia won by almost a half million votes.

Two LaGuardia allies were also victorious. Newbold Morris became the first City Council president, the legislative body created to replace the Board of Aldermen, and Thomas E. Dewey became the New York County (Manhattan) district attorney. Governor Lehman had appointed Dewey to the post of special prosecutor in 1935. Dewey had zeroed in on Dutch Schultz, but the investigation came to an abrupt end the night the Dutchman was sent to his grave—a fate, it was later learned, ordered by Salvatore Lucania, a.k.a. Charles "Lucky" Luciano.

"Lucky" had acquired his unique moniker years before, when he had been "taken for a ride" to a wooded section of Staten Island. The rival gangsters had thrown his battered body into a roadside ditch and left him for dead. Somehow Lucania had managed to crawl up to the roadway, where he was spotted by a passing patrolman who transported him to the hospital. From that point on he was "Lucky" Luciano.

Luciano established a successful corporate business model for organized crime involving everything from illegal gambling and bootlegging to narcotics and numbers. It was said that one of the reasons he lasted so long was that unlike his rivals, Luciano paid his taxes—at least on a portion of his ill-gotten earnings. It did not hurt that he also spread money around to politicians in both parties. But his luck ran out when he went up against Dewey.

Luciano got word in late March 1936 that Dewey was after him. He immediately fled to Hot Springs, Arkansas, to lie low. The last thing he expected was that an NYPD detective visiting the city on unrelated business would happen to spot him. Luciano was arrested the next day and extradited to New York on a warrant issued by Dewey. His trial lasted more than a month, and when it was finally over, on June 16, 1936, the jury found him guilty on sixty-one counts. Luciano received a fifty-year sentence, while Dewey went on to become governor of New York. During World War II Luciano made available his Sicilian connections to help the U.S. government. In return Governor Dewey commuted his sentence. Luciano was released shortly after the war and deported to Sicily, where he died in 1962 at age sixty-four.

On February 12, 1938, a thirty-one-year-old off-duty black patrolman named John A. Holt was alerted by his neighbor that an apartment in the building was being ransacked. Holt took out his revolver and immediately went to investigate. He spotted the burglar in the hallway and ordered him to stop. When the suspect failed to comply, Holt opened fire. The suspect darted up the stairs and out onto the roof. Holt gave chase, but the suspect escaped via an adjoining building.

Unbeknown to Holt, another neighbor had called the police. Two officers from the Thirty-Second Precinct on radio motor patrol were dispatched to the location to investigate a burglary in progress. They entered the building just as Holt discharged his weapon and were unaware that he was a cop. When Holt came down the stairs with the gun still in his hand, the officers mistook him for the burglar. They shot and killed him.

Two days later the police arrested the burglary suspect and recovered the stolen property. District Attorney Dewey investigated the shooting and determined it had been an accident. The officers were cleared of any wrongdoing.

Patrolman Holt left behind a wife and three young children. He became the first black officer in the department to receive an inspector's funeral. During the service he was remembered by his colleagues as a "fleet-footed colored lad" for his unparalleled skills on the basketball court as a key player on the official NYPD team.

The advent of radio motor patrol soon proved to be a deadly double-edged sword for the department. The specially equipped police cars were crashing in record numbers as they raced to crimes in progress, maiming and killing patrolmen and citizens alike. Part of the blame was attributed to the color of the police cars. They were either dark green or black and virtually indistinguishable from every other car on the road. To remedy the problem in February 1938 the department purchased new two-door Plymouth coupes (among the least expensive cars on the market) that featured green bodies, black fenders, and white tops. The distinctive tricolor paint scheme lasted until the early 1970s, when the NYPD began to phase in two-toned blue and white radio cars to take their place.

The police department's original Air Services Division had been grounded in 1933 by Mayor O'Brien as a cost-cutting measure. By the summer of 1939 the city's financial situation had improved enough to reinstate the division in a hanger at Floyd Bennett Field in Brooklyn and rename it the Aviation Bureau.

The department's new fleet consisted of two ultra-modern 450-horsepower Stinson fixed-wing aircraft purchased with the help of aviator Howard Hughes, at a cost of approximately $34,000. Each airplane could carry up to five passengers, attain cruising speeds of 160 miles per hour, and maintain two-way radio contact with the ground crew. Inspector Arthur W. Wallander returned to command the small but prestigious bureau. He had achieved fame during the unit's earlier incarnation, when he had piloted an airplane to follow a carrier pigeon that was flying a ransom note to a kidnapper.

During the dedication ceremony LaGuardia remarked, "We will find before long that the Aviation Unit will be performing such valuable and essential work that we will wonder how we got along without it." Then the mayor, a former pilot himself; Police Commissioner Valentine; and New York Yankee pitcher Lefty Gomez climbed aboard one of the airplanes as passengers in its inaugural flight.

LaGuardia's relationship with the police force got better as the years passed. He had come to see firsthand the fine service the NYPD provided to the citizens of New York and wanted their efforts to be formally recognized. In 1939 he authorized a private committee to raise funds to erect a memorial dedicated to the city's police officers. His vision resulted in the creation of the department's most iconic image, a larger-than-life bronze statue produced by the mayor's longtime friend and sculptor, Atillio Piccirilli.

The statue depicts a patrolman holding an American flag with one hand and cradling a young boy with the other. The models Piccirilli used for the statue were Patrolman Martin J. Gillen of the Twentieth Precinct and LaGuardia's young adopted son, Eric. The statue was originally intended to be put on display at a site near the Firemen's Monument, at West 100th Street and Riverside Drive, but the plan for a memorial was scuttled at the onset of World War II. For the next twenty-two years the three-thousand-pound statue languished in a city warehouse until it was placed at the entrance of the Police Camp. When the facility was sold, the statue was relocated to the Memorial Lobby inside the entrance to One Police Plaza, where it remains to this day impressing visitors to Police Headquarters.

By the spring of 1940 it had become evident to the administration that the same events in Europe that had prevented the police memorial from becoming a reality would soon have an impact on the lives of all Americans. LaGuardia had made it clear since his earliest days as mayor that he was no admirer of Adolf Hitler. His feelings, however, were not shared by all six hundred thousand of the city's German residents. Since it was not always politically expedient for him to publicly voice his opposition to the Nazis, LaGuardia employed a number of creative methods to get his message across. For example, during a visit to the city by high-ranking Nazi officials, LaGuardia instructed Valentine to assign a detail of Jewish patrolmen as their escorts. The Nazis were appalled by LaGuardia's actions and lodged an official protest with the State Department. When informed of their complaint, LaGuardia said that what he had done to them was nothing in comparison to their mistreatment of Jews in Nazi Germany.

While news of the atrocities taking place in Europe was being reported on a daily basis, the New York World's Fair proved to be a popular distraction at home. Former police commissioner Grover Whalen had been instrumental in getting the international fair off the ground and was president of the Fair Corporation during its first year in operation. He stepped down the following year but continued to host dignitaries and luminaries visiting the exposition.

Dedicated to "Building the World of Tomorrow," the fair, situated at the expansive grounds in Flushing Meadows Park, was dominated by a pair of giant, gleaming, white futuristic structures called the Trylon and Perisphere. In 1939 32 million people visited the fair. Remarkably the Queens district attorney reported that only two criminal indictments were handed down for the entire season. The unusually low crime rate was due in large measure to the independent police force of approximately one thousand special patrolmen working at the fair under the supervision of former police inspector Richard Sheridan.

Tragedy struck during the fair's second season; New Yorkers were awakened from their indifferent slumber when terrorists targeted the British Pavilion. British officials at the fair received several unfounded bomb threats in June 1940. As a precaution Valentine posted several detectives in the vicinity of the exhibition hall during the Fourth of July celebration. Despite the increased police presence, the pavilion's switchboard operator received yet another anonymous telephone threat. The caller said that the place was going to blow up and that she should "get out." The operator duly notified her superiors, who in turn contacted the police.

During a search of the premises, a suspicious valise was found by an electrician in a ventilation room on the top floor of the pavilion. Detective William Federer carried it to a secluded area at the edge of the fairgrounds behind the Polish Pavilion. Bomb Squad detectives Joseph Lynch and Ferdinand Socha were called in from home to the scene. As the two investigators examined the satchel, Lynch told his partner it was the real thing. The bomb inside suddenly detonated. The powerful blast, later determined to be the equivalent of twelve sticks of dynamite, killed Lynch and Socha instantly and severely injured three other detectives and a patrolman standing nearby.

Detective Lynch left a wife and five young children. At the time there were no pension benefits for widows and orphans. To help her get by the Police Relief Fund paid Mrs. Lynch fifty dollars a month to change the bed linen in the dormitory of the commanding officer of the Fiftieth Precinct. She could keep getting the money as long as she did not get married again. The Sochas had no children. Socha's wife eventually remarried and moved to Maryland with her second husband.

Patrolman Emil Vyskocil was busy shooing away bystanders when the bomb exploded. The metal shards that lodged in his ankles were too small to locate even with an X-ray machine. He suffered terrible leg pain for two years until a doctor and a New York City Transit engineer developed a primitive metal detector that enabled surgeons to pinpoint the exact location of the tiny metal fragments. Vyskocil's operation was deemed a success. The device was subsequently shipped to Pearl Harbor, where it was used to treat thousands of similarly injured servicemen.

Immediately after the bombing Valentine ordered his men to round up every known Bundist, Fascist, anarchist, and Christian Front member they could find. Unfortunately no significant information resulted from the mass arrests, even after detectives employed the third degree on several of the more promising suspects.

The Board of Estimate authorized a $25,000 reward for the capture of the bomber. The Detectives Endowment Association kicked in another $1,000. Although the department conducted a most thorough investigation, no perpetrator was ever charged with committing the heinous act.

After the deaths of Lynch and Socha the commanding officer of the Bomb Squad, Lieutenant James Pyke, realized that the methods the department utilized for transporting and examining suspicious infernal devices needed to be improved for the safety of all concerned. It was with this in mind that Pyke designed the LaGuardia-Pyke Bomb Carrier, the first of three specially constructed bomb-proof containers fashioned out of ⅝-inch steel elevator cable. Each carrier cost approximately $15,000 to build and was about the size of a small shed. A carrier was mounted onto a flatbed trailer so that it could be driven directly to the location of any suspicious device, which could be placed inside it. If the bomb went off, the innovative mesh design allowed explosive gasses to pass through tiny spaces between the cables but prevented lethal projectiles from escaping. The success of these containers set the standard for bomb-removal equipment for years to come.

The act of terrorism at the 1940 World's Fair made it clear to both LaGuardia and Valentine that the NYPD was going to be on the front line of the home defense. The recently elected president of the Patrolmen's Benevolent Association, Joseph Burkhard, agreed with them. He declared, "The organized policemen of this State and city are now ready to better the fifth columnists by the formation of our own combat unit [members of the PBA], to be taken henceforth as the sixth column."

This was a distinct change from the position Burkhard had taken previously, when Valentine had attempted to determine how many members of the department belonged to subversive organizations such as the Christian Front or the German-American Bund. Valentine's need to know arose after several members of the Christian Front had been arrested in Brooklyn and were charged with attempting to make explosives. The incarcerated leader of the Brooklyn chapter alleged that several hundred New York City police officers were active members of the organization. In an attempt to determine to what extent (if any) this was true, Valentine circulated a questionnaire that required members of the force to divulge their association with any dissident group.

As their union leader, Burkhard rallied to the defense of six patrolmen who refused to fill out the questionnaire on the grounds that it was a violation of their constitutional rights for the department to ask for such information. Nevertheless, over four hundred other officers freely admitted to having applied for membership in the Christian Front. Twenty-seven more confessed that they were active members of the organization. LaGuardia reminded them that the very nature of their duties as sworn policemen required that they always remain neutral and advised them to sever their relationship with the organization, and they did. He left it up to Valentine to decide how to discipline the six malcontents.

As a result of the steps LaGuardia took to safeguard the city, President Franklin Roosevelt named him the national director of the newly established Federal Office of Civilian Defense in April 1941. In turn the mayor appointed Valentine as police defense coordinator for New York City. The public responded enthusiastically to the police commissioner's call for voluntary service. During June and July 1941 precinct personnel enrolled eighty-one thousand volunteers as civil defense air raid wardens. Soon other civilian defense branches were created such as Fire Watchers, Auxiliary Firemen, Emergency Welfare, Messenger Corps, Diver Corps, Emergency Repair, Canteen Service, and the Medical Rescue Squad, all supervised by members of the NYPD.

Meanwhile, Valentine was struggling with an internal dilemma that had reached epidemic proportions on his watch. Officers were committing suicide in record numbers. In April 1941 Patrolman Rudolph Christopal, age thirty, became the 115th member of the force to take his life since Valentine had become police commissioner. In comparison, only thirty-four officers had been killed in the line of duty over that same period. The suicides were not confined to just the lower ranks. In July 1939 Inspector Charles Neidig killed himself after being banished to an outer borough command for a minor infraction. Two months later an officer described as one of Valentine's most brilliant aides, Inspector Lewis Rosenfeld, pressed his .38 caliber service revolver to his head and pulled the trigger. He was only forty-six years old. His wife reported that just moments before he shot himself, he shouted, "I can't take it any more."

The suicide rate for the NYPD during the 1940s was six times the national average. The press, always anxious to find an angle, blamed the suicides on Valentine's strict disciplinary regime. This sentiment was apparently borne out during a meeting with officers from all ranks convened to discuss the matter. When Valentine asked his men, "What makes you so jittery? Who are you afraid of?" an anonymous voice in the back of the audience shouted out, "The speaker!"

Although the rash of police suicides provided excellent fodder for the newspapers, there still remained the business of policing the city and

LaGuardia's attempt for an unprecedented third consecutive term in office. Hylan had sought to be the first mayor to serve three consecutive terms, but he had lost out when Tammany Hall went with Jimmy Walker instead. Even the mayor's good friend, Judge Seabury, thought two terms were enough for any man and urged him to step down, but LaGuardia sensed that the city would need him more than ever if the United States entered the war overseas.

LaGuardia's Democratic opponent in the 1941 mayoral election was William O'Dwyer, a former patrolman (1917–24) who had left the force to become a lawyer. Since then he had risen to prominence, first as a judge (appointed by interim mayor Joseph McKee) and then as the district attorney of Kings County (Brooklyn), where he prosecuted a syndicate the press dubbed "Murder Incorporated." Although O'Dwyer had sent four men to the electric chair, his failure to net the so-called big fish proved to be his Achilles heel.

O'Dwyer made an appeal to the large Jewish population in the borough of Brooklyn. The ethnic bloc controlled 30 percent of the vote and was thought to be the key to winning any citywide election. O'Dwyer maligned Valentine and claimed that the police department had showed favoritism to anti-Semitic groups. Despite O'Dwyer's harsh criticism of the police department with which he once served, Jews regarded the mayor as one of their own, even though he referred to his Hebrew blood as not being enough to brag about.

The election was close, but LaGuardia carried the day with 52 percent of the vote. After he lost, O'Dwyer took a page from LaGuardia's book and took a leave of absence from city government to join the army. He was commissioned a major and stationed in Italy, just like LaGuardia had been. His strategy would pay off four years later.

Barely a month after the election, the country was stunned by the Japanese sneak attack on Pearl Harbor. New York City civil defense volunteers sprang into action when LaGuardia ordered nightly citywide blackouts.

In an address to 192 graduates from the Police Academy several days after the declaration of war on the Axis powers, LaGuardia informed the rookies that he would not support the same draft exemption for them that he did for firemen. "I want to give it to you straight," he said. "If you are called into the Army, you must go. The reason is we can replace vacancies in the Police Department, but we need more experienced firemen because of the technique of modern (incendiary bomb) warfare. If you are called into the Army, your places will be kept for you."

The Patrolmen's Benevolent Association cited his position, along with a reduction in the starting salary for probationary patrolmen from $2,000 to $1,200 two years earlier as evidence that the mayor favored fireman over cops, but LaGuardia insisted that his reasons were rooted in simple logic. As director of the Office of Civil Defense, he had direct knowledge of the devastating toll Nazi firebombs had taken on London. LaGuardia thought it important to keep enough firemen in service to prevent the same thing from happening to New York in the event of a similar type of raid.

Ironically shortly after the United States entered the war, it became apparent to President Roosevelt that LaGuardia could not effectively discharge his responsibilities as both mayor and director of the Office of Civil Defense. He asked him to choose one or the other. LaGuardia resigned his position as head of the Office of Civil Defense for, as he put it, the benefit of the people who had reelected him.

In January 1942 the police department began to enlist additional volunteers to protect the bridges, ferries, and waterfront as part of the new City Patrol Corps, which was to take over for the old Police Reserve that Police Commissioner O'Ryan had disbanded in 1934. The City Patrol Corps's main function was to prevent pedestrians from carrying onto bridges small bombs that could be dropped onto ships leaving the harbor. The success of this group (which at its peak had 7,125 members) and its predecessors provided the foundation for a permanent cadre of civilian volunteers known as the Auxiliary Police.

Once the draft exemption was removed for police officers, the number of NYPD members in the armed forces climbed from just one hundred in March 1942 to over a thousand uniformed(as compared to seven hundred during World War I) and a handful of civilian employees by the end of the war. Fortunately only fifteen were killed in action. Patrolmen and ranking officers serving overseas managed to stay in touch with their colleagues back home through the pages of *Spring 3100*. But because of censorship, the letters were often postmarked as coming from nondescript locations such as "Somewhere in the South Pacific" or "Somewhere in New Guinea."

Patrolman Fred Steiner, a captain in the army, complained about the poor quality of beer overseas. He wrote his buddies, "Next time you hoist a tall one, have another for the guy from the 9th Precinct who hopes it won't be too long before this rotten business is ended and he'll be able to join with you in person, in knocking an odd one or two, back there in the greatest town of them all." Navy chief specialist "G" Paul B. Weston, a sergeant from the Police Academy stationed on a ship, confessed, "For a guy that can't swim too well I am optimistic, eh?" He went on to profess his renewed faith in God. Corporal Wilbur Ehrlich, a patrolman from the Seventy-Eighth Precinct, managed to get a message to his friends all the way from Kriegsgfangenpost, Germany, on November 7, 1943: "As you can see, I've got a new address. I was captured as a prisoner of war in September. I was wounded slightly about the arms and back but I am as healthy as ever now and looking forward to the time when I'll be returning to get back to work. Regards to the boys." Ehrlich's POW camp was liberated by the Allies near the end of the war, and he returned home to resume his police career.

Meanwhile, back in New York police officers supported their colleagues fighting on the front by purchasing $16 million worth of war bonds. It was an astonishing amount of money considering that the average weekly salary for a patrolman at the time was only $48.90. The War Department used the capital to buy eighty fighter planes and a B-25 bomber. In recognition of their proud sponsors, the Army Air Corps painted "City of New York Police" and "City of New York Patrol" on the fuselages of the aircraft funded by the force.

During the war the department's manning level dropped to just 15,000 men, some 4,000 men below the authorized staffing quota. To supplement the force LaGuardia hired 254 temporary patrolmen for a period to last no more than six months past the end of the war. Each man was paid $2,000 per year but received no pension benefits. Despite their important contribution in alleviating personnel shortages, the temporary patrolmen drew the mayor's wrath when they formed their own benevolent association and sought to become permanent members of the NYPD. The action upset LaGuardia so much that he ordered Valentine to immediately dismiss their spokesman from the force.

With fewer police available to enforce traffic regulations, one would have thought that there would have been a rise in traffic-related fatalities, but the strict rationing of gasoline and the ban on weekend pleasure driving substantially reduced the volume of traffic on New York City streets. Fewer cars resulted in fewer fatal accidents. According to police statistics, there were 857 traffic fatalities in 1942. When the rationing rules went into effect in 1943, the number of traffic deaths dropped to 742.

While the vast majority of Americans willingly mobilized to help defeat the Axis powers, there were others who saw no hope for their situation at home, no matter what the outcome of the war. Across the United States urban areas were experiencing violent race riots. LaGuardia was particularly concerned that a second outbreak would occur in Harlem. In an effort to keep neighborhood residents from rising up, he regularly met with prominent black leaders and pledged to assign more black patrolmen to their community. But meetings and promises still could not prevent another deadly riot from taking place. On August 1, 1943, a black woman named Marjorie Polite complained that the accommodations at the Hotel Braddock on West 126th Street were unsatisfactory and decided to leave. During the checkout process she demanded that the elevator operator return the dollar tip she had given him earlier for helping with her luggage. The elevator operator refused. Patrolman James Collins, whose post included the hotel, was called to resolve the dispute. When Mrs. Polite turned on him, he arrested her for disorderly conduct.

Two other people in the hotel lobby, Mrs. Florine Roberts and her son, army private Robert Bandy, thought Patrolman Collins had overreacted and rushed to Mrs. Polite's defense. Bandy tried to prevent Collins from taking Mrs. Polite into custody. A scuffle ensued. Bandy grabbed Collins's nightstick and hit him in the head. As Bandy started to flee, Collins fired one round from his revolver. The bullet grazed Bandy's left shoulder. It caused a minor injury, but local activists with their own agendas began to circulate a deliberate lie throughout the neighborhood that a white cop had murdered an innocent black soldier.

As soon as he received the first reports of wanton looting, Valentine sealed off all of the streets leading into Harlem and flooded the area with six thousand patrolmen. He banned liquor sales and put a mandatory 11 p.m. curfew into effect. Both Valentine and LaGuardia remained on the scene for the next two days. Despite their constant presence there was enormous property damage, and six black men lost their lives. As bad as the disturbance was, a race riot in Detroit in June 1943 had left thirty-four dead and required federal intervention. Adam Clayton Powell Jr., the black pastor of Harlem's Abyssinian Baptist Church and a staunch critic of the mayor, conceded that LaGuardia's leadership had helped to stem the violence.

In September 1943 policewomen were issued new stylish leather shoulder bags, courtesy of former police commissioner Grover Whalen. The bags were specially designed to conceal their revolvers but also had compartments for a compact and a tube of lipstick. LaGuardia playfully teased the policewomen as he presented them with the new equipment: "Use your gun as you would your lipstick—only when you need it."

In January 1944 LaGuardia offered all city employees a onetime $420 bonus in lieu of a recurring pay increase. Most city workers had not seen their salary go up in the ten years that LaGuardia had been in office. In fact new patrolmen made less money than before LaGuardia had become mayor because he had lowered their starting salary by $800 and added an extra step for them to reach top salary. As a result new police officers began their careers at a pay rate of just $25.00 per week and took seven years to reach top pay.

The leadership of the Patrolmen's Benevolent Association preferred that the bonus be part of a permanent raise. The matter was a hot topic for discussion at the next union meeting. Thirty-eight delegates walked out in protest after a majority of delegates voted to accept the bonus, even though LaGuardia said he was giving it to them in exchange for future productivity gains.

When police employees were queried by *Spring 3100* about how they intended to spend the extra cash, a twenty-six-year-old policewoman named Gertrude Schimmel replied, "I'm planning to buy War Bonds. After my hubby comes back from the war, we're going on a second honeymoon to Arizona and Mexico." It is not known whether Schimmel ever followed through with her travel plans, but by the time she retired, she had achieved the highest rank of any woman in the NYPD. Early in her career Schimmel was assigned to perform undercover work infiltrating illegal gambling establishments. (As a result of those experiences, Schimmel became such a good card player that later in life she traveled to Las Vegas to partake in professional high-stakes poker tournaments.) In 1971 Schimmel became the first female captain in department history. In recognition of her groundbreaking achievement, Mayor John Lindsey personally pinned on her shoulder bars. In 1978 she was promoted to deputy chief and retired at that rank in 1981 after completing thirty-seven years of service.

As an allied victory loomed on the horizon, LaGuardia and Valentine began to ponder their futures after the war. LaGuardia hinted that he might run for an unprecedented fourth term as mayor. He mulled over the idea for several months before announcing on May 6, 1945, during his weekly Sunday morning radio show that he would not seek office again.

Valentine waited until September 1945 to disclose that he intended to retire, even though the leading candidate to replace LaGuardia, Democrat William O'Dwyer, since discharged from the military, graciously offered to let him stay on as police commissioner for as long as he wanted. During his farewell address to the force Valentine stated that he expected to be lonesome in his retirement, but just the opposite turned out to be true. He was so in demand after he left the job that he had to hire the famed William Morris Agency to handle his schedule of personal appearances.

With Valentine's departure LaGuardia, despite being a lame duck mayor, was in the position of being able to appoint Valentine's successor to a five-year term, for the vast part of which he himself would not be in office. Although none of the mayoral candidates issued a public statement concerning their preferences, LaGuardia's selection of Deputy Chief Arthur Wallander as the city's new police commissioner was made with O'Dwyer's blessing.

The fifty-three-year-old Wallander was born in New York City in February 1882 and raised in the Bronx. He had joined the department in 1914 and had distinguished himself during his thirty-one-year career as a physical fitness instructor, a police pilot, the commanding officer of the prestigious Emergency Service Division, and (most important in LaGuardia's eyes) the chief of staff for defense, supervising upward of 425,000 civilian defense volunteers during the war.

Wallander's swearing-in ceremony on September 23, 1945, was broadcast live over the radio. Afterward Wallander pledged never to disgrace the city, to fight for ideals, and to endeavor to make the police department greater and the city better and more beautiful than ever.

O'Dwyer and Wallander knew each other from their early days together on the force. Their bond was so strong that after O'Dwyer won the mayoral election and was told that Wallander had an offer to become an airline executive, he said, "He won't. As soon as he leaves headquarters, I'll have him locked up."

Despite his impressive qualifications, Wallander was replacing a legend. Valentine was recognized as the premier police administrator in the country. After the war in the Pacific ended, General Douglas MacArthur selected him to go to Japan to transform the national police from an arm of the military to a civilian-controlled police force. In between his travels and his duties as host of the weekly radio show *Gang Busters* Valentine managed to find time to write his autobiography, appropriately titled *Nightstick*. Sadly, however, the "Honest Cop" died on December 16, 1946, just fifteen short months after retirement. His life story was published posthumously in 1947. As for LaGuardia, before he left City Hall, he commended the NYPD for its service during his twelve years in office:

> For the first time in four years we celebrate Christmas in a country at peace. For this gift we give our thanks to Almighty God and to the men who fought and died on land, on the sea, and in the air to make it possible. For the peace abroad we are indebted to the Army, Navy and Air Force, but for the peace in our own City we owe our thanks to you men of the Police Force, who, although shorthanded because of war conditions, and with civilian defense and anti-sabotage responsibilities added to your regular duties, did everything that was demanded of you and maintained a magnificent record for which you can be justly proud. This is also the last of twelve Christmases in which I can address you as your Mayor. As Mayor let me say that I am proud of you and the City of New York is proud of you. There is no finer police force in the world and none that commands a greater respect from the people it serves. We have come a long way together and I shall miss you. I wish you all a Merry Christmas and a Happy New Year.

On December 31, 1945, Mayor LaGuardia left office with a wave of his top hat and a smile as big as all New York. Over the next year and half he kept busy with his weekly radio broadcasts, penning his autobiography (only partially completed at the time of his death), and touring Europe as director of the United Nations Relief and Rehabilitation Administration.

Like Valentine, with whom he had shared so much, LaGuardia was battling his own health crisis, pancreatic cancer. His final days were spent confined in a bed at his residence in the Riverdale section of the Bronx. LaGuardia lapsed into a coma on September 16, 1947. Although doctors remained by his bedside around the clock and millions of New Yorkers prayed for his recovery, the Little Flower died peacefully in his sleep on September 20, 1947. At 8:15 that morning an order went out over the police teletype network informing members of the force of his death. His longtime friend and adviser, Samuel Seabury, lamented, "The greatest mayor in the history of New York is dead." Police estimated that fifty thousand people viewed his remains in an open casket at the Cathedral of St. John the Divine before LaGuardia was laid to rest in Woodlawn Cemetery in the Bronx.

Forgotten by most New Yorkers was the man who had stepped aside in 1933 so that LaGuardia could become mayor. John O'Ryan never returned to public life except for a brief tenure as New York State's director of civilian defense in 1941. He continued to practice law and write books on military topics. O'Ryan, LaGuardia's first police commissioner, died in 1961 at the age of eighty-five.

During the reign of these men the NYPD set a standard of professionalism by which all succeeding police administrations would be judged. When they came on board, the public viewed the police force as a greedy, self-serving organization that catered unabashedly to the will of the city's politicians. With LaGuardia's full support and Valentine's sheer will to root out corruption and dismiss those he found guilty of misconduct, the department appeared for the time to have cleansed itself. However, not all leaders in the future would be as steadfastly vigilant. Without these dedicated reformers organized corruption involving members of the police force would soon return, and even some of the most successful strategies employed by Valentine during his almost twelve years in office would be called into question.

Still the NYPD had shown that it could protect the city in times of crisis. The department had also made great technological strides in the continuing battle against crime. Most important, the men and women of the nation's largest police department had shown America during its darkest hour why they were called New York's Finest.

ACKNOWLEDGMENTS

This book would not have been possible without the important contributions of the following people: Mr. Robert Wilson, agent; Mr. David Doorey, research assistant; Mrs. Mary Whalen, research assistant; Ms. Bridget Barry, editor, University of Nebraska Press; Ms. Sabrina Ehmke Sergeant, assistant editor, University of Nebraska Press; Ms. Sara Springsteen, associate project editor, University of Nebraska Press; Ms. Bojana Ristich, copyeditor, University of Nebraska Press; Ms. Tish Fobben and Ms. Acacia Gentrup, marketing, University of Nebraska Press; Mr. Leif Milliken, rights and contracts, University of Nebraska Press; Ms. Elizabeth Demmers, Potomac Books; William Bratton, police commissioner, NYPD; John Beirne, deputy commissioner, NYPD Office of Labor Relations; David Cohen, deputy commissioner, labor counsel, NYPD; Stephen Davis, deputy commissioner, public information, NYPD; James Dean, inspector (retired), Emergency Service Unit, NYPD; E. James, lieutenant, NYPD, editor, *Spring 3100*; Paul McCullagh, agency attorney, NYPD Office of Labor Relations; Edward Dagostino, police officer, NYPD Office of Labor Relations; Frank Caruso, director, NYPD Fleet Services Division; Thomas Doepfner, assistant deputy commissioner, NYPD Legal Bureau; Ms. Lesa Moore, agency attorney, NYPD Legal Bureau; Patrick Lynch, president, Patrolmen's Benevolent Association; John Puglisi, vice president, Patrolmen's Benevolent Association; David Nicholson, attorney, Patrolmen's Benevolent Association; Joseph Mancini, editor, *Finest Magazine*, Patrolmen's Benevolent Association; Greg Longworth, attorney, Patrolmen's Benevolent Association; Michael Palladino, president, Detectives Endowment Association; Paul DiGiacomo, vice president, Detectives Endowment Association; Ms. Sam Katz, Detectives Endowment Association; Edward Mullins, president, Sergeants Benevolent Association; Robert Ganley, vice president, Sergeants Benevolent Association; Robert Maladivich, editor, *Sergeants Benevolent Association Magazine*; Anthony Garvey, former president, Lieutenants Benevolent Association; Lou Turco, president, Lieutenants Benevolent Association; William Larney, Lieutenants Benevolent Association; Dylan McCarthy, NYPD intern, summer 2012; John Timoney, former first deputy, NYPD; George Grasso, judge and former first deputy, NYPD; Ms. Colleen Scully, William Bratton's personal assistant; Mrs. Easter Miles, daughter of Detective Joseph Lynch; Mr. Emil Vyskocil Jr., son of Patrolman Emil Vyskocil; Mr. Joshua Ruff, curator, New York City Police Museum; Ms. Christine Bruzzese, supervising reference librarian, Municipal Reference and Research Center; Ms. Janet Isaac, librarian, Municipal Reference and Research Center; Mr. Daniel Altari, proofreader; Mr. Charles Murphy; Professor David Ignato; and our families: Laura Whalen, Melissa Whalen, and the late Vera Whalen.

APPENDIX

TABLE 1. TWO-PLATOON–FOUR-SECTION DUTY SYSTEM USED BY THE NYPD IN 1898

	DAY 1					DAY 2				
	6 a.m.–8 a.m.	8 a.m.–1 p.m.	1 p.m.–6 p.m.	6 p.m.–12 a.m.	12 a.m.–6 a.m.	6 a.m.–8 a.m.	8 a.m.–1 p.m.	1 p.m.–6 p.m.	6 p.m.–12 a.m.	12 a.m.–6 a.m.
1st Section	P	R	P	R	P				P	
2nd Section		P	R	R	P				P	R
3rd Section				P	R	P	R	P	R	P
4th Section				P			P	R	R	P

	DAY 3					DAY 4				
	6 a.m.–8 a.m.	8 a.m.–1 p.m.	1 p.m.–6 p.m.	6 p.m.–12 a.m.	12 a.m.–6 a.m.	6 a.m.–8 a.m.	8 a.m.–1 p.m.	1 p.m.–6 p.m.	6 p.m.–12 a.m.	12 a.m.–6 a.m.
1st Section		P	R	R	P				P	R
2nd Section	P	R	P	R	P				P	
3rd Section				P			P	R	R	P
4th Section				P	R	P	R	P	R	P

P — Patrol
R — Reserve
— Home time

217

TABLE 2. THREE-PLATOON DUTY SYSTEM USED BY THE NYPD IN 1904

SQUAD	DAY 1			DAY 2			DAY 3		
	1ST PLATOON 8 a.m.–4.pm.	2ND PLATOON 4 p.m.–12 a.m.	3RD PLATOON 12 a.m.–8 a.m.	1ST PLATOON 8 a.m.–4.pm.	2ND PLATOON 4 p.m.–12 a.m.	3RD PLATOON 12 a.m.–8 a.m.	1ST PLATOON 8 a.m.–4.pm.	2ND PLATOON 4 p.m.–12 a.m.	3RD PLATOON 12 a.m.–8 a.m.
1A	P	R		P			P		
1B	P			P	R		P		
1C	P			P			P	R	
2A		P	R		P			P	
2B		P			P	R		P	
2C		P			P			P	R
3A			P	R		P			P
3B			P			P	R		P
3C	R		P			P			P

P	Patrol
R	Reserve
	Home time

Patrolmen performed the duty as follows: 1st platoon: 8 a.m.–4 p.m. for two weeks; 2nd platoon: 4 p.m.–12 a.m. for two weeks; 3rd platoon: 12 a.m.–8 a.m. for two weeks; then the rotation started again.

TABLE 3. 1906 NYPD DUTY CHART

DAY 1   **DAY 2**

6 a.m.–8 a.m.	8 a.m.–1 p.m.	1 p.m.–6 p.m.	6 p.m.–12 a.m.	12 a.m.–6 a.m.	6 a.m.–8 a.m.	8 a.m.–1 p.m.	1 p.m.–6 p.m.	6 p.m.–12 a.m	12 a.m.–6 a.m.
1	1	1	1	1				1	
	2	2	2	2				2	2
			3	3	3	3	3	3	3
			4		4	4	4	4	4

DAY 3   **DAY 4**

6 a.m.–8 a.m.	8 a.m.–1 p.m.	1 p.m.–6 p.m.	6 p.m.–12 a.m.	12 a.m.–6 a.m.	6 a.m.–8 a.m.	8 a.m.–1 p.m.	1 p.m.–6 p.m.	6 p.m.–12 a.m.	12 a.m.–6 a.m.
	1	1	1	1				1	1
2	2	2	2	2				2	
			3		3	3	3	3	3
			4	4	4	4	4	4	4

Darkened numbered boxes indicate squad and hours scheduled to patrol; lightened numbered boxes indicate squad and hours scheduled to be on reserve; boxes without numbers indicate home time (off-duty hours).

The chart rotates every 4 days (96 hours); of the 96 hours, 36 hours are on patrol, 28 hours are on reserve, and 32 hours are home (off) time.

Distribution of patrol force during each shift of the 24-hour day: 6 a.m.–8 a.m. (2 hours)—25 percent scheduled to patrol and 75 percent off; 8 a.m.–1 p.m. (5 hours)—25 percent scheduled to patrol, 25 percent scheduled for reserve, and 50 percent off; 1 p.m.–6 p.m. (5 hours)—25 percent scheduled to patrol, 25 percent scheduled for reserve, and 50 percent off; 6 p.m.–12 a.m. (6 hours)—50 percent scheduled to patrol and 50 percent scheduled for reserve; 12 a.m.–6 a.m. (6 hours)—50 percent scheduled to patrol, 25 percent scheduled for reserve, and 25 percent off.

Nights off granted as follows: roundsmen and patrolmen: 1 night off every 12 days or 3 rotations; doormen and matrons: 1 night off every 30 days or 7.5 rotations. Nights off commence at the finish of a short-day tour of patrol duty and after return roll call at 1:30 p.m.

Rotation: 6 hours patrol, 6 hours reserve, 2 hours patrol, 5 hours reserve, 5 hours patrol, 6 hours reserve, 6 hours patrol, 12 hours off, 6 hours patrol, 8 hours off, 5 hours patrol, 11 hours reserve, 6 hours patrol, 12 hours off; 1-hour meal periods.

TABLE 4. ANNUAL VACATION ACCRUAL
RATES BY RANK IN 1906

Sergeant and detective sergeant	15 days with pay
Roundsman	12 days with pay or 20 days with half-pay
Patrolman, doorman, and matron	10 days with pay or 18 days with half-pay

TABLE 5. ANNUAL VACATION ACCRUAL
RATES BY RANK IN 1920

Deputy commissioner and chief inspector	30 days
Borough inspector, chief of staff, and chief surgeon	28 days
Inspector, surgeon, and chaplain	26 days
Captain and acting captain	24 days
Lieutenant, acting lieutenant, and detective sergeant first grade	22 days
Sergeant, acting sergeant, and detective sergeant second grade	20 days
Patrolman, policewoman, and patrolwoman	18 days
Civilian staff member	25 days

Only one captain in each district could be on vacation at the same time. Only one lieutenant, sergeant, and matron in each precinct could be on vacation at the same time. Not more than 9 percent of the total compliment of patrolmen in each precinct could be on vacation at the same time. No more than two patrolmen in each squad could be on vacation at the same time.

TABLE 6. ANNUAL POLICE SALARIES IN 1918 AND 1928

POSITION	1918	1928
Patrolman	$1,200–$1,650	$2,500
Sergeant	$1,900	$3,000
First-grade detective	NA	$3,500
Lieutenant	$2,450	$3,500
Captain	$3,120	$4,500
Deputy inspector	NA	$5,000
District inspector	$3,900	NA
Inspector	NA	$5,400
Borough inspector	$4,300	NA
Deputy chief inspector	NA	$5,800
Chief inspector	$6,000	$8,000
Deputy commissioner	$6,000	NA
Police commissioner	$7,500	$10,000

TABLE 7. COST OF EQUIPMENT FOR PATROLMEN IN 1914 AND 1919

ITEM	1914	1919
Summer blouse	$12.00	$27.00
Winter blouse	$18.00	$35.00
Trousers	$6.00	$16.00
Shoes	$4.00	$9.00
Cap	$1.35	$2.00
Gloves	$1.00	$4.00
Pistol	$14.00	$19.00

TABLE 8. ADDITIONAL EXPENSES IN 1919

Change of bed sheets	$1.00 per month
Shoe shine	$1.00 per month
Pension*	$35.00 per year
Insurance	$14.45 per month, broken down as follows:

Patrolmen's Benevolent Association	$0.55
Patrolmen's Association of Greater New York	$1.65
Police Endowment Fund	$2.55
Municipal Police Mutual Association	$1.55
Mutual Benevolent Association	$2.55
Patrolmen's Endowment Organization	$2.80
Police Volunteer Association	$2.80

* Mandatory. Member eligible for half-pay retirement pension after reaching 55 years of age or achieving 25 years of service.

TABLE 9. EXPENSES FOR PATROLMEN DURING
FIRST YEAR OF SERVICE IN 1913

Overcoat	$25.00
Winter trousers	$6.50
Winter blouse	$16.75
Winter cap	$1.75
Summer cap	$1.47
Leather belt	$1.70
Cord and tassel	$0.45
Locust nightstick	$0.30
Billet	$0.33
Rawhide straps	$0.10
Whistle	$0.35
Nippers and holders	$0.50
Revolver and cartridges	$12.50
Plates for clubs	$0.08
Cap device	$0.20
Precinct numbers	$0.24
Buckskin gloves	$1.30
White gloves (3 pairs)	$0.60
Rubber cap cover	$0.40
Rubber cap cape	$0.35
Rubber coat	$3.75
Rubber boots	$3.50
Rubber holster	$0.20
Single mattress	$5.00
Four sheets ($0.78 each)	$3.12
Two bedspreads	$4.50
Four pillow cases ($0.30 each)	$1.20
Two double blankets	$10.00
One comforter	$3.00
One pillow	$2.25
Total	$120.09

TABLE 10. PRECINCT NUMBERING SYSTEM AND REPORTED STAFFING IN 1898

BOROUGH OF MANHATTAN

New Precinct Number	Old Precinct Number	Location	Staffing
Central Office	NA	300 Mulberry St.	144
First	First	Old Slip	119
Second	Second	Liberty St. & Church St.	139
Third	Third	City Hall	104
Fourth	Bridge	Brooklyn Bridge	128
Fifth	Fourth	9 Oak St.	134
Sixth	Sixth	19 Elizabeth St.	98
Seventh	Seventh	247 Madison St.	95
Eighth	Fifth	19 Leonard St.	134
Ninth	Ninth	135 Charles St.	130
Tenth	Eighth	24 MacDougal St.	157
Eleventh	Tenth	205 Mulberry St.	80
Twelfth	Eleventh	105 Eldridge St.	113
Thirteenth	Twelfth	Attorney St. & Delancy St.	66
Fourteenth	Thirteenth	Union Market–Hudson St. & Delancy St.	77
Fifteenth	Fourteenth	1st Ave. & 5th St.	109
Sixteenth	Fifteenth	253 Mercer St.	117
Seventeenth	Sixteenth	230 W. 20th St.	105
Eighteenth	Eighteenth	327 E. 22nd St.	122
Nineteenth	Nineteenth	137 W. 30th St.	197
Twentieth	Twentieth	434 W. 35th St.	117
Twenty-First	Twenty-First	160 E. 35th St.	102
Twenty-Second	Twenty-Second	345 W. 47th St.	140
Twenty-Third	Seventeenth	Grand Central Depot	44
Twenty-Fourth	Twenty-Third	163 E. 51st St.	133
Twenty-Fifth	Twenty-Fifth	153 E. 67th St.	151
Twenty-Sixth	Twenty-Fourth	150 W. 68th St.	121
Twenty-Seventh	Central Park	The Arsenal, Central Park	180

Twenty-Eighth	Twenty-Seventh	432 E. 88th St.	116
Twenty-Ninth	Twenty Eighth	177 E. 104th St.	122
Thirtieth	Twenty-Sixth	134 W. 100th St.	108
Thirty-First	Thirtieth	428 W. 125th St.	163
Thirty-Second	Twenty-Ninth	148 E. 126th St.	144
Thirty-Third	Thirty-Second	150th St. & Amsterdam Ave.	137
Criminal Court Squad	NA	Franklin St. & Centre St.	172
Second Court Squad	NA	W. 10th St. & 6th Ave.	NA
Third Court Squad	NA	69 Essex St.	NA
Fourth Court Squad	NA	151 E. 57th St.	NA
Fifth Court Squad	NA	170 E. 121st St.	NA
Sixth Court Squad	NA	185th St. & 3rd Ave.	NA
Seventh Court Squad	NA	314 W. 54th St.	NA
Detective Bureau	NA	300 Mulberry St.	138
Bureau of Information	NA	300 Mulberry St.	NA
Boiler Squad	NA	300 Mulberry St.	NA
Health Squad	NA	Franklin St. & Centre St.	82
Bicycle Squad	NA	1867 Broadway	90
House of Detention	NA	203 Mulberry St.	9

BOROUGH OF THE BRONX

Thirty-Fourth	Thirty-First	High Bridge	66
Thirty-Fifth	Thirty-Seventh	138th St. & Alexander Ave.	118
Thirty-Sixth	Thirty-Third	160th St. & 3rd Ave.	122
Thirty-Seventh	Thirty-Fourth	177th St. & Bathgate Ave.	66
Thirty-Eighth	Thirty-Eighth	Main St. & Westchester Ave.	78
Thirty-Ninth	Thirty-Eighth Sub	Wakefield	47
Fortieth	Thirty-Fifth	Kingsbridge	69
Forty-First	Bronx Park	Bronx Park	57
Forty-Second	Thirty-Sixth	Pier "A"–North River	65

Forty-Third	Eighteenth	43rd St. & 4th Ave.	65
Forty-Fourth	Eighth	16th St. & 8th Ave.	69
Forty-Fifth	Eleventh	Richard Ave. & Rapelye St.	74
Forty-Sixth	Tenth	Bergen St. & 6th Ave.	61
Forty-Seventh	Third	17 Butler St.	73
Forty-Eighth	Fifteenth	Emmet St. & Amity St.	42
Forty-Ninth	First	318 Adams St.	97
Fiftieth	Second	49 Fulton St.	53
Fifty-First	Twenty-Second	Grand Ave. & Park Place	42
Fifty-Second	Twelfth	Atlantic Ave. & Schenectady Aves.	53
Fifty-Third	Seventeenth	Lee Ave. & Clymer St.	71
Fifty-Fourth	Fourteenth	Ralph Ave. & Quincey St.	69
Fifty-Fifth	Ninth	Gates Ave. & Troop Ave.	89
Fifty-Sixth	Fourth	Dekalb Ave. & Classon Ave.	67
Fifty-Seventh	Twenty-First	Clermont Ave. & Flushing Ave.	49
Fifty-Eighth	Thirteenth	Tompkins Ave. & Vernon Ave.	45
Fifty-Ninth	Sixteenth	Lee Ave. & Clymer St.	74
Sixtieth	Fifth	Bedford Ave. & N. First St.	78
Sixty-First	Seventh	Manhattan Ave. & Greenpoint Ave.	64
Sixty-Second	Nineteenth	Humbolt Ave. & Herbert St.	52
Sixty-Third	Sixth	Stagg St. & Bushwick Ave.	65
Sixty-Fourth	Twentieth	DeKalb Ave. & Hamburg Ave.	73
Sixty-Fifth	Twenty-Seventh	Eastern Pky. near Osborne St.	34

Sixty-Sixth	Twenty-Sixth	Canarsie Village	34
Sixty-Seventh	Twenty-Third	Grand St. near Flatbush Ave.	46
Sixty-Eighth	Twenty-Eighth	Voorches Ave. & Shore Rd.	32
Sixty-Ninth	Twenty-Fourth	W. 8th St. & Surf Ave.	48
Seventieth	Twenty-Ninth	29th Ave.–Bath & Benson Aves.	33
Seventy-First	Twenty-Fifth	86th St. & Fort Hamilton Ave.	35
Seventy-Second	Thirtieth	Foster Ave. near Coney Island Ave.	32
Seventy-Third	Prospect Park	Prospect Park	72
Detective Bureau	NA	Municipal Building–Joralemon St.	15
License Squad	NA	Borough Hall–Fulton St. Entrance	14

BOROUGH OF QUEENS

Headquarters, Borough of Queens	NA	No. 142 East End Ave.	NA
Seventy-Fourth	First, Long Island City	Crescent St. & Grand Ave.	39
Seventy-Fifth	Second, Long Island City	4th St. & Vernon Ave.	51
Seventy-Sixth	Flushing	Linden Ave. & Broadway	38
Seventy-Sixth (First Sub)	College Point	2nd Ave. near 6th St.	NA
Seventy-Sixth (Second Sub)	Whitestone	8th Ave. & 18th St.	NA
Seventy-Seventh	Newtown	Grand Ave. & Court St.	19
Seventy-Eighth	Jamaica	Flushing Ave. & Fulton St.	38
Seventy-Eighth (Sub)	Richmond Hill	Johnson Ave. & Jamaica Ave.	NA
Seventy-Ninth	Far Rockaway	Mott Ave. & Central Ave.	31
Seventy-Ninth (Sub)	Rockaway Beach	Seaside Ave. & Henry St.	NA

Headquarters, Borough of Richmond	NA	19 Beach St. Stapleton	NA
Eightieth	First (Staten Island)	19 Beach St. Stapleton	65
Eighty-First (Sub)	Second (Staten Island)	Richmond Terrace & W. New Brighton	NA
Eighty-Second (Sub)	Third (Staten Island)	E. Broadway & Tottenville	NA
Eighty-Third (Sub)	Fourth (Staten Island)	Rockland Ave. & New Springfield	NA

OTHER COMMANDS

Detective Bureau Manhattan	NA	NA	123
Detective Bureau Brooklyn	NA	NA	15
Central Office Squad	NA	NA	144
Telegraph Squad	NA	NA	21
Court Squads	NA	NA	172
Total Staffing			7,431

TABLE 11. STAFFING OF INDIVIDUAL POLICE DEPARTMENTS CONSOLIDATED IN 1898

DEPARTMENT	STAFFING
Manhattan and the Bronx	
New York City Police Department	5,280
New York City Park Police	337
Brooklyn	
City of Brooklyn Police Department	1,831
City of Brooklyn Park Police	126
City of Brooklyn Bridge Police	102
Queens	
Long Island City Police Department	86
Town of Flushing, Constables	0
Village of Flushing Police Department	13
Village of College Point Police Department	8
Village of Whitestone Police Department	4
Village of Arverne Police Department	3
Village of Far Rockaway Police Department	15
Village of Rockaway Beach Police Department	10
Town of Jamaica, Constables	0
Village of Jamaica, Constables	0
Village of Richmond Hills Police Department	8
Town of Newtown, Constables	0
Staten Island	
Richmond County Police Department	70

	1898 VAN WYCK	1902 LOW	1904 MCCLELLAN	1910 GAYNOR
Police Board	4 bipartisan commissioners			
Police commissioner		1	1	1
First deputy		1	1	1
Second deputy		1	1	1
Third deputy				1
Fourth deputy				1
Fifth deputy				
Chief of police	1			
Chief inspector				1
Assistant chief				
Deputy chief	5			
Inspector	10	14	16	18
Deputy inspector				
Captain	72	77	85	87
Lieutenant				614
Sergeant	324	398	409	568
Detective sergeant	88	121	263	
Roundsman	361	394	427	
Patrolman	6,396	6,393	6,776	8,374
Patrolwoman				
Policewoman				
Doorman	153	176	186	192
Matron		61		70
Surgeon	21	21	23	24
Total*	7,457	7,673	8,292	10,177

* Total includes probationary patrolmen and civilian staff not listed individually by rank or title. The ranks of roundsman, detective sergeant, patrolwoman, matron, and doorman were eliminated. Roundsmen became sergeants. Sergeants and detective sergeants became lieutenants. Matrons and patrolwomen became policewomen. Doormen became patrolmen. Other ranks such as deputy inspector and assistant chief were added.

1914 MITCHEL	1918 HYLAN	1926 WALKER	1932 LAGUARDIA	1946 O'DWYER
1	1	1	1	1
1	1	1	1	1
1	1	1	1	1
1	1	1	1	1
1	1	1	1	1
		1	1	1
1	1	1	1	1
			1	6
	3	7	9	15
18	22	15	28	33
		15	27	30
97	90	94	105	135
524	524	543	648	628
726	769	964	1,072	1,047
9,387	9,387	14,153	17,253	12,991
	10	30		
70	65	95	155	155
24	17	23	27	22
10,707	10,858	15,950	19,331	15,068

SELECTED BIBLIOGRAPHY

While hundreds of sources were used to write this book, the authors found the index of the *New York Times* most helpful in chronicling the day-to-day goings on in the NYPD during the time period covered. Once an outline was completed, it was possible to use the information provided by the index to search and locate other sources. These sources included biographies of the main characters, magazine articles, and internal police department documents from which many of the quotes cited in the text were drawn.

ARCHIVAL SOURCES

Charter of the City of New York.

Committee of Fourteen Records, 1905–32. New York Public Library Manuscripts and Archives Division. Melanie A. Yolles, curator. May 1985. Rev. July 2000.

Department of Health. *Annual Report,* 1919.

General Laws of the State of New York, 1911.

General Laws of the State of New York, 1920.

International Police Conference. Third Annual Meeting, New York City, April 30–May 5, 1923.

Laws of New York State, 1902–7.

NYPD. *Annual Reports,* 1898–1946.

——. Circulars, 1898–1946.

——. General Orders, 1898–1946.

——. "Rules and Regulations and Manual of Procedure." Rev. December 6, 1940.

——. "Rules and Regulations of the Police Department, City of New York," 1908.

——. Special Orders, 1898–1946.

Transcripts of Police Commissioner Richard Enright's Radio Broadcasts 1923. New York Municipal Reference Library.

"Barnum in Modern Dress—Grover Whalen 'America's Greatest Greeter' Presents the World of Tomorrow." *Harper's Magazine*, October 1938.

"The Best Administration New York Ever Had." *Campaign Book of the Citizen's Union*, September 1903.

Bingham, Theodore (General). "Policing Our Lawless Cities." *Hampton's Magazine*, 1909.

Brodsky, Alyn. *The Great Mayor*. New York: St. Martin's Press, 2003.

Brown, Peter Megaree. *Riot of the Century: The New York City Draft Riots of July 1863*. New York: Benchmark Press, 1998.

Bryk, William. *The Last Police Chief*. New York: Gotham Center for New York City, CUNY, April 2010.

Cahalane, Cornelius J. (Inspector, New York Police). *Police Duty: A Course of Study for Policemen Everywhere*. New York: Chief Publishing, 1912.

———. *Police Practice and Procedure*. New York: E. F. Dutton, 1914.

Caliendo, Ralph. *New York City Mayors*. Xlibris, 2010.

Clump, Irving. *The Boys' Book of Policemen*. New York: Dodd, Mead, 1917.

Curran, Henry H. *Pillar to Post*. New York: Charles Scribner's Sons, 1941.

Donnelly, Jim. "NYPD Green: History of New York City Police Cars 1917–1973." *Classic Car*, May 2014.

Eno, William Phelps. *Street Traffic Regulation*. New York: Rider and Driver Publishing, July 1909.

Fowler, Gene. *Beau James: The Life and Times of Jimmy Walker*. New York: Viking Press, 1949.

Fuller, Hector. *Abroad with Mayor Walker*. New York: Shields Publishing, 1928.

Gribetz, Louis, and Joseph Kaye. *Jimmy Walker: The Story of Personality*. New York: Dial Press, 1932.

Griffen, Henry Farrand. "The Policeman and Public Safety." *The Outlook*, May–August 1911.

Hickey, John. *Our Police Guardians, by Officer "787" John J. Hickey*. Self-published, 1925.

Hylan, John J. *Autobiography of John Francis Hylan, Mayor New York*. New York: Polary Press, 1922.

Keire, Mara L. *Vice in American Cities 1890–1925: The Committee of Fourteen and Saloon Reform in New York City, 1905–1920*. N.p., n.d.

Kessner, Thomas. *Fiorello H. LaGuardia and the Making of Modern New York*. New York: McGraw-Hill, 1989.

Kurland, Gerald. *Seth Low: The Reformer in an Urban and Industrial Age*. New York: Twayne Publishers, 1971.

Lewinson, Edwin R. *John Purroy Mitchel: The Boy Mayor of New York*. New York: Astra Books, 1965.

Leyson, Burr W. (Captain). *Fighting Crime: The New York City Police Department in Action*. New York: E. P. Dutton, 1948.

Limpus, Lowell M. *Honest Cop*. New York: E. P. Dutton, 1939.

———, and Burr W. Leyson. *This Man LaGuardia*. New York: E. P. Dutton, 1938.

McAdoo, William. *Guarding a Great City*. New York: Harper and Brothers, 1906.

McClellan, George, Jr. *The Gentleman and the Tiger: The Autobiography of George B. McClellan Jr.* New York: J. P. Lippincott, 1956.

Mittgang, Herbert. *The Man Who Rode the Tiger: The Life and Times of Judge Samuel Seabury*. New York: J. B. Lippincott, 1963.

"Police Inquiry Constructive." *Gaynor Charter on Police*, September 30, 1912.

Pretzel, Notker A. "How McLaughlin Is Meeting New York's Peculiar Police Questions." *Police Journal*, August 1926.

Repetto, Thomas. *American Mafia: A History of Its Rise to Power*. New York: Henry Holt, 2004.

Riss, Jacob A. "The Police Department of New York." *The Outlook*, September–December 1898.

"Rosenthal Murder's Lesson." *Gaynor Charter on Police*, July 30, 1912.

Ruff, Joshua, and Michael Cronin. *Images of America: New York City Police*. Charleston SC: Arcadia Publishing, 2012.

Stowe, L. B. "The New York Police." *The Outlook*, 1907.

Valentine, Lewis J. *Nightstick*. New York: Dial Press, 1947.

Van Wagner, Ernest. *New York Detective*. Binghamton NY: Vail-Ballou Press, 1938.

Wallach, Julia, and Isabel Richman Wallach. *Good Citizenship*. New York: American Book, 1908.

Wallander, Arthur W. (Sergeant, Training School Police Department, City of New York). *Physical Training Manual*. New York: Siebel Press, 1925.

Waller, George. *Kidnap: The Story of the Lindberg Case*. New York: Dial Press, 1961.

Whalen, Grover. *Mr. New York: The Autobiography of Grover Whalen.* New York: G. P. Putnam's Sons, 1955.

"What's the Matter with the Police?" *Gaynor Charter on Police*, April–May 1919.

Woods, Arthur. *Crime Prevention.* New York: Bibliobazaar. (Reprint.)

———. *Policeman and Public.* New York: Arno Press and the *New York Times*, 1971.

INDEX

bomb-removal equipment, 204
Bomb Squad, 203–4
Booraem, Alfred, 55
Boston police strike, 111
Brady, James, 151
Broderick, James, 133–34
Buda, Mario, 113
buffs, 72
Bugher, Frederick, 55, 64, 66, 105–7, 124
Bullock, William, 148
Bureau of Crime Prevention, 155, 163, 175
Bureau of Criminal Identification, 90
Bureau of Criminal Science, 130
Bureau of Detectives. *See* Detective Bureau
Bureau of Homicide, 147–48
Bureau of Missing Persons, 97, 102
Bureau of Narcotics, 185
Bureau of Policewomen, 114, 132, 151
Bureau of Street Traffic Regulations, 44
Bureau of Unemployment Relief, 163
burglary cataloguing, 51
Burkhard, Joseph, 204
Businessmen's League, 146
buttons scandal, 16
Byrd, Richard, 155

call boxes, 29, 80
captain position, 5, 8
Carbone, Charles, 91–92
Carey, Arthur, 147–48
Catholic Church, investigation of, 94–95
chain of command, 5–6
Chamberlain, Arthur, 157
Chamber of Commerce, New York, 45, 49–50
Charity Organization Society, 22
Charter Revision Committee, 12–13, 14, 19
chief inspector position, 27

Christian Front, 204
Christmas donations, 95, 163
Christopal, Rudolph, 205
Cirofici, "Dago" Frank, 75–76
Citizen Soldiers Training Camp, 97–98
Citizens' Union, 2, 15, 19, 21–22, 109, 116
City Charter: Charter Revision Committee and, 12–13, 19; mayor and, 12, 79, 84, 103; police department and, 2–3, 4, 7, 10, 19, 119, 163
City Patrol Corps, 207
civil defense, 205, 206–7, 211
civilianization of police department, 197–98, 207
civil service rules, 8
Cobb, Moses, 72
Cocchi, Alfred, 95–97
Cody, Edward, 69
College of the Police Department, 152, 157
Collins, James, 209
Columbia University, 19
Combat Cross, 186
Communists, 157–58, 160, 193
community-based policing, 102
Compton, Betty, 143, 166
Condon, John, 165
Confidential Squad, 133, 136, 147, 164
consolidation of counties, 1, 229
Coolidge, Calvin, 111
Cordes, John, 138–39, 149
Corrigan, Joseph, 120
Cortright, Moses, 27
Costello, Frank, 185–86
Costigan, Daniel, 28, 75, 86–87, 106–9, 132
Costuma, Louis, 163
Coughlin, John, 138, 144, 147, 149
Crain, Thomas, 120, 161
Crater, Joseph Force, 160–61
Crime Prevention Bureau, 155, 163, 175
crime scene investigating, 50

crime statistics, 72, 148, 152, 191
Criminal Identification Bureau, 90
Criminal Science Bureau, 130
Croker, Richard, 2–3, 7–8, 12, 13, 14, 16, 17, 127
Cropsey, James C., 67–70, 72, 82, 132–33
Cross, Adam, 23–24, 25–26
Cruger, Ruth, 95–97, 106–7
Crybaby Bandits, 133–34
Culliver, Louis, 120
Cunningham, Charles, 61–62
Curran, Henry H., 77, 115–16
Curran Committee, 77
Curry, John, 169
Curtis, Edwin, 111

Daily News, 172
DB13 cards, 97
Democratic Party: clubhouse raid of, 136–37; county merger and, 1; elections of 1898–1921 and, 2, 16, 31, 35, 116; elections of 1925–33 and, 122, 128, 154, 169, 179
Depression, the, 163, 175, 177, 185, 191, 197
Detective Bureau: under Arthur Woods, 88, 89; under Douglas McKay, 86; under John McCullagh, 5–6; under Theodore Bingham, 49, 50; under William Devery, 10–11; under William Flynn, 67–68; under William McAdoo, 45
Detective Division, 130, 188–89
detective sergeant position, 5–6, 10–11, 45, 50
Devery, William: about, 8, 13, 17; as chief of police, 8–9, 10–12; as first deputy commissioner, 14, 15, 20, 49; on Francis Greene, 27; as mayoral candidate, 31
Dewey, Thomas E., 199, 200

Dillon, James, 101, 104–5, 122–23
dispatchers, 192
Donohue, Raymond, 193
Dougherty, George, 70, 73–74, 86
Dougherty Brothers gang, 139
draft, the, 206–7
Drennan, William, 24
Driscoll, Clement J., 67, 69
Duffy, George, 54, 60
duty systems, 217–19; and six-section schedule, 27–28; ten-squad, 110; three-platoon, 15, 21, 24, 41, 49, 71–72, 110, 218; two-platoon, 21, 24, 27–28, 49, 110, 217
dynamite, 92

Ederle, Gertrude, 134–35
Edwards, William, 65
Eighteenth Amendment, 112
Election Bureau, 12–13
election fraud, 12
elections, mayoral. *See* mayoral elections
electronic traffic control, 114–15
Ellison, William B., 91
Emergency Service Division, 158, 175, 193, 211
Emergency Service Unit, 102, 175
Enright, Richard: about, 91, 107–8, 110, 124–25; and becoming police commissioner, 106; corruption accusations against, 115, 131; final police commissioner days of, 123–24, 129–30; International Police Conference and, 117–18; "Into the Net," 121; James Dillon and, 122–23; Ku Klux Klan and, 117; Lewis Valentine and, 132; as mayoral candidate, 153; police movies of, 121; police personnel and training and, 121–22; Police Recreation Center and, 113–14; police reforms of, 107–11, 116, 151–52; Police Riot

Raines Liquor Tax Law, 21–22, 27, 31
ranks, police, 5, 8–9, 50, 122. *See also*
    specific ranks
regulations, police, 5, 151–52
Republican Party: county merger
    and, 1; elections of 1897–1905 and,
    2, 3, 30, 46, 55–56, 178; elections
    of 1917–33 and, 99, 115–16, 124,
    179–80; Police Board and, 8, 14, 15;
    police commissioners and, 25
R. Hoe and Co., 22–23
Riis, Jacob: *How the Other Half Lives*,
    178
riots: Communist, 158, 160; Harlem,
    192–94, 209–10; Home Defense
    League involvement in, 99;
    between Irish and blacks, 11–12;
    Jewish, 23–24, 25–26; taxi, 183–84
Ritter, John, 24
Rivera, Lino, 193–94
Roberts, Charles, 194
Roberts, Florine, 209
Roosevelt, Franklin D., 161, 164, 166,
    167, 173, 205, 207
Roosevelt, Theodore, 4, 8, 12, 40, 107
Rose, Jack, 75–76, 77–78
Rosenberg, Lefty Louis, 75–76
Rosenfeld, Lewis, 205
Rosenthal, Herman, 75–76, 78
Rothstein, Arnold, 143–44, 147, 148,
    149, 154–55
roundsmen position, 5, 6, 45, 50
Roundsmen's Benevolent Association,
    45, 107
Rubin, Robert, 86
Russell, John, 54
Ruth, Babe, 163

Sacco, Nicola, 113, 141–42
salaries: of detectives, 121; of lieuten-
    ants, 50; of patrolmen, 10, 154;
    of police commissioners, 3; of
    precinct doormen, 24–25; of

roundsmen, 50; of sergeants, 121;
    under Fiorello LaGuardia, 210;
    under Joseph McKee, 167; under
    Richard Enright, 110–11
Sanger, Margaret, 150–51; *Family Limi-
    tation*, 150
San Juan Hill riot, 99
Saunders, Jefferson, 29
Scharlin, Abraham, 138–39
Schimmel, Gertrude, 210–11
Schmittberger, Max, 40, 67, 81, 101
School of Instruction, 7, 28, 57, 122, 152
Schultz, Dutch, 185, 191, 199
Seabury, Samuel, 78, 161–66, 171–73,
    206, 213
sergeant position, 5, 6, 50, 121, 195. *See
    also* detective sergeant position
Sexton, John, 3, 7–8, 13
Seymour, Horatio, 59
Shepard, Edward, 16
Sheridan, Richard, 202
shields, police personnel, 50
shoofly system, 5, 45–46, 108
signal boxes, 80, 89, 118–19, 195
Sisto, J. A., 166
six-section schedules, 27–28
Slattery, Daniel, 54
slot machines, 185–86
Smith, Al, 128, 129, 136, 167
Smith, Jean, 110
Socha, Ferdinand, 203
Soderman, Harry, 186
Special Duty Division, 108, 114
Special Orders, 63
Special Services Division, 120, 130, 133
specialty squads, 89–90, 98, 123, 130.
    See also specific squads
Spellman, Francis, 172
Spirit of St. Louis, 155–56
Spring-Rice, Cecil, 93
Spring 3100, 157, 174, 196, 207, 210
Square Deal Party, 124, 153
staffing levels, 230–31